COMPARATIVE AND INTERNATIONAL EDUCATION SERIES

Volume 7

The Revival of Values Education in Asia and the West

COMPARATIVE AND INTERNATIONAL EDUCATION

Volume 1   WAGNER: The Future of Literacy in a Changing World

Volume 2   EISEMON: Benefiting from Basic Education, School Quality and
Functional Literacy in Kenya

Volume 3   TARROW: Human Rights and Education

Volume 4   THOMAS & KOBAYASHI: Educational Technology—Its Creation,
Development and Cross-Cultural Transfer

Volume 5   BRAY with LILLIS: Community Financing Education: Issues and
Policy Implications in Less Developed Countries

Volume 6   LAUGLO & LILLIS: Vocationalizing Education: An International
Perspective

Volume 7   CUMMINGS, GOPINATHAN & TOMODA: The Revival of Values
Education in Asia and the West

NOTICE TO READERS

Dear Reader

An invitation to Publish and Recommend the Placing of a Standing Order to Volumes
Published in this Valuable Series.

If your library is not already a standing/continuation order customer to this series, may we
recommend that you place a standing/continuation order to receive immediately upon
publication all new volumes. Should you find that these volumes no longer serve
your needs, your order can be cancelled at any time without notice.

The Editors and the Publisher will be glad to receive suggestions or outlines of suitable
titles, reviews or symposia for editorial consideration: if found acceptable, rapid
publication is guaranteed.

ROBERT MAXWELL
Publisher at Pergamon Press

The Revival of Values Education in Asia and the West

Edited by

WILLIAM K. CUMMINGS
Harvard University, USA

S. GOPINATHAN
Institute of Education, Singapore

and

YASUMASA TOMODA
Osaka University, Japan

PERGAMON PRESS   1988

OXFORD · NEW YORK · BEIJING · FRANKFURT
SÃO PAULO · SYDNEY · TOKYO · TORONTO

UK	Pergamon Press plc, Headington Hill Hall, Oxford OX3 0BW, England
USA	Pergamon Press, Inc., Maxwell House, Fairview Park, Elmsford, New York 10523, USA
PEOPLE'S REPUBLIC OF CHINA	Pergamon Press, Room 4037, Qianmen Hotel, Beijing, People's Republic of China
FEDERAL REPUBLIC OF GERMANY	Pergamon Press GmbH, Hammerweg 6, D-6242 Kronberg, Federal Republic of Germany
BRAZIL	Pergamon Editora Ltda, Rua Eça de Queiros, 346, CEP 04011, Paraiso, São Paulo, Brazil
AUSTRALIA	Pergamon Press Australia Pty Ltd., P.O. Box 544, Potts Point, N.S.W. 2011, Australia
JAPAN	Pergamon Press, 5th Floor, Matsuoka Central Building, 1-7-1 Nishishinjuku, Shinjuku-ku, Tokyo 160, Japan
CANADA	Pergamon Press Canada Ltd., Suite No. 271, 253 College Street, Toronto, Ontario, Canada M5T 1R5

First edition 1988

Library of Congress Cataloging in Publication Data
The Revival of values education in Asia and the West / edited by William K. Cummings, S. Gopinathan, and Yasumasa Tomoda. — 1st ed. p. cm. — (Comparative and International education series : v. 7)
1. Moral education—Cross-cultural studies.
I. Cummings, William K.   II. Gopinathan, Saravanan.
III. Tomoda, Yasumasa, 1940– .   IV. Series
LC268.R49 1988   370.11'4—0019   88-14037

British Library Cataloguing in Publication Data
The Revival of values education in Asia and the west.—
(Comparative and international education series; v. 7).
1. Education—comparative studies
I. Cummings, William K.   II. Gopinathan, Saravanan
III. Tomoda, Yasumasa   IV. Series
370.19'5
ISBN 0-08-035854-3 Hardcover
ISBN 0-08-035853-5 Flexicover

Printed in Great Britain by
Hazell Watson & Viney Limited
Member of BPCC plc
Aylesbury, Bucks, England

Introduction to Series

The Comparative and International Education Series is dedicated to inquiry and analysis on educational issues in an interdisciplinary cross-national framework. As education affects larger populations and educational issues are increasingly complex and, at the same time, international in scope, this series presents research and analysis aimed at understanding contemporary educational issues. The series brings the best scholarship to topics which have direct relevance to educators, policymakers and scholars, in a format that stresses the international links among educational issues. Comparative education not only focuses on the development of educational systems and policies around the world, but also stresses the relevance of an international understanding of the particular problems and dilemmas that face educational systems in individual countries.

Interdisciplinarity is a hallmark of comparative education and this series will feature studies based on a variety of disciplinary, methodological and ideological underpinnings. Our concern is for relevance and the best in scholarship.

The series will combine careful monographic studies that will help policymakers and others obtain a needed depth for enlightened analysis with wider-ranging volumes that may be useful to educators and students in a variety of contexts. Books in the series will reflect on policy and practice in a range of educational settings from pre-primary to post-secondary. In addition, we are concerned with non-formal education and with the societal impact of educational policies and practices. In short, the scope of the Comparative and International Education Series is interdisciplinary and contemporary.

I wish to thank the assistance of a distinguished editorial advisory board including:

Professor Suma Chitnis, Tata University of Social Sciences, Bombay, India.

Professor Kazayuki Kitamura, Research Institute of Higher Education, Hiroshima University, Japan.

Professor Gail P. Kelly, State University of New York at Buffalo, USA.

Dean Thomas LaBelle, University of Pittsburgh, USA.

Dr S. Gopinathan, Institute of Education, Singapore.

Professor Guy Neave, Institute of Education, London.

PHILIP G. ALTBACH

Acknowledgments

The prospect for this book evolved over many years as the editors came to know each other, first in Japan and later in Southeast Asia and the United States. Gradually the circle of acquaintances broadened until all of those who have prepared chapters agreed to join in the common endeavor. Hidetoshi Kato, currently President of Japan's University of the Air, invited William Cummings to bring the group into a broader project on Environmental Education sponsored by the Nippon Life Insurance Foundation. Through the generous sponsorship of this Foundation, it was possible for several of the authors to get together in Kyoto and share viewpoints. Martha Metzler of the Harvard Graduate School of Education has provided valuable assistance in preparing the manuscript. The editors wish to extend their deep-felt appreciation to all who have cooperated in this project.

Contents

Part 1. Introduction

1. The Revival of Values Education
   WILLIAM K. CUMMINGS, S. GOPINATHAN AND YASUMASA TOMODA   3

2. Values Education in the Curriculum: Some Comparative
   Empirical Data
   YUN-KYUNG CHA, SUK-YING WONG AND JOHN W. MEYER   11

Part 2. The West

3. Values Education in the Western European Tradition
   JUDITH TORNEY-PURTA AND CAROLE H. HAHN   31

4. The Good Citizen—A Threatened Species?
   MORRIS JANOWITZ   59

Part 3. Asia

5. Politics and Moral Education in Japan
   YASUMASA TOMODA   75

6. Ideologies in Korea's Morals and Social Studies Texts:
   A Content Analysis
   SOOYEON C. SUH   93

7. A Subtle and Silent Transformation: Moral Education in
   Taiwan and the People's Republic of China
   JEFFREY F. MEYER   109

8. Being and Becoming: Education for Values in Singapore
   S. GOPINATHAN   131

9. Moral Education in a Developing Society: The Malaysian Case
   HENA MUKHERJEE   147

Part 4. Conclusion

10. Policy Options for Values Education
    WILLIAM K. CUMMINGS   165

Index   181

PART 1

Introduction

CHAPTER 1

The Revival of Values Education

WILLIAM K. CUMMINGS, S. GOPINATHAN AND YASUMASA
TOMODO

Periodically, critics assert a weakening in the moral fabric of their societies.
Walter Lippman, writing in 1955 about the meaning of freedom in Western
democracies, observed as follows:

> Originally it was founded on the postulate that there was a universal order on which all
> reasonable men were agreed: within that public agreement on the fundamentals and on the
> ultimates, it was safe to permit and it would be desirable to encourage, dissent and dispute.
> But with the disappearance of the public philosophy—and of a consensus on the first and
> last thing—there was opened up a great vacuum in the public mind (Lippman, 1955, p. 100).

Through the 1960s, this pessimism tended to be dismissed, at least by
national opinion leaders and prominent intellectuals, as the reaction of out-
of-phase moralists who were being displaced by the progressive changes
associated with the transition to post-industrial society. Talcott Parsons and
Winston White (1961, p. 210; see also the essays by Lipset and Lowenthal
in that volume) wrote, concerning the family's role in values education,
that there had occurred "a quite definite upgrading process, not, as is so
frequently suggested, a downgrading process".

But over the past decade the tide of opinion has shifted. Americans have
become attuned to the repeated urging of Secretary of Education William
J. Bennett (1987, p. 13) that we "get down to, and back to, the business of
the moral education of the young". Gallup polls in the US indicate that
parents are as concerned that schools help students to develop standards of
right and wrong as to teach them to speak, think, write and count. And
most states and local districts have developed or are instituting programmes
in values education (*US News and World Report*, 1977, p. 43). A surprising
indication of the new mood was the instant best-seller status achieved by
the liberal philosopher Allan Bloom's treatise on *The Closing of the American Mind* (1987), wherein it is argued that contemporary youth are deprived
of "the experience of really believing" and hence are unable to form critical
judgements of truth, beauty, or love.

The upsurge of interest in values education is certainly not restricted to
the United States. A 1980 study indicated that official public policies on
moral education had been adopted in all but one of the Canadian provinces

(for a thoughtful review of recent Canadian developments see Gow, 1980). Religious education, long a standard subject in English primary schools, has achieved new emphasis, and, as reported in chapter 3, similar revivalist trends are evident in the Federal Republic of Germany, the Netherlands, Sweden and Denmark. Indeed, as the essays of this volume indicate, values education is receiving prominence in school and community education throughout the modern world.

The Significance of the Past

Contemporary writings on the subject and the enthusiasms of its proponents sound as if this concern is a newly discovered goal of education. This is, of course, not so. Education has always concerned itself with the issue of the values to be transmitted to the young. It has been argued, for instance, that the advent of mass education in the US was triggered by mass immigration and the desire to draw the migrants into the mainstream of American life. Whether education has been little more than to socialize pupils into the conventional morality of their societies or whether, following the Socratic injunction that an unexamined life is not worth living, educational effort has been directed into readiness for the making of choices, into questioning common usage and redefining the notions of obedience and responsibility, no effort worthy of the name of education has ignored this aspect. Often schools have taught values almost unconsciously, by the behaviours they have rewarded and proscribed or by their everyday routines, but at other times they have made specific curriculum provisions by introducing such subjects as religion and ethics, civics, current affairs and character education.

The practice of values education in contemporary educational institutions is clearly influenced by earlier practice. The openness of English schools to religious education was prepared by the Anglican Church's firm role in the promotion of popular education during the nineteenth century. The stress on civic education in the US schools as well as the avoidance of religious and moral education is a reflection of the strong influence of Enlightenment thought on America's founding fathers. "Eastern morality" was introduced by the modernizing government of Meiji Japan into the school curriculum in order to stem the potentially negative influences of "Western technology" and thought; despite US attempts during the post-World War II Occupation to erase moral education from the Japanese school curriculum, Japanese educators remain firmly committed to transmitting a core of moral and civic values through the schools. The exploration of those early events and conditions that channelled distinctive national traditions of values education is one of the central themes in the several national case studies reported in this volume.

The Critical Questions

The extensive literature on values education and the existence of several well-established scholarly journals testify that values education is an established *sub-discipline*.[1] The major questions that values education poses can be stated thus: what is to be understood by the term "values education" and what are the objectives of values education? What values, secular and non-secular, should form the content of values education? What institutions are to be responsible for establishing values and for inculcating them? What age cohorts and social groups are most likely to be influenced by values education? If education is a primary vehicle of socialization what aspects of schooling, as between the formal curriculum, the school ethos, the administrative structure, or other elements, are most important? What is the role of the teacher, how is s/he to be selected and trained, and what pedagogical practices are to be approved? And finally, how is the effectiveness of the programme to be ascertained?

The chapters of this volume suggest the range of possible answers to these questions, and it would be presumptuous to attempt a summary in this introductory chapter. However, we would like to point to two strands in the answers which have led us to highlight in the title of this volume the distinction between Asia and the West. First, a broad distinction can be drawn in values education between values clarification and values instruction. Proponents of values clarification assume that young people are or should be capable of making their own decisions concerning appropriate values and hence advocate a pedagogy designed to facilitate or stimulate these decisions. Proponents of values instruction believe that the responsibility for identifying appropriate values lies with the schools, the adult community and/or the state, and thus the task of values education is to meaningfully convey the socially approved values to young people. Second, while the potential scope of values education is broad, some pedagogues focus primarily on those values guiding the relation of individuals to the state and polity, what in the West is often called civic education, while others, especially in Asia and the developing world, place greater stress on interpersonal or moral values.

Until recently, Western writers have tended to dominate the professional literature on values education, and partly as a result of this the field seems to place greater credence on those values education approaches which favour the clarification of civic values. Through the inclusion in this book of studies from both Asia and the West, we hope to illustrate that the implicit assumptions of the field deserve re-examination.

---

[1] See the extensive literature reviewed in Leming (1983).

Values Education in Developing Societies

Many of the questions and relationships considered by values education have been explicated with data derived from stable, industrially developed societies. On the other hand, there has been little systematic research into the problems of values education in developing societies. In 1981 UNESCO sponsored a series of workshops on values education in Asia but there has been little follow-up activity (UNESCO–NIER, 1981). Given the differences in political structure, degree of plurality, low degree of social cohesion and of the different and complex functions that education systems have in developing countries, it is vitally necessary to supplement our understanding of values education processes in cross-national contexts.

Developing multi-ethnic societies face a set of unique challenges. There is often in these societies poorly developed social institutions and civic traditions which can be utilized to hold *disparate* social groups together. The state is the major actor and arbiter. However, as the last two decades have shown, the state, or more precisely the political elite, often does not enjoy full legitimacy for a variety of reasons. Many members of the elite, though often educated in foreign schools, in the interests of social control and feeding on anti-colonial sentiment, look to the use of ethnic traditions as a unifying factor. The successful use of such a preservation strategy may in its turn assist in the perpetuation of the elite. It is for such reasons that cultural policies have a great significance in developing plural societies. The use of indigenous languages, the designation of a national religion, the adoption of symbols drawn from indigenous tradition, renewal of interest in folklore and traditional arts and crafts are, substantially, those things that pass for cultural policy-making in many countries.

Pedagogues in contemporary advanced societies are often dismayed and sometimes outraged at the tendency of leaders in developing countries to portray values education as a means for strengthening national solidarity and the authority of the ruling elites. This directive thrust contrasts sharply with the prevailing tendency among Western educators to see values education as a vehicle for assisting young people to clarify their goals and develop critical perspectives on social issues. But as the chapters in this book on the United States and Western Europe indicate, more restrictive concerns were at the core of values education in the earlier stages of Western development. Similarly, through World War II the main thrust of Japanese values education was to strengthen the ideology of the Imperial family-state (*tenno-shugi*). Thus we can see that attention to a nation's development stage should be an important consideration in a review of policies and approaches to values education.

The Selection of Values

A revealing national variation concerns the approach to selecting values for educational programmes. Western societies, as we have noted, tend to place predominant stress on civic values, though in the case of most European societies these are supplemented by religious and moral values. Japan tends to place greater stress on moral than on civic values. Regardless of the area of stress, the particular combinations that advanced nations settle on flow from centuries of cumulative tradition.

In developing societies, especially those in which governments have chosen to emphasize ethnic heritage, the task of value selection is more problematic. Not only is there selection to be made between competing indigenous traditions but often with a Western-oriented modernizing tradition as well. It often takes a very strong state presence to make the selection process work.

The essential societal problem is most newly independent societies is not the protection of pluralism but the enhancement of solidarity. In many countries of sub-Saharan Africa and on the Indian sub-continent the resurgence of tribalism and the failure of political cohesion and societal consensus have been of major concern to political elites. The concern with shared values is a response to a fragmenting social polity. In part the fragmentation has been caused by the rapid push to industrialization and modernization. Caught up with the stresses in social and personal life that the new processes bring, there has been, in nations such as Iran, Malaysia and Indonesia, a revival of the power of religion of a fundamentalist kind. The strictures of Islam, its view of an ordered political and social system with answers to problems grounded in an authoritative text, the Koran, appeals to those yearning for a simpler, surer, better understood code of behaviour. Such fundamentalist pressures are, of course, not without problems for the political leadership, especially in a plural state.

The Primacy of Schools

It is not uncommon for the discourse on values education to include consideration of various institutions including the church and even the mass media. Voluntary service and other related experiences may also be treated as elements in the process of values education. However, as each of these voluntary institutions is under separate control and, except for the schools, is largely out of the reach of public policy, it is difficult to foster extended discussion about the efficacy of extra-school institutions in values education. Thus in advanced countries, where most of the policy research on values education has been carried out, the primary focus is on the role of schools.

The school system in Asia and the developing societies, even when poorly developed, is an important state institution for it is a major source of mobility in the newly emerging market economies. Equally important, even though it does not always do this well enough, it is an important instrument of secondary socialization, imparting new knowledge and preparing pupils for new attachments. The other major competing institution, the family, is often seen in contradictory terms. It is seen as too rooted in its traditions and customs and thus in opposition to new state ideologies, yet the family is also thought to be potentially supportive, since school-taught attachments cannot be sustained without some family support. Further, governments in developing societies keep a wary eye on such other groups as religious organizations, uncertain as to their impact on moral education policies. Thus the belief in the efficacy of the school and in the potency of schooling processes appears to be far stronger in Asia and many developing countries than is currently acknowledged in the West.

Other policy options are, of course, turned to in Asia and the developing countries to bring about value change including the mobilization of the mass media, youth organizations and public campaigns. In both Singapore and Korea, obligatory military service is viewed as a key mechanism for values education. In Indonesia, the Pramuka youth movement as well as voluntary social service by university students is looked to as a means for reinforcing official values. Nevertheless, it is the schools especially that are looked to for the realization of values education policies.

The Plan of this Book

This introductory chapter has highlighted several of the complexities involved in the selection of values and the reliance on schools as the primary vehicle for values education. It is clear from cross-national investigation that the concern with values education is well-nigh universal but that national approaches to the critical questions confronting value educators are extraordinarily diverse. In the face of this diversity, some years ago the group of individuals who have joined forces in this book began discussions, first through correspondence and later through joint meetings, to prepare a volume illustrating at least part of the spectrum. This book is the outcome.

The first concern of the group was to examine the context of the revival, why is it that values education is gaining new impact in national and local educational systems? Secondly, the group sought to understand the nature of that impact. Chapter 2 helps to locate values education in its historical time and place; the case studies presented in chapters 3–9 provide examples of the major variations in national practice in Asia and the West; and the concluding chapter identifies many of the options open to educational leaders. The authors of this book wish to provide both practitioners and scholars with insights into the latest developments, so that they can approach their work with broader vision and compassion.

References

Bennett, W. J. (1987) About character. *Human Events*, 31 January.

Bloom, A. (1987) *The closing of the American mind: How higher education has failed democracy and impoverished the souls of today's students.* New York: Simon & Schuster.

Gow, K. M. (1980) *Yes Virginia, there is right and wrong: Values education survival kit.* Toronto: John Wiley and Sons Canada.

Leming, J. S. (1983) *Foundations of moral education: An annotated bibliography.* Westport, Conn.: Greenwood Press.

Lippman, W. (1955) *Essays in the public philosophy.* Boston: Little, Brown, and Co.

Parsons, T. and White, W. (1961) The link between character and social structure. In S. M. Lipset and L. Lowenthal (Eds.), *Culture and social character.* New York: Free Press of Glencoe.

UNESCO–NIER (1981) *Moral education in Asia*, Research Bulletin of the National Institute of Educational Research, Japan, No. 20.

US News and World Report (1977), "Mind bending" in the schools stirs growing protest, 4 July.

CHAPTER 2

Values Education in the Curriculum: Some Comparative Empirical Data

YUN-KYUNG CHA, SUK-YING WONG AND JOHN W. MEYER

In modern and modernizing societies, public problems and concerns tend sooner or later to float into the agendas of the mass educational system. Concerns about economic efficiency or effectiveness may appear in a renewed emphasis on science or mathematics or vocational training. Concerns about national integration turn out to involve perceived needs for instruction in national language and culture. Problems of order may call for revisions in social studies, history or civics curricula. It is often difficult to trace specific linkages, since so many different causal paths connect public life with the school system: linkages may involve pressures from local communities and parents; a variety of professional elites; or the authorities of the national state. In one way or another, school curricula reflect prevailing social, cultural and political concepts whether implicitly or explicitly: different attitudes toward children and childhood, taken-for-granted definitions of the "educated individual", the institutional methods through which the "ideal" education takes place, the relation of the individual to society and to the state, and the like. They may also reflect worldwide processes, as crises in central countries in the world system lead to perceived problem-definitions, educational reflections, and then through the diffusion around the world of standardized models of problems and solutions. In a forty-year period that may now be ending, the United States has been a central place on the world educational (as well as economic) map, and American problems and the associated educational agendas have affected educational changes in many other countries. In a world society that is now rather more decentralized, more diversity in educational problems and solutions may arise.

Authorship is equal. The research reported here was supported by funds from the National Science Foundation (Grant No. NSF-SES-8512561) and from the Center for the Study of Youth Development, Stanford University. It is part of a larger project we are carrying out with two other researchers—Aaron Benavot and David Kamens. We are grateful to Professors Benavot and Kamens for their help on the research reported here. Our work has also benefited from our continuing collaboration with other members of the Stanford comparative education project.

In this chapter, we trace empirically—using data collected on elementary school curricula in many countries over recent decades—the educational career of the subjects moral and religious education, showing where and when they appear in the official curriculum. For reasons we note, they have never appeared prominently in the American curriculum, but have nonetheless survived in a good many countries over many decades of expansion and institutionalization of mass education. There seems, now, to be a renewed concern with the subjects, for reasons on which we will attempt to shed light. In many countries there are discussions of the need for more attention to the subjects, and a concern to rethink the curriculum in this area. Our data can provide some evidence on how this is occurring, and perhaps, where it may lead.

Background

The socialization of the student as a moral being has been a core concern of mass education since its rise in the eighteenth and nineteenth centuries. There is no period or place in which education is conceived to be a narrowly technical enterprise, involving knowledge and competence in language or mathematics independent of broader socialization into the moral order. Even at the present time, producing the "morally mature" individual through the harmonious development of the child's intellectual, spiritual and physical potentials is one of the ultimate goals of education in many countries (especially in Asia). Early curricula in the West are filled with moral and religious content of one sort or another, and, as their primitive forms evolve and differentiate, this content never disappears, but is located in increasingly specific categories: history, social studies, civics, religion, philosophy and ethics, and moral education. Similar concerns evolve outside the formal curriculum itself, in conceptions for life in the bigger society through discipline, participation and the extracurriculum.

While researchers in the field have paid much attention to examining curricular effectiveness at the classroom level and adopting more case study approaches, little, of a general historical or comparative sort, is known about this evolution. There may be a tendency to generalize from the unique histories of a few central educational systems such as the American one—a tendency that, as we note above, may have had a perverse self-fulfilling character during a period of educational hegemony. Such a line of thought might lead to the expectation that very general processes of secularization would lead to the slow disappearance of specialized moral or religious instruction, and to the rise of more "progressive" emphases on civics and social studies as naturally embodying the necessary moral development of the child. But we have no way of knowing that this is really true, and for all we know we may be making the typical mistake in the analysis of educational systems of treating idiosyncratic American customs as representing a general model of educational progress.

Radical Society

Consider the American case as an exception, rather than a guide to progress. It has a political system, first of all, disconnected from a religious tradition embodied in a single church—there is no single guide or legal statement to moral socialization built into established organizational authority. By the mid-1970s, only sixteen states specifically addressed the necessity of including some sort of moral values in the general curriculum whereas other states dealt with the task of character building in a very general way (Edelman, 1976). Second, the American polity lacks a traditional, or "feudal", base in social authority to which reference can be made as a basis of unified moral instruction (Hartz, 1955). Third, in all social domains, a strong legitimization of moral authority as rooted in individual choice and exchange is sustained, in an extraordinarily successful and penetrative economy based on market principles, polity based on democratic participation and choice, and cultural system based on a very high level of free religious involvement (Tocqueville, 1969; Bellah *et al.* 1985). A history of success and later hegemony continually intensifies faith in individual involvement in society itself as the root of moral conduct and moral order—a history developing from radical liberal (i.e. republican) conceptions in the nineteenth century to the progressive construction of the organized society in the twentieth, with the attendant development of an elaborate sociological and social psychological "social control" theory of moral behaviour as rooted in natural involvement in the good society. (Mead, 1934; Dewey, 1964, 1975; Cooley, 1983; Hamilton and Sutton, 19870

In this tradition of radical liberalism, moral instruction is difficult to ground in missing organized traditions of either religious or social authority. Absent an established religion, attempts to build in religious instruction seem sectarian. Absent an established tradition of social authority, attempts to build in traditional moral instruction seem to reflect only the illegitimate dominance of an elite "subculture". (The same Americans who have always had an obsession with learning manners have always had deeply populist suspicions of tradition as elite pretence). So, in the case of America, the issue of any forms of moral and religious instruction has always been more an issue of local political struggle rather than constitutional (Tyack and Thomas, 1987).

The solution has been to teach neither religion nor morals in the curriculum, but to immerse the pupil in (a) knowledge of society and polity and how they work, and (b) participation as a young citizen in the school as a little social system. Consider the two issues separately. First, if proper conduct is rooted in the natural relations of society itself, then it can be enhanced by instructing the child in how society works—in civics, social science, psychology, economics and history. In the educational system of radical liberalism, a better understanding of how society works will generate more competent, effective and properly conforming persons. Understanding the workings of the virtuous natural economy, polity and social relationship system will help the student understand both his/her own role and the proper roles of others. In the classic American theory of interactionism, the socially controlled self incorporates such understandings as part of its constitution. In good part, this theory contains no idea that individuals have recalcitrant selves at odds with society (the Freudian id)—thus improper conduct reflects ignorance, not the studied pursuit of improper goals.

Second, the ideology of radical liberalism, the school itself is to be a little social system replicating the bigger one, not simply a formal organization. The child will learn moral conduct in society by participating as a citizen in proper conduct in the school itself. Thus, much moral socialization should occur, not in the curriculum but in participation in the life of the classroom and school itself, with reflections of all the wider social institutions—cooperative work participation, political choice through the rituals of elections, social responsibility for order, and the like. Citizenship and conduct are managed in participation in school life, more than in the formal curriculum itself: analogous to the larger society in which religious and association participation over and above narrowly political and economic roles is a central desideratum.

In few other loci around the world would one expect to find such a polity and such an ideology. An important exception might be another sort of radical regime, in which society is conceived to have its own natural laws controlling individual conduct—societies dominated by communist regimes. Here too there is a *social* (rather than traditional or religious) theory of authority and moral conduct. And here too one might expect to find emphases on general curricular instruction in the natural laws of proper social, economic and political life, rather than distinctive elements of moral or religious education. And one would expect to find an emphasis, similar to the American one, on the individual student as a responsible participant and citizen in the school as a microcosmic social system, rather than simply a formal organization for instruction (Bronfenbrenner, 1970). The effort, quite outside the curriculum, would be to build a school in which proper social orientations and conformity would naturally result from participation, comparable to the wider attempt to construct the good society in which proper consciousness would naturally obtain.

Thus, we approach our cross-national comparisons with an initial idea:

1. Radical regimes will de-emphasize both moral and religious education,

in preference to broader instruction in social science and for emphases on participation in school as a matter of citizenship (more than organizational discipline).

More Typical Alternatives

This line of thought suggests that moral and religious education might be the more common case. In most modern societies, society is seen as linked to religious or social traditions, which carry more of the burden of sustaining the moral order and instruction which is seen as beneficial to proper moral conduct.

In many modern societies, an explicit link to an organized religious tradition is maintained through some sort of public or state religion. Individual behaviour as well as public life is socially controlled by this religious system, not simply by participation in public life. Where this is the case, we expect to find religious instruction in the curriculum:

2. Societies with established organized religions will emphasize religious instruction in the curriculum.

But many modern societies, while retaining an emphasis on cultural traditions and their authority, either lack a unified religious tradition or have politically disestablished such a tradition. In either case, we expect to find a curricular emphasis on moral education, as a slightly secularized version of established traditions, customs, and their authority. This may especially be the case in societies, such as the Latin ones, in which bitter struggles have disestablished a unifying religious tradition, but left a conception of society as requiring unified moral authority in place: these should be the more common loci, among developed countries, of moral education in the curriculum. A good example of this can be found in a series of educational reforms during the period 1880–1883 in France. Showing strong bitterness toward the clergy's participation in the anti-republican agitation of 1876, the new republican curriculum substituted civic and moral instruction for religious education and a catechism of republican principles for the catechism of the church (Hughes and Klemm, 1907).

3. Societies built around a tradition of collective authority, but lacking an established religion, will emphasize moral education in the curriculum.

The Modern Third World

Most of the world's educational systems are in very new states that have arisen since World War II and are by and large in the social and economic peripheries of the world. In these systems, as is commonly noted, nation-building is a critical problem. It is less commonly noted that in most of these societies, nation-building on the basis of the legitimation and incorporation of present social arrangements is not feasible (Meyer, 1980, pp. 109–137). The state tends to be built up and legitimated according to exogenous world standards, and a modern civil society is something to be constructed as a project in the future. Society as it now is tends to be seen as inadequate— inefficient, archaic, corrupt and "undeveloped". The needed new citizen-members will not arise from the normal operation of this society: they must be built by purposive political and educational action. At the same time, modernizing elites in these countries are confronted with strong social pressures for the preservation of some elements of tradition. Also, the social fabrics of these countries are largely based on traditional authoritative social relations. What we have called the standard "radical" educational solutions to this—immersing the child in knowledge of the operation of normal society, and in participation in a school that is its microcosm—is unlikely to work. A more directive and future-oriented programme of moral socialization, managed by state and educational authority, seems called for. In such societies, we imagine, perceptions of the need for special and authoritative instruction in the emergent religious and moral values will be common:

4. Emerging societies and states will tend to construct or maintain distinctive programme of moral or religious education, apart from mainstream instruction in civics or social life.

Overall

Our review of the possibilities involved suggests as a conclusion the general notion that religious and moral education will retain their strength in the evolution of national educational systems in the contemporary world system. There is no reason to imagine that radical secularization is likely to be a dominant trend—in a wide variety of societies and educational systems distinctive programmes in moral or religious socialization would seem ideologically appropriate. We can put this idea in a conservative way, to guide our later examination of the data:

5. There is no reason to expect a secular decline in the frequency of moral or religious education in modern national schooling systems.

The guiding ideas above provide some suggestions in terms of which to look at the descriptive data we present below. We do not propose rigorous tests, since we are exploring new types of data not previously worked through by researchers, but imagine that in interpreting the descriptive material the general ideas above will be useful.

Data

We have systematically collected, for many countries at several points in time, official national elementary educational timetables, listing subjects to be taught and proportions of time to be devoted to them. For the period 1975 to the present, we have collected data for about ninety countries, mainly by corresponding with national Ministries of Education, but also from other source books (especially from Massialas and Jarrar, 1983; UNESCO Regional Office for Education in Asia and Pacific, 1984; and Sheikha al-Misnad, 1985). For the period 1945–1974, we collected about 164 timetables, mainly from the World Survey of Education compiled by UNESCO (1958), Sasnett and Sepmeyer (1966), UNESCO–NIER (1970) and from the UNESCO Regional Office for Education in Asia (1966). For the period 1920–1944, we collected about sixty-four timetables from a wide variety of sources, mainly from the Educational Yearbook series published by Columbia University (1924–1944) and from Kandel (1933). Some caveats:

(1) The data are, of course, official statements of policy. We have no way of knowing how these policies are put into practice, though both formal research and informal observation suggest that there is a great deal of decoupling here, especially as one moves to peripheral countries (see Weick, 1976). On the other hand, official statements of policy are interesting ideological forms in their own right, and may suggest the nature and loci of various prevailing doctrines.

(2) For many timetables, we do not know the length in hours of the school work. Thus we can show in the tables below the percentages of curricula time to be devoted to various subjects, but do not know the exact number of hours involved.

(3) We define as a "country" any entity with a national educational system. In some periods, thus, we are referring in part to colonies—an important issue in the analysis below. By the period of 1975 to the present, of course, almost all the entities involved in our data have come to be defined as independent nation-states.

(4) For some countries at some time points, we know whether or not a subject is included in the official curriculum, but we do not know how much time is to be devoted to it: our case bases when we report the existence of a topic in the curriculum are larger than when we report amounts of time devoted to this topic.

(5) Sometimes, official curricula report that a certain amount of time is to be devoted to a combined set of subjects (e.g. "moral and religious education"). In such cases, we treat the amount of time as split equally between the listed subjects.

(6) Occasionally, we have more than one timetable for a country during a given period. This is usually not a problem, since official curricula tend to

change rather slowly. When there are discrepancies, we choose the time-table closer to each target year: 1935, 1960 and 1985.

(7) We have tried to collect timetables for as many countries as possible in each period. We have been much more successful than we or others had imagined possible—it turns out that communication about national educational systems in the world system is much more common than might have been anticipated. But our data does not represent in any strict sense samples of countries. In general, our data for the 1920–1944 period represent especially countries in Europe and Latin America. Our data for the 1945–1974 period are relatively complete. Our data for the 1975–present period under-represent Eastern Europe and Latin America.

(8) To simplify the presentation and analysis of the data, our measures combine data for all the years ordinarily included in elementary education. In order to standardize this as much as possible, we have chosen to code the curricula in grades 1–6 of the national system. In some instances, in which elementary education covers fewer grades than this, we have included results for the first year or two of the lower secondary cycle in order to approximate the standard six-year curriculum. Our results are not greatly affected by this decision.

Results

A first and obvious question is how common moral and religious education are among national educational systems. We report relevant results in Table 2.1, including, for comparative purposes, time allocated to instruction in the related fields of civics and social studies.

TABLE 2.1 *The Prevalence of Instruction in Moral Education,*
Religious Education, Civics and Social Studies in Recent Periods:
Means or Proportions (Number of Cases in Parentheses)

(a) All countries for which data are available

	1920–1944	1945–1974	1975–present
Mean percentages of instructional time given to subject			
Moral Ed.	0.78 (41)	1.05 (138)	0.96 (86)
Religion	5.07 (49)	3.66 (125)	4.51 (82)
Civics	0.92 (43)	0.94 (135)	0.52 (86)
Soc. Stud.	0.19 (57)	1.77 (119)	4.96 (66)
Proportion of countries including subject			
Moral Ed.	0.41 (58)	0.35 (158)	0.26 (88)
Religion	0.60 (58)	0.55 (158)	0.64 (88)
Civics	0.48 (58)	0.42 (158)	0.17 (88)
Soc. Stud.	0.04 (57)	0.26 (129)	0.68 (69)

(b) Constant panels of countries*

		1920–1944	1945–1974	1975–present
Mean percentages of instructional time				
Moral Ed.	(*N*=21)	0.71	1.12	1.05
Religion	(*N*=19)	4.16	3.62	3.21
Civics	(*N*=20)	1.14	0.82	0.49
Soc. Stud.	(*N*=15)	0.09	2.48	4.38
Moral Ed.	(*N*=37)	0.87	0.85	—
Religion	(*N*=43)	5.09	4.25	—
Civics	(*N*=36)	1.07	0.97	—
Soc. Stud.	(*N*=47)	0.23	1.43	—
Moral Ed.	(*N*=69)	—	0.98	0.99
Religion	(*N*=52)	—	4.52	4.21
Civics	(*N*=60)	—	1.23	0.51
Soc. Stud.	(*N*=41)	—	2.06	4.50
Proportions of countries giving subject				
Moral Ed.	(*N*=26)	0.31	0.31	0.27
Religion	(*N*=26)	0.50	0.54	0.50
Civics	(*N*=26)	0.46	0.46	0.15
Soc. Stud.	(*N*=17)	0.06	0.35	0.71
Moral Ed.	(*N*=54)	0.43	0.35	—
Religion	(*N*=54)	0.57	0.57	—
Civics	(*N*=54)	0.52	0.52	—
Soc. Stud.	(*N*=49)	0.04	0.20	—
Moral Ed.	(*N*=73)	—	0.22	0.26
Religion	(*N*=73)	—	0.62	0.63
Civics	(*N*=73)	—	0.41	0.19
Soc. Stud.	(*N*=46)	—	0.30	0.67

*Data used only for those countries where measurement is available for all 3 time periods.

Table 2.1a reports the data for all the countries in our data set, and thus for differing numbers of countries at each time period. The first section shows the mean percentage of time allocated to each subject. The overall results suggest the following: first, very small amounts of time—about 1 per cent of the curriculum—are devoted to moral education. Civics gets even less than 1 per cent. More time, on the average, is devoted to religious instruction. Social studies has increased, in the most recent period, to about 5 per cent of the curriculum. The data suggest slight changes over time in moral education and religious instruction. In the most recent period, civics has declined sharply (from 0.92 to 0.52) and social studies has increased dramatically (from 0.19 to 4.96).

The second section of Table 2.1a shows the data in terms of proportions of the curricula containing a given topic, rather than amounts of time devoted. Here, there is a suggestion that moral education has declined in frequency over time (from 0.41 to 0.26), while religious instruction occurs in a constant proportion of countries (about 60 per cent). Civics has declined sharply (from 0.48 to 0.17), and social studies has increased sharply (from 0.04 to 0.68).

Table 2.1b reports the same data, but in a way that permits more precise comparisons over time: we report the data only for the few cases where we have data at all three points in time, or for two successive points in time. Naturally, we have fewer such cases. But the results permit conclusions about time changes, they show that moral education has remained relatively constant over time, that the proportions of countries giving religious education have also remained constant over time (but the average amount of time devoted to religious education has declined a little over the period). Civics has declined in both mean precentage of the curricula time (from 1.14 to 0.49) and frequency (from 0.46 to 0.15) in the three-time-point comparison.

TABLE 2.2 *Correlations Between Particular Curricular Emphases on Values Over Time: Moral Education, Religious Education, Civics and Social Studies (Number of Cases in Parentheses)*

(a) Intercorrelations between periods: Percentages of time devoted to subject

		1920–1944	1945–1974	1975–present
Moral Ed.	1920–1944	1.00	0.43	0.50
	1945–1974	(37)	1.00	0.19
	1975–present	(21)	(69)	1.00
Religion	1920–1944	1.00	0.68	0.50
	1945–1974	(43)	1.00	0.88
	1975–present	(21)	(52)	1.00
Civics	1920–1944	1.00	−0.23	−0.03
	1945–1974	(36)	1.00	0.11
	1975–present	(20)	(60)	1.00
Soc. Stud.	1920–1944	1.00	−0.07	−0.27
	1945–1974	(47)	1.00	0.33
	1975–present	(17)	(41)	1.00

(b) Intercorrelations between periods: Presence or absence of subject

		1920–1944	1945–1974	1975–present
Moral Ed.	1920–1944	1.00	0.62	−0.03
	1945–1974	(54)	1.00	0.36
	1975–present	(26)	(73)	1.00
Religion	1920–1944	1.00	0.47	0.38
	1945–1974	(54)	1.00	0.80
	1975–present	(26)	(73)	1.00
Civics	1920–1944	1.00	−0.04	0.03
	1945–1974	(54)	1.00	0.09
	1975–present	(26)	(73)	1.00
Soc. Stud.	1920–1944	1.00	−0.10	−0.39
	1945–1974	(49)	1.00	0.36
	1975–present	(18)	(46)	1.00

Social studies has dramatically increased in both mean percentage of curricula time (from 0.09 to 4.38) and frequency (from 0.06 to 0.71). These trends are more prominent when data for two successive time points are compared.

Both moral education and religious instruction show a rough aggregate consistency over time. A second question is whether the same countries are involved. Do countries emphasizing moral or religious education in one period also do so in the next? We naturally expect positive correlations here—for one thing, elementary curricula often remain constant for long periods of time—but the question is how large they are, or how much the inclination to have instruction in one of these areas is a consistent national characteristic. Table 2.2 shows the correlation matrices for each subject over time. Table 2.2a shows the correlations in terms of percentage of curricular time devoted to each subject. Table 2.2b shows the correlation in terms of the simple dichotomy of whether the subject is taught or not. Overall, the results show that religious instruction is a more consistent national property over time, with very substantial correlations between each period and the others. Moral education varies more over time—the countries that teach it in one period are not so much more likely than others to teach it in the next. For instance, as Table 2.2b shows, the correlation between moral education in the 1920–1944 period and 1975–present is -0.03. This implies that many countries that taught moral education during the 1920–1944 period do not teach it at the present time.

A third question has to do with the relationships between instruction in these subjects—are countries that have religious instruction less likely to give time to moral education? A number of ideas discussed at the outset suggest that in part these subjects are partial trade-offs for each other, and that moral education will be found especially in countries without an organized and established religion or set of religions. Table 2.3 presents the correlations between percentages of time given over to moral education, religion and (for comparison) civics and social studies. The results show, consistently across the three time periods, a modest negative correlation between the percentages of time devoted to religious instruction and that devoted to moral education, as we might expect. They also show fewer relations between either subject and civics or social studies (except for anomalous results in the 1945–1974 period, for which we have no explanation). Incidentally, the results also show a negative correlation in the current period between instruction in social studies and in civics—a historical curricular replacement that is marginal to our present interests (Suk-ying Wong, 1987).

TABLE 2.3. *Intercorrelations Between Percentages of Curricular Time Devoted to Moral Education, Religious Education, Civics and Social Studies: Three Different Time Periods (Number of Cases in Parentheses)*

	Moral Ed.	Religion	Civics	Soc. Stud.
1920–1944				
Moral Ed.	1.00	−0.25	−0.07	−0.07
Religion	(38)	1.00	0.04	−0.13
Civics	(38)	(40)	1.00	−0.08
Soc. Stud.	(36)	(42)	(37)	1.00
1945–1974				
Moral Ed.	1.00	−0.22	0.58	0.34
Religion	(113)	1.00	0.04	−0.22
Civics	(126)	(111)	1.00	−0.14
Soc. Stud.	(105)	(103)	(100)	1.00
1975–present				
Moral Ed.	1.00	−0.26	0.01	0.08
Religion	(82)	1.00	−0.12	−0.18
Civics	(84)	(80)	1.00	−0.32
Soc. Stud.	(64)	(62)	(62)	1.00

The consistent negative relationship between time given to religion and time given to moral education reveals the partially equivalent nature of these subjects in their role in the curriculum. It is especially striking because, in a number of countries, the two subjects are taught together as one general topic (which in our method of coding generates an automatically positive association). Of the countries giving moral education, 20.8 per cent paired it with religious instruction in the 1920–1944 period (five out of twenty-four cases); 14.5 per cent (eight out of fifty-five cases) did so in the 1945–1974 period; and 30.4 per cent (seven out of twenty-three cases) did so in the 1970-present period. Moral education is less often paired with other subjects in a common curricular element (moral education, however, is sometimes combined with civics: 29.2, 34.5 and 13.0 per cent in each time period).

A fourth research question concerns the general relation between moral and religious instruction and indices of social and economic development. Our arguments above lead us to expect a weak relation, rejecting any notion that instruction in these subjects is concentrated in less developed areas. To study this, we show the correlations in each period between the percentage of time given to the subject and two different indices of development: GNP per capita in 1950, 1960 and 1980 and Urbanization (defined as the proportion of the population in cities over 1,000,000 in 1930 and 1960) (Banks, 1975; United Nations, 1975). The results are shown in Table 2.4. Very clearly, the relationship between development measures and curricular emphases on moral or religious instruction is slight. Countries high on GNP per capita in the later periods are a little more likely to have religious instruction (0.24 and 0.28 in the 1945–1974 and 1975–present time periods), but the Urbanization variable shows no tendency (−0.07 and 0.04 respectively during the same periods). It seems obvious that no general argument about, say, negative effects of development on instruction in these areas can be sustained: the later GNP per capita correlation reflects a special tendency of Western countries to have religious instruction, as seen below.

TABLE 2.4 *Correlations Between Measures of National Development and Percentages of Curricular Time Devoted to Values Education (Number of Cases in Parentheses)*

	GNP per capita	*Urbanization*
1920–1944	*1950*	*1930*
Moral Ed.	−0.14 (25)	−0.08 (25)
Religion	0.02 (29)	0.06 (30)
Civics	−0.09 (25)	−0.43 (23)
Soc. Stud.	0.19 (33)	0.45 (35)
1945–1974	*1960*	*1960*
Moral Ed.	−0.16 (89)	−0.07 (110)
Religion	0.24 (81)	0.07 (101)
Civics	−0.05 (86)	−0.01 (105)
Soc. Stud.	−0.08 (78)	−0.03 (100)
1975–present	*1980*	*1960*
Moral Ed.	−0.22 (65)	0.04 (66)
Religion	0.28 (62)	−0.17 (62)
Civics	−0.07 (66)	0.09 (67)
Soc. Stud.	−0.01 (49)	0.07 (50)

Finally, in order to approach our ideas about the types of countries most likely to employ moral or religious instruction, we present information on countries classified by a simple world region scheme:

1. Sub-Saharan Africa.
2. Middle East and North Africa, including most Islamic countries.
3. Asia.
4. Latin America and the Caribbean.
5. Eastern Europe.
6. The West, including Western Europe, the United States, Australia, New Zealand and Former British colonies in North America.

The results of this classification, in terms of mean percentages of instructional time given to moral and religious instruction at each time point, are given in Table 2.5. Obviously, in many cells we have very few cases, so the results should be examined with great caution.

TABLE 2.5. *World Regions and Percentages of Curricular Time Devoted to Values Education (Number of Cases in Parentheses)*

	Sub-Saharan Africa	Middle East & N. Africa	Latin America & Caribbean	East Europe	West	Asia
Moral Ed.						
1920–1944	—	0.30	0.87	0.00	0.53	3.16
		(5)	(3)	(5)	(17)	(6)
1945–1974	0.82	1.41	2.57	0.00	0.18	1.09
	(31)	(16)	(23)	(9)	(22)	(22)
1975–present	0.45	· 0.15	0.78	0.00	0.07	3.24
	(16)	(11)	(18)	(4)	(14)	(18)
Religion						
1920–1944	0.00	11.17	0.79	5.49	6.18	0.00
	(2)	(8)	(8)	(5)	(16)	(6)
1945-1974	2.78	10.14	1.56	0.00	6.50	2.67
	(25)	(15)	(25)	(8)	(19)	(18)
1975–present	4.16	11.10	2.48	0.00	5.20	3.12
	(16)	(11)	(17)	(4)	(12)	(17)
Civics						
1920–1944	0.00	0.95	1.93	2.46	0.79	0.88
	(2)	(7)	(3)	(4)	(15)	(6)
1945–1974	0.53	1.27	1.41	0.06	0.90	1.58
	(34)	(16)	(22)	(9)	(21)	(19)
1975–present	0.52	0.00	0.51	0.50	0.48	0.75
	(15)	(11)	(18)	(4)	(16)	(18)
Soc. Stud.						
1920–1944	0.00	0.00	0.00	0.23	0.52	0.00
	(2)	(9)	(10)	(6)	(18)	(4)
1945–1974	1.06	0.21	3.21	0.00	0.74	3.88
	(21)	(16)	(23)	(9)	(23)	(18)
1975–present	3.59	5.96	7.52	0.00	4.83	4.79
	(17)	(5)	(15)	(3)	(11)	(11)

Given the limited number of cases, the consistency of the findings is remarkable. The subjects are found in most regions fairly consistently across time, despite changes in the case bases. Only a few figures stand out. First, Eastern European countries, as we might expect, give almost no time in the recent periods (i.e. after the current regimes came into power) to either moral or religious education. Second, Latin American countries—most of which have gone through sharp separations of state and religion—tend to score highly on moral education over time compared to other regions of the world: they were the countries that devoted the highest percentage of time to it during the 1945–1974 period (2.57) and came second to Asia during the 1920–1944 and 1975–present periods (0.87 and 0.78 respectively). Third, Asian countries—many of which lack a clearly established organized religion—tend to emphasize moral education; the region devotes the highest percentage of time to the subject of all the regions both in the earliest and the latest periods (3.16 and 3.24 respectively) and it came second to Latin

America during the 1945–1974 period (1.09). Fourth, Western countries, in many of which this separation is more limited, devote a fairly high percentage of curricular religious time to instruction (6.18, 6.50 and 5.20 respectively from the earliest to the latest periods). Fifth, religious instruction is especially high in the Islamic countries of North Africa and the Middle East—in fact, the highest values in our data come from countries in this region (11.17, 10.14 and 11.10 respectively). Finally, the other regions, sub-Saharan Africa, Asia, and Latin America and the Caribbean devote a fairly low proportion of curricular time to religious instruction. There exists a notable anomaly in Table 2.4: countries in this area devote substantial percentages of time to religion, which seems to be contrary to our previous discussion. This is due to the fact that this region, in our data set, contains many former British Caribbean colonies (see Appendix, p. 27).

These observations encourage reflection along the lines with which we began the chapter. In both developed and developing worlds, instruction along moral or religious lines is common, and moral education tends to be especially prominent where a state-linked religion is missing.

TABLE 2.6 *Former Colonial Power and Percentage of Time Devoted to Values Education: Former Colonies Only (Number of Cases in Parentheses)*

		Former colonial power	
		Anglo–US	*France or Spain*
Moral Ed.			
	1920–1944	*0.00 (N=9)*	2.26 (N=3)
	1945–1974	0.22 (N=50)	2.62 (N=33)
	1975–Present	0.69 (N=44)	1.22 (N=13)
Religion			
	1920–1944	8.86 (N=9)	0.48 (N=12)
	1945–1974	5.45 (N=36)	1.49 (N=40)
	1975–Present	5.57 (N=41)	1.33 (N=12)
Civics			
	1920–1944	0.60 (N=9)	0.6 (N=6)
	1945–1974	0.46 (N=42)	1.53 (N=33)
	1975–Present	0.51 (N=44)	0.68 (N=13)
Soc. Stud.			
	1920–1944	1.03 (N=9)	0.00 (N=14)
	1945–1974	2.46 (N=33)	1.38 (N=32)
	1975–Present	5.50 (N=36)	4.62 (N=9)

To inquire further into this issue, we have classified those countries with a colonial background by the metropolitan power which controlled them. Our notion was that former French or Spanish colonies, deeply affected by the disestablishment of religion in the French Revolution, might be especially prominent loci of moral education as a kind of substitute. We thought further that former British colonies, reflecting a tighter linkage between national religion and polity, might have more religious, and less moral, emphasis in education. The results of this classification appear in Table 2.6 which strongly supports the argument. Table 2.6 shows that the mean percentage of time devoted to moral education is consistently higher in the former French or Spanish colonies compared to former British colonies, and that quite the opposite trend is true for religious education. This observation, as with that of the special emphasis on moral education in Asian countries, encourages us to take seriously the notion that an emphasis on moral education reflects traditions of considerable social authority separated from an explicit religious system.

Conclusions

We find that a curricular focus on moral education is quite common in national educational systems, and shows no signs of declining. Less time tends to be given to it than is given to religious instruction, and there is something of a negative relation between the two. They are partially substitutes for each other. Moral education is a less stable curricular component over time than is religion, presumably because it is rooted less clearly in definite organizational linkages. Both kinds of instruction are found about equally in developed and less developed societies.

But pronounced regional differences, presumably reflecting differences in political organization and ideology, appear. Communist countries, as with what we call the radical liberalism of the American polity, emphasize neither moral nor religious education as separate curricular components. Islamic societies, and many Western ones, emphasize religion. Asian countries, along with Latin American ones lacking an established religious linkage, tend to be especially prominent loci of moral education. Along the same line of thought, former colonies tend to reflect the patterns of metropolitan powers: former British colonies emphasize religious education, while former French and Spanish ones emphasize moral education.

Overall, our data suggest that some sort of distinctive emphasis on socializing the child to normative compliance with social authority remains strong in the modern system. In the core of the world, it reflects established traditions. In much of the Third World, it presumably reflects a perceived requirement for forms of individual submission to collective social authority over and above the natural operation of society.

Appendix

Data set (x) for periods 1 (1920–1944), 2 (1945–1974) and 3 (1975–present)

Country	1	2	3
Afghanistan	x		
Albania	x		
Algeria	x	x	
Angola	x		
Argentina	x	x	x
Australia	x	x	
Austria	x	x	
Bahamas	x		
Bahrain	x	x	
Bangladesh			x
Barbados	x	x	
Belgium	x	x	
Belize			x
Bermuda	x	x	
Bhutan	x		
Bolivia	x		
Botswana	x	x	
Brazil	x		
Brunei	x	x	
Bulgaria	x	x	
Burma	x		
Burundi	x		
Byel. Russ.	x		
Central Africa Rep.	x		
Cameroon	x		
Canada	x	x	x
Cape Verde	x		
Chile	x	x	
China (PRC)	x	x	x
Columbia	x	x	
Congo	x		
Cook Is.	x		
Costa Rica	x	x	
Cuba	x	x	x
Cyprus	x	x	
Czechoslovakia	x	x	
Denmark	x	x	
Djibouti	x		
Domin. Rep.	x	x	
Dominica			x
Dutch E. Indies	x		
Ecuador	x	x	x
Egypt	x	x	x
El Salvador	x		
England	x	x	x
Estonia	x		
Ethiopia	x	x	

Country	1	2	3
Fiji			x
Finland	x	x	
Fr. Guiana			x
France	x	x	
Gabon			x
Gambia			x
Germany	x		
Germ.(FRG)		x	x
Germ.(GDR)		x	x
Ghana		x	x
Gibraltar			x
Greece	x	x	
Greenland	x	x	x
Grenada			x
Guadeloupe		x	x
Guam		x	x
Guatemala	x		
Guin. Bissau	x		
Guinea	x		
Guyana		x	x
Haiti	x	x	
Honduras	x	x	
Hong Kong		x	x
Hungary	x	x	x
Iceland		x	x
India	x	x	x
Indonesia		x	x
Iran	x	x	
Iraq	x	x	x
Ireland	x	x	x
Israel		x	x
Ital. Comal.	x		
Italy	x	x	
Ivory Coast			x
Jamaica	x	x	x
Japan	x	x	x
Jordan		x	x
Kampuchea	x		
Kenya		x	x
Kiribati			x
Korea Rep.	x	x	x
Kuwait		x	x
Lao	x		
Latvia	x		
Lebanon	x		
Lesotho		x	x
Liberia	x	x	

Country	1	2	3
Libya	x	x	x
Lithuania	x		
Luxembourg	x	x	
Macao			x
Madagascar	x	x	
Malawi		x	x
Malaysia	x	x	x
Maldives			x
Mali	x		
Malta		x	x
Martinique			x
Mauritius			x
Mexico	x	x	
Monaco	x		
Mongolia	x		
Morocco	x	x	
Mozambique			x
N. Ireland	x	x	
Namibia		x	x
Nepal		x	x
Netherlands	x	x	x
New Zealand	x	x	
Nicaragua	x	x	x
Niger		x	x
Nigeria		x	x
Niue Island			x
Norway	x	x	x
Oman		x	x
P. N. Guinea			x
Pacific Is.	x		
Pakistan		x	x
Palestine	x		
Pan. Canal	x		
Panama	x	x	
Paraguay	x		
Peru	x	x	
Philippines	x	x	
Poland	x	x	
Portugal	x	x	
Puerto Rico	x		
Quatar		x	x
Reunion	x		
Romania	x	x	
Rwanda		x	x
Ryukyu		x	
S. Africa	x	x	x
S. Rhodesia	x		

Country	1	2	3
S. Vietnam	x		
Sao Tome			x
Saudi Arabia	x	x	
Scotland	x	x	
Senegal		x	x
Servia	x		
Seychelles		x	x
Sierra Leone		x	x
Singapore		x	x
Somalia		x	
Spain	x	x	x
Sri Lanka		x	x
St. Chris.			x
St. Lucia			x
St. Pierre	x		
Sudan	x		
Suriname	x		
Swaziland	x		
Sweden	x	x	x
Switzerland	x	x	
Syria	x		
Taiwan		x	x
Tanzania		x	x
Thailand		x	x
Togo	x	x	
Tr. Tobago			x
Tunisia	x	x	x
Turkey	x	x	x
Uganda	x		
Ukrain. SSR	x		
Upper Volta	x		
Uruguay	x	x	
US Samoa	x		
USA	x	x	x
USSR	x	x	x
Vanuatu			x
Venezuela	x		
Vietnam		x	x
W. Samoa	x		
Yemen Rep.		x	x
Yugoslavia		x	x
Zaire	x		
Zambia	x		
Zanzi./Pem.	x		
Zimbabwe			x

References

Banks, A. (1975) *Cross-national time series data archive*. Binghamton: Center for Comparative Political Research, State University of New York. United Nations (1975). *Statistical yearbook*. New York: United Nations.

Bellah, R. N., Madsen, R., Sullivan, W., Swidler, A. and Tipton, S. (1985) *Habits of the heart*. Berkeley: University of California Press.

Bronfenbrenner, U. (1970) *The worlds of childhood: US and USSR*. New York: Russel Sage Foundation.

Cooley, C. H. (1983) *Human nature and the social order*. New Brunswick: Transaction Books.

Dewey, J. (1964) *On education*. Chicago: University of Chicago Press.

Dewey, J. (1975) *Moral principles in education*. Carbondale: Southern Illinois University Press.

Edelman, L. F. (1976) Basic American. *NOLPE School Law Journal*, **6**, 83–123.

Hamilton, G. and Sutton, J. (1987) *The problem of control in the weak state: Domination in the US, 1880–1920*. Davis: Department of Sociology, University of California.

Hartz, L. (1955) *Liberal political tradition in America*. New York: Harcourt, Brace.

Hughes, J. and Klemm, L. R. (1907) *Progress of education in the century*. Toronto: Linscott.

Kandel, I. L. (1933) *Comparative education*. New York: Houghton Mifflin.

Massialas, B. G. and Jarrar, S. A. (1983) *Education in the Arab World*. New York: Praeger.

Mead, G. H. (1934) *Mind, self and society*. Chicago: University of Chicago Press.

Meyer, J. W. (1980) The world polity and the authority of the nation-state. In Albert Bergesen (Ed.), *Studies of the modern world-system*. New York: Academic Press.

Sasnett, M. and Sepmeyer, I. (1966) *Educational systems of Africa*. Berkeley: University of California Press.

Sheikha al-Misnad. (1985) *The development of modern education in the Gulf*. London: Ithaca Press.

Suk-ying Wong (1987) The evolution and organization of the social studies curriculum: A comparative and longitudinal study, 1900–1980. Unpublished Ph.D. Dissertation. Stanford University.

Tocqueville, A. (1969) In Lawrence (Trans.), J. P. Mayer (Ed.), *Democracy in America*. New York: Doubleday, Anchor Books.

Tyack, D. and Thomas, J. (1987) Moral majorities and the school curriculum: Historical perspectives on the legalization of virtue. In D. Tyack, J. Thomas and A. Benovat (Eds.) *Law and the shaping of public schools, 1785–1954*. Madison: University of Wisconsin Press.

UNESCO (1958), *World survey of education*, Vol. II. Paris: UNESCO.

UNESCO–NIER (National Institute for Educational Research) (1970) *Asian Study of Curriculum*, Vols. I–III. Tokyo: NIER.

UNESCO Regional Office for Education in Asia (1966). *Curriculum, methods of teaching, evaluation and textbooks in primary schools in Asia*. Bangkok: UNESCO Regional Office for Education in Asia.

UNESCO Regional Office for Education in Asia and Pacific (1984). *Country Studies*. Bangkok: UNESCO Regional Office for Education in Asia and Pacific.

Weick, K. E. (1976) Educational organizations as loosely coupled systems. *Administrative Science Quarterly* **21**, 1–19.

PART 2

The West

CHAPTER 3

Values Education in the Western European Tradition

JUDITH TORNEY-PURTA AND CAROLE H. HAHN

There is a diverse set of values from which to choose in discussing the impact of education on students' values, ranging from civic values (such as support for the right to vote and practice of the duty to vote) to values connected with personal character. The values which relate the individual to social groups, in particular to the society and the civic community, are of special importance in the Western European tradition. In this chapter, the focus will be on five countries of Northern Europe which share this tradition: Denmark, the Federal Republic of Germany (FRG), the Netherlands, Sweden and the United Kingdom (UK). These countries have been selected because with their shared yet distinctive histories they offer an interesting mix of similarities and differences in regard to values education within this tradition.

Since the days of the Romans, the Saxons, the Vikings and the early Christians, similar yet distinctive cultures have evolved in these contiguous lands. Ideas growing out of the Protestant Reformation, the Renaissance, the Enlightenment and the Industrial Revolution contributed to the evolution of cultural values and institutions. Today one sees similar commitments in these countries to maintaining Parliamentary democracy, a Christian heritage together with respect for religious pluralism, and compulsory free public education for all children to the age of sixteen. With the exception of the FRG, these countries have had long-established rights of citizens to participate in government and to criticize policy. These countries confer

Although Judith Torney-Purta is listed as the senior author, both authors contributed equally to the chapter. The conceptualization and the model were the responsibility of Judith Torney-Purta; she also collected the data in Sweden in 1987 during a sabbatical leave from the University of Maryland with support from the Swedish National Board of Education. The observational and interview data in Denmark, the FRG, the Netherlands, and the UK were collected in the 1985–1987 by Carole Hahn, with financial support and released time from Emory University. The authors wish to thank Roy Williams and Roger Homans in the UK, Hans Hooghoff and Hans Dieteren in the Netherlands, Ingrid Dreyer and Jorgen Lerche Nielsen in Denmark, Dieter Grebe in the FRG, and Gunilla Svingby, Margot Blom and Tomas Englund in Sweden for reviewing parts of the manuscript. Any inaccuracies which remain are the responsibility of the authors.

31

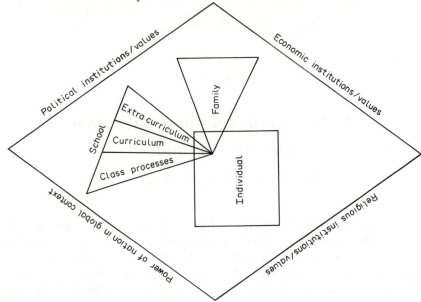

FIG. 3.1. Influences Upon Values Education

upon adults the freedom to make value decisions for themselves and upon parents the freedom to educate their children into their preferred value system. In the 1980s these societies struggle with economic, security and political issues including those which face liberal democracies everywhere. Moreover, they all face the challenge of preparing young people to live satisfying lives in an increasingly integrated global society; they seek to pass on values associated with both their shared cultural heritage and their unique national identities. In many of these countries there has recently been a resurgence of interest in the role of educational institutions in moral and values education. Further, in Northern Europe there are both within- and between-country variations which illustrate a set of categories for understanding values education, particularly factors of the political context. The conceptual model which follows is potentially useful in understanding values education in national settings outside Europe as well as in that region.

A Model Depicting Influences upon Values Education

The visualization of the categories of a model for understanding influences on values education is found in Fig. 3.1. The centre of the model is the individual young person, with special attention given to the role of the family and the school in values education. These three units are shown within a large national/cultural/community context which sets the bound- aries within which the school and family exert their influence. The purpose of these categories is to organize a discussion of influences upon the acquisition of social and civic values by young people and the role of individual characteristics, schools and families in that process. The purpose is not to draw a conclusion that one source of influence is more important than others, but to assess these factors as they interact with each other and to raise issues for discussion.

The particular situation with respect to values acquisition in five Northern European countries will be described using data collected during 1985–1987 in Denmark, the UK, the FRG and the Netherlands, and in 1987 in Sweden. In a concluding section the implications of these data and this model for values education processes will be explored.

The Four Dimensions of Context

There are a number of institutions that set the parameters for individuals' acquisition of values relating to social groups, society and the civic community. Four of these contextual parameters are domestic political institutions and their associated values, economic institutions and their associated values, religious institutions and their associated values and the international system. Although for the purpose of this discussion Figure 3.1 is drawn in a functionalist form, with the young person at the centre as the recipient of influence, it could also be "turned inside out" to depict the influence of individuals on schools, families or societal institutions or the conflict between those institutions. This chapter is not meant to argue that these institutions should set such parameters, only that in Northern European societies values education can be understood best by considering these parameters. In many respects these institutions are implicit rather than explicit in their influence upon the values education which takes place in schools and families and through other agents of socialization, such as the mass media.

This chapter focuses on the impact which families and schools have upon all individuals who spend a significant part of their childhood or adolescence in a given society. Little attention is paid to individual differences in values acquisition such as those mediated by gender, cognitive ability or level of moral development as defined in theoretical systems such as that of Kohlberg. Figure 3.1 does list some of these important individual factors.

Family

Central to all studies of the influence of parents on social or civic values are socio-economic status, educational level, ethnic or immigrant background and left or right political orientation (often linked with political party membership). These factors are important in the acquisition of many values which relate the individual to the society and social groups—e.g.

values relating to the role of worker in the economic system and to the role of citizen in the political system. Some of the influence of families is explicit and some implicit.

Conceptual models are most useful when they suggest how demographic factors, such as parental education, have an impact on young people. Are better-educated parents more likely to consider it important to transmit certain values to their children, rather than leaving values education to institutions outside the home, such as church or school? Are children in the homes of better-educated parents more likely to hear a diversity of points of view discussed or to find reading materials such as newspapers readily available? Are parents of higher educational or social status levels more likely to have the time and resources to take on active participant roles in the community or to discuss reasons for the moral decisions they make, thereby providing models for their children? These processes deserve further exploration but would require research which was as extensive cross-nationally in its study of parents as this research is of schools.

There is another important set of factors which is infrequently given attention in studies of civic or societal attitudes. That is the religious background and values of the family and their relation to values education. This is obvious when one studies countries such as the Netherlands where schooling is segregated on a religious basis. One might ask, for example, how much emphasis the family places on the child adopting values associated with religious beliefs without exploring alternatives?

School

The contribution of the school to values education is the main focus of the chapter. Three major aspects of the school will be considered. First, there is the content of the specified and taught curriculum, especially courses in social studies, history, civic education, language, religion and literature. The taught curriculum may differ for students in different tracks or streams. Second, there are in-class and in-school processes, including how much respect is shown for the opinions of students, how free they are to disagree with the teacher and the styles of presenting problems and asking questions used in classes. The influence of peers on each others' in-school behaviour is included here. Extracurricular activities form the third dimension—for example, out-of-school clubs, student government, charity drives. The diversity in these dimensions in five countries will be explored. Within each of these dimensions further questions are important, for example, what groups participate in the debate on curricular content; to what extent do individual students actually participate in available activities; how much and how is the school influenced by the family and other agencies of socialization?

Questions and Sources of Information

The purpose of the study was to examine the role of schooling in values acquisition in five Northern European countries. Four questions were addressed:

1. In what similar ways are schools teaching values in the five countries?
2. What are the major differences in approaches to values education among the five countries?
3. Is there renewed interest in values education and if so, what are the major reasons for it?
4. What policy and research issues might be addressed in regard to values education?

The material used to answer these questions represents the weaving together of three sources. One is quantitative empirical data, including the IEA Civic Education Survey (International Association for the Evaluation of Educational Achievement) in which large stratified random samples of fourteen-year-olds and students in the last year of secondary education were tested in 1971 in the following Northern European countries: Finland, the FRG, Ireland, the Netherlands and Sweden (see Torney *et al.*, 1975 for a description of the findings as a whole, and Torney-Purta and Schwille, 1986).

The second source of data is more qualitative and was collected more recently. Interviews with educators and classroom observations were conducted in 1985–1987 in the UK, Denmark, the Netherlands and the FRG by Carole Hahn, University professors and others in the four countries who had previously published articles and papers on political and social education were contacted. They were interviewed and asked to recommend other individuals who might provide further insights into understanding these issues in their national context. Further, all contacts were asked to recommend secondary schools and classroom teachers who would permit a visitor to observe classes in political and/or social education and other classes in which students might discuss value issues. Observations were made in nine secondary schools in England, eight in Denmark, seven in the Netherlands and four in the FRG. These schools were primarily in suburban areas or middle-sized towns. In addition surveys were administered to over 1000 students to measure civic attitudes and experiences. While the data from the surveys are not directly relevant to the topic of this chapter, they did provide insights into some issues addressed here. Data from these sources are reinforced by contemporary news articles and documents published by ministries of education.

The data reported here for Sweden were collected in 1987 by Judith Torney-Purta, who interviewed approximately twenty educators in the Stockholm, Uppsala, Malmo and Gothenberg areas. They included individuals employed by the National Board of Education and the Education Ministry as well as faculty members specializing in curriculum theory, civic education and religious education at universities and teacher training colleges and one group of teachers. One school visit was made to two classes of fourteen-year-olds.

Common Themes of Values Education

The countries of Western Europe, sharing as they do a common tradition, also share many themes of values education. Values are not taught in Northern Europe in a separate course labelled "moral education", as they are in some countries of Asia. Rather, values are transmitted as an implicit dimension of many subjects and by means of school ethos and what is sometimes called "the hidden curriculum". The subjects in which values are most clearly transmitted are religion, history, social studies or civic education, and literature. The arts courses and, to a lesser extent, foreign languages, geography, sciences and mathematics are also vehicles for values instruction.

Religious education is a part of the school curriculum in the five countries studied but it does not necessarily take up many hours of instruction. Traditionally, religious education in Northern Europe was expected to convey Judeo-Christian values, but as all of the countries have experienced an influx of other religious groups, the content of those courses has been re-examined. Still in many primary schools, lessons relate to Bible stories. Primary school teachers attempt to teach honesty and respect for authority, for law and for other individuals. Values are taught through precept and example; holidays such as Christmas and Easter are a focus for values education. Religious studies in secondary schools teach about specific religious beliefs (often in a comparison of different religions) and the application of ethical principles to societal issues. Much of the values education which takes place in these various courses assumes that the content of certain values can be taught, although many teachers also stress the process of considering life questions and making value choices or decisions.

Values teaching may be less obvious in language and history lessons, but it is perhaps more influential because of the amount of time given to those subjects. A substantial part of the primary school curriculum is devoted to learning national and cultural values through primary language instruction and history. British children spend many hours absorbing their national heritage and cultural values in history and English literature lessons. Similarly, German, Dutch, Swedish and Danish children come to internalize their national values through hearing the stories of their people in language, literature and history lessons. At the secondary school level those subjects continue to be given importance both in the timetable and, in countries with national examinations, on these exams.

Since World War II, a course similar to North American "social studies" has been added to the secondary curriculum in the five countries. While generally accepting the need for some social and civic education, policy-makers, educators and the public have not usually given this course the status of more traditional courses, such as history and geography. Social or political education is frequently one of the few non-examined courses (in systems with examinations) and it generally receives relatively little time in a student's timetable. But even given those limitations, social and political education has both explicit and implicit value dimensions which are influential for many students.

Other components of the formal curriculum also contribute to values education. Arts classes deal with aesthetic values, while mathematics and science courses teach positivistic values and the importance of the scientific enterprise. Those values are not, however, the focus of this book.

There is evidence that the content of the formal curriculum is only effective in instilling values if the classroom and school climate provide appropriate reinforcement of those values. That is, students learn as much or more from what they experience and from the models they see as from what is told to them. The IEA study of civic attitudes described previously concluded that when students regularly participate in classroom discussions in which they are encouraged to express their opinions, they are more politically knowledgeable, more politically interested and less authoritarian. On the other hand, students who receive most of their civics instruction by way of lectures and recitation and through patriotic rituals are less knowledgeable about politics and tend to be more authoritarian (Turney *et al.*, 1975). The amount of freedom secondary students have to develop and express their own opinions on civic and social issues is important. The role of school experience and classroom climate in the formation of values relating to personal morality is also illustrated by Kohlberg's research on ways of enhancing moral development using discussions with peers, especially work which deals with the context provided in the just community school (Kohlberg and Higgins, 1987).

In these five Northern European countries the liberal democratic tradition emphasizes that adult citizens be encouraged to inquire into issues; however, the extent to which that tradition is reflected in school practice varies. Interviews and observations indicated that some teachers lead more open discussions into controversial issues than do others, even in the same district using the same curriculum guidelines. Type of discussion also varies by subject taught, age of students, community expectations and how comfortable the individual teacher feels handling controversial issues. One is most likely to see open discussion of these issues in upper secondary social studies, religion or literature classes in communities where the values of constituents are more liberal. But the variables that may be most significant here are the individual teacher's commitment to promoting open-ended inquiry into issues on which controversy exists and the extent to which he or she believes that students are capable of actively constructing and reflecting on their own value systems.

In all five countries in our study, teachers were aware that some topics were especially sensitive in their communities; teachers would be especially careful about those issues, and some would choose not to bring those topics up in the classroom at all. Only in Denmark did the majority of teachers say that they were comfortable discussing all controversial issues with their students. In Sweden, the national syllabus which was in place until 1980 proclaimed that all issues should be dealt with scientifically, objectively and in a neutral fashion. Such structures tended to inhibit teachers dealing with controversial issues. Since these constraints were removed in the 1980 syllabus, most agree that teachers now feel that they have permission to hold such discussions. It is also the case that most do not believe that there is as much discussion of controversial issues in Sweden as there is in Denmark, however.

In our survey of secondary students in four countries (not including Sweden), those in the FRG were the most likely to agree with the statement "in our classes we often discuss controversial issues" while the students in England were most likely to disagree with that statement. However, it was the Dutch students who were the least likely to agree with statements such as these: "our teachers respect our opinions and encourage us to express them", "in this class, pupils are encouraged to make up their own minds about issues", "pupils feel free to disagree openly with their teachers" and "teachers try to get pupils to speak freely and openly in class". Students in the other three countries gave moderate support to those statements, suggesting that students perceive classrooms to be less conducive to open discussion of controversial issues than teachers believe them to be or than many educators in these four liberal democracies recommend.

Another informal means by which values are transmitted in schools is through the guidance system. Teachers, particularly at the primary school level, are expected to be concerned about students' welfare, and counsellors are assigned to secondary students to be available to help with personal problems as well as educational and career counselling. In Denmark the pupil has the same class teacher from the first to the ninth grade. This helps class teachers to know the child and his or her family so that guidance and support can be given. In Sweden pupils have the same teacher for three years in a given subject (such as social sciences), and a system of continuity of teachers similar to that in Denmark is being debated. In the UK, the "pastoral system" is especially strong as form teachers work closely with pupils to deal with real-life dilemmas related to personal values.

Informal processes and norms, sometimes called the hidden curriculum, are another means by which values are transmitted. This is particularly true of values related to gender equity. Secondary school authorities and ministers of education are predominantly males. Observations of classroom interaction reveal that female students are less verbally assertive and less likely to take risks than males except in the FRG. In the UK there have been some curricular units developed to raise the issue of gender equity. In Denmark there is widespread acceptance of women in non-traditional careers but even there young women report that inequities continue to exist. Traditional expectations for women in occupations and in politics are reinforced by school patterns in all five countries. These observations corroborate the IEA data gathered in 1971. That research indicated that differences between male and female adolescents' political attitudes were of substantially the same magnitude regardless of the general level of tolerance for women's rights or number of women in positions of political power in the country (Torney-Purta, 1984). For example, in Sweden, which is well known for its gender equality, recent studies still show males at the secondary school level out-performing females on tests measuring knowledge of politics and economics (Lindquist *et al.*, 1987).

In addition to formal subjects and informal processes of classroom and school climate, extracurricular activities are an important part of citizenship education in these five Northern European democracies. Schools have student councils, but teachers and students almost without exception say that the councils are restricted to planning social events and charity drives, or to tackling problems such as litter on school grounds. In Germany some student groups have recently organized demonstrations opposing change toward more conservative policies proposed by ministries of education, but such student activism has become relatively rare. In most secondary schools there are also student clubs, which could be seen as parallel to adult interest groups except that they usually do not have clearly developed interests in the political sense and do not try to influence school decision-making except on a narrow band of issues. Charity drives for animal and environmental protection and to alleviate world hunger teach values of altruism and citizen action. Although only a small percentage of students belong to youth political clubs, such as Young Conservatives or the Social Democrats, those organizations teach values and skills associated with political activism to those students who are involved. Many more students are taught values of cooperation, leadership and working for the good of the whole through team sports.

The avenues by which values are taught are thus quite similar across these five nations. The particular core values that are taught are also similar—the work ethic, values rooted in Judeo-Christian religious teachings, democratic values of citizen participation and some blend of individualism and concern for the common good. In the IEA study the structure of attitudes was almost identical in all the countries tested, even though students from different countries differed on the actual level of support for these attitudes. There have been some attempts within Europe to arrive at what might be called a short-list of common core values on which educators and the public can agree and which includes such things as honesty, support for the rule of law and respect for others.[1] Of all of these five countries, Sweden appears to have gone the farthest to explore the explicit identification of a list of agreed-upon core values.

Many dimensions of influence outlined in the model are also similar across these countries. Recent pressures to improve values education seem to have similar roots as well, suggesting that a concern for values may be a part of the global scene which transcends national boundaries. There are also, however, important national distinctions which remind us that education cannot be understood apart from the national political, economic and cultural context which has substantial differences across countries.

Differences in Approaches to Values Education

Some differences between these countries are visible and explicit, others more hidden and implicit. For example, British classes are visibly different from those in the other three countries in that students wear school colours and in some cases school uniforms. British children appear to be most respectful of authority. In many schools pupils approach teachers with "Miss . . ." or "Sir . . ." and then wait to continue speaking until they are encouraged to do so. Secondary students spend more time writing than speaking in classes—in contrast to students in the other four countries.

The UK has traditionally had a decentralized system of education, with each local education authority (LEA), and sometimes each school, determining its curriculum. That is why one school may require social and vocational education, while another teaches general studies, and a third has no course in political or social education. While religious instruction and a daily religious assembly were mandated by the Education Act of 1944, their content has been left up to the LEA. In reality, despite the tradition of autonomy there has been much similarity in the content of the curriculum across schools because of the influence of the national examinations which most students take at age sixteen, and for the 30 per cent who stay in school beyond that, at A (advanced) levels. The new General Secondary Certificate of Education examination system may bring about further uniformity in a theoretically autonomous system. It proposes a national core curriculum which, if implemented, is most likely to reduce diversity across

[1] See regularly issued publications of the Council for Cultural Cooperation of the Council of Europe dealing with preparation for life in democratic society and education against intolerance, as well as discussion in Torney-Purta and Schwille (1986). For general information about these educational systems see Elvin (1981).

LEAs. It is estimated that 90 per cent of a school's timetable will be determined by the core curriculum objectives and assessment.

Seven per cent of the students in the UK attend independent schools called "public schools". Privately run, and privately financed, public schools give a high priority to values education. Many have mandatory chapel as well as religion courses. Much emphasis is put on sports. Traditionally, many political and business leaders have come out of public schools where presumably they learned values of public service and entrepreneurship as well as leadership skills. British public schools set a model that, some believe, state schools should emulate with regard to the teaching of manners and values.

The FRG is a federated system in which the responsibility for education rests with the Ministries of Education for each of the eleven Länder. For example, history or religion in all schools in Nordhein–Westfalen follows the curriculum guidelines for that Land but it is different from that in Bayern or Hessen, which have their own guidelines. The political context or climate in each Land seems to influence the handling of value issues. For example, in the 1970s and early 1980s there appeared to be more discussion of controversial issues in classrooms in Hessen than in traditionally conservative-dominated Lander. But when the centre-right coalition came to power in Hessen in 1987, they began moving away from the philosophy and organizational patterns of comprehensive schooling popular under the Social Democrats. It is possible that a shift in attitudes about controversial issue discussion in schools will follow.

In the Netherlands the various tiers of government—the state, the provinces and the municipalities—have different responsibilities toward education. There is a considerable amount of national legislation on education, including Acts of Parliament and decrees implementing them. The principal pieces of legislation—the Primary Education Act and the Secondary Education Act—include regulations on standards for curriculum and examinations. The authorities for secondary education are the Minister of Education for state schools, the municipal executive for local authority schools, and the school board in Catholic, Protestant or non-denominational private schools. Such a diversity in authority could result in different approaches to values education but those differences are not as great as one might expect. For example, teachers in all three types of school can be observed leading discussions of controversial value issues. Some self-selection takes place so that teachers who would be uncomfortable with the emphasis in a Protestant or a Catholic school are not likely to apply to teach there.

Teaching the work ethic is an important part of values education in many Dutch schools. Those students not enrolled in a school which prepares them for university entrance (a *gymnasia athenea* or *lycea*) are likely to be taking some vocational instruction. Students in the general secondary schools (*havos*, *mavos* or *lavos*) usually take vocational courses as well as general education subjects. Other post-primary students are enrolled in vocational schools or apprenticeship training. A significant part of many secondary school students' days, and a substantial part of the nation's education budget, is spent on preparation for work.

Since 1968, all Dutch schools teach *maatschaapijleer* (similar to social studies), which is a non-examined subject, in addition to separate courses in history and geography which are examined. *Maatschaapijleer* has six thematic fields—education, home and environment, work and leisure, state and society, technology and society, and international relations. Proposals were made in early 1987 by more conservative members of the parliament to set minimum hours for basic courses for the first three years of secondary school but no minima were included for *maatschaapijleer*.

Denmark has a centralized system of education. The Ministry of Education publishes broad curricular guidelines which are non-binding for primary schools, but detailed and obligatory for secondary schools. Among the five nations studied, Denmark appears to put the greatest stress on individualism, but feeling for the class as a group is strong. Unique to Denmark is the fact that children stay together with the same group of pupils and the same class teacher for the first nine years of school. Danish history, geography, Christian studies (based on principles of the Danish Lutheran Church) and the Danish language are taught throughout the grades. By grade 7, contemporary studies is added. It is an issue-centred subject, with student input into the selection of topics to be studied. Examples of issues which were selected for study in grade 9 in 1987 were video violence and youth culture. In upper secondary schools studies of East–West relations and economic development in the Third World are often topics of study.

The discussion of controversial value issues in Danish schools is a generally accepted practice and takes place in many subjects. The principle aim of the *Folkeskole* (grades 1–9 or 10) as stated in the Education Act of 1975 is "to give pupils the opportunity to acquire knowledge, skills and working methods and ways of expressing themselves . . . to create opportunities for experience and self expression which allow pupils to . . . develop their ability to make independent assessments and evaluations and to form opinions" (Danish Ministry of Education, 1983). One period each week is scheduled for *klassens-time* or the class meeting where pupils discuss problems in the class, issues facing the student council and plans for class parties or the annual trip. Encouraging students to express their opinions in open classroom discussions goes beyond a single subject such as contemporary studies.

Student councils and class governments seem to have considerable power in Denmark. Danish school law says that a purpose of schools is to teach democracy through practice in decision-making and responsibility. In addition to having active student councils and teacher involvement in school decision-making, Danish students and teachers also elect representatives to the School Council, on which the headteacher and parent representatives sit as members. This contrasts with the other countries in which the headmaster (and in rare cases the headmistress) in the UK, or the director in the FRG, retain most of the decision-making power. Authority structures are reinforced in other ways. Danish students call their teachers by their first names while in the other countries teachers and administrators are addressed formally.

Sweden has a centralized system of education in which the National Board of Education, after extensive consultation with educational, political and community groups writes curriculum goals and guidelines and a syllabus for each subject area to fulfil the general curriculum goals which have been debated and passed by the Parliament. These documents are sent to schools along with material providing advice on implementation. A new curriculum for the comprehensive school was passed in 1980.

The curriculum in Sweden prescribes that at all grades a formal weekly meeting of the class council should be held (including all class members with a designated chair, secretary and parliamentarian and written minutes). This is seen as preparation for the practice of democratic group process, and may be particularly significant in Sweden because of the tendency for group consultation on issues to be highly valued in society as a whole. The class councils in the early grades, when children are seven to ten years of age, are especially valuable as a way for a teacher to build a group spirit. These councils deal with issues ranging from raising money to plant trees in Ethiopia to disregard of school rules. In the early grades the class will frequently be split in half to discuss in a group of twelve to fifteen the moral issues raised in selections from literature read aloud to the class.

The major explicit attention to values is found in the social studies syllabus, and especially in a course in civic education, one of the orientation subjects taught one to three hours weekly during grades 7–9. There is some flexibility in curriculum implementation at the school level, since each school prepares locally based timetables which concretize the requirements in the syllabus and may also emphasize certain topics. Although there are no national examinations and only a small number of school inspectors, there is a tradition of adherence to the centrally prescribed curriculum in Sweden.

The 1980 curriculum explicitly states a number of values which the school is obliged to teach. For example, "instruction must help to inculcate in pupils an understanding for other people and their conditions as a foundation for a desire for equality and solidarity". The themes of equality and solidarity are important aspects of the organization of schools as well as for the explicit teaching of values. Some parts of the curriculum deal with study about religion, which is prescribed at every level of schooling. In general, Lutheran beliefs regarding the nature of the human being and of society are the source historically for much of what is now taught in the social sciences. Curriculum plans since 1919 have moved steadily away from instruction in Lutheranism and the catechism to instruction about religion. In religious education, the 1980 curriculum notes: "schools are to help pupils to contemplate questions concerning life and its meaning . . . and [give] a wider knowledge of the Christian religion" (National Swedish Board of Education, 1980a, pp. 7 and 9).

Considerable debate surrounded the passage of the 1980 curriculum, especially the continuing change from instruction in religion to instruction about religion (a course with emphasis on comparative religions and existential questions). Another major change in 1980 was the prescription of explicit attention to teaching about conflict and controversy as a preparation for citizenship in democracy. The 1969 curriculum had so clearly stressed the objectivity and neutrality of "scientifically based" teaching in the social sciences, that most teachers avoided discussion of controversial issues entirely. In contrast, the 1980 curriculum noted:

> Neutrality and empiricism demand that society should not be portrayed as harmonious and free from conflicts. Instead, it is important that children be made to realize the connection between human, social and national conflicts and, on the other hand, aggression, violence, and war. Schools must make their pupils realize that different people live in different economic, social, and cultural conditions and that this can give rise to antipathies between different groups. The discussion of conflicts and their resolution . . . applies to the teaching of all subjects, to class committee meetings, and to other contexts involving discussion of human relationships (National Swedish Board of Education, 1980b, p. 25).

As a result of the inclusion of statements like this in the curriculum, most teachers seem to feel that they have permission to discuss controversial issues, although there remains a great deal of concern about balanced presentation. However, many teachers, especially those trained to teach in the academic or "theoretical" subjects for grades 7–9, are paying only a little more attention to controversial issues and discussions of conflict than they were before 1980. The inculcation of a sense of community within which conflict is mediated and moderated is still of great importance.[2]

Although the curriculum notes that "printed teaching materials must be engagingly written and must invite a critical debate", the textbook series used in the large majority of Swedish schools is not especially effective in doing that. The books place primary emphasis in their reading selections on descriptive material, while the questions at the end of selections ask for recall of information from the text and not for discussion of contemporary problems.

At the upper secondary school a new curriculum has been under development and debate since 1981. Its stress is upon helping the pupils build upon their current knowledge and interest by discussing societal questions or issues in order to stimulate the search for and analysis of factual information

[2] For a discussion of contemporary and historical Swedish trends in civic education and the role of conflict perspectives see England (1986).

from different sources, the consideration of values held by different groups, and action.

The particular programmes in these five countries are illustrative of the several channels through which schools influence student values, the way in which school practices reflect decisions about schooling more generally, and the continuing impact of the political, economic and religious context both explicitly and implicitly. Clearly, while there are important similarities in values education, there are also unique features in each country which help to explain why a renewed interest in values education takes a slightly different form in each country.

Renewed Interest in Values Education

In the 1980s there has been a renewed interest in values education in the UK, the FRG, the Netherlands and Denmark, and to some extent in Sweden. Some of the groups expressing this interest feel that too much laxity in the schools followed the student movements of the 1960s. The desire is expressed to return to an emphasis on knowledge of the national language, history and mathematics. The fact that these countries continue to experience large migrations of families from cultures outside of Northern Europe focuses attention on differences in traditional religious, political and economic values. Elections of conservative politicians have reflected concern in the public mind about the need to return to traditional values associated with the more homogeneous cultures which existed in the past. These more conservative politicians have then placed into positions of educational leadership individuals who give high priority to these values.

In the UK the reawakening interest in values education received impetus from the mid-1970s through a number of Department of Education and Science (DES) publications which reviewed and reappraised the school curriculum. Values education was embedded in the Great Debate on Education launched by Prime Minister Callaghan in 1976 and continued under Prime Minister Thatcher. Concerns were expressed about education's role *vis-à-vis* the UK's place in Europe and the world, as well as the pervasive impact on the mass media on cultural identity and heritage (Department of Education and Science, 1977, 1979, 1980a, 1980b, 1981; Her Majesty's Inspectorate, 1977).

In the early years of the debate politicians were calling for more political education, but in recent years they have been calling for less. The political education movement of the 1970s grew out of a concern for the lack of political awareness of school-leavers. It emphasized the need to develop "political literacy", which was defined as a knowledge of politics in everyday life, understanding of political concepts such as power, liberty and authority, and support for procedural democratic values such as freedom, tolerance, fairness and respect for truth and evidencial reasoning. Advocates of political education in the 1970s argued that the traditional courses in history were not effective in developing sufficient political knowledge in the masses of youth, noting that a course in the British constitution was taken by only a very few academic students (Heater, 1969; Stradling, 1975; Crick and Lister, 1978; Crick and Porter, 1978). In the 1970s politicians from both major political parties joined educational leaders in supporting the work of the Politics Association to promote political literacy. Her Majesty's Inspectorate gave official backing to the movement in 1977 by recommending "political competence" as a curricular goal in its publication *Curriculum 11–16*. By 1980 interest in political education had peaked. In a national survey, most schools reported that they taught units in political and social issues in the general (non-examined) courses titled general studies, social studies, social education or social and vocational education (Stradling and Noctor, 1986).

In the 1980s the interest of social educators in the UK shifted to promoting world studies, education about developing countries, multicultural and anti-racist education, peace education, environmental education and human rights education. All have explicit curricular objectives regarding values (Lister, 1986). Peace education has been attacked by the New Right in Britain, who refer to it as "appeasement education" (noted by Heater, 1986).

British Conservatives have been calling for a return to "Victorian values", such as an emphasis on the family linked with a strict moral code for behaviour, patriotism, humble pride, tradition, the Protestant work ethic, self-help, thrift and Christian virtues. There is also much concern with stimulating the economy with hard work and a spirit of enterprise. In a period when the Department of Education and Science budgets have been drastically cut, Government money remains available to schools through the Department of Employment for manpower training and technical and vocational education. A major purpose of the vocational programmes is to instil in youth values such as punctuality, discipline, pride in doing a job well and hard work.

Values education is also being debated in Britain with regard to religious education (RE) in a multicultural society. Most RE still takes the form of biblical stories in primary classes, assemblies based on a reading of the Scriptures, and in secondary schools the presentation of Christian positions on social issues. However, some RE teachers, particularly those in areas with many immigrant pupils, have shifted the emphasis of their courses from confessional Anglican Church instruction to a comparative religion approach. But their efforts are subject to attack, sometimes as too little and sometimes as too much. Some Muslim and Jewish parents feel that multi-faith RE is inadequate and they are requesting separate schools for their children. On the other hand, some critics call for the schools to reassert the Anglican Christian heritage of British society. Thus, religious as well as economic and political value conflicts are being played out in the debate over the schools' curriculum. The differing views are likely to become more visible if the national curriculum, proposed in 1987, is given to schools to implement in diverse communities.

Similar arguments over values education are heard in the Netherlands but within the unique Dutch context of "pillarization". Pillarization is the tradition which recognizes the religious pluralism of Dutch society as the basis for the organization of education. There are separate state-supported Protestant, Catholic and non-denominational schools, with their associated school boards, teachers' unions, teacher training institutes and curriculum development centres. As a result, Catholic values can be taught throughout the formal and informal curriculum of Catholic schools and Protestant values can be taught in Protestant schools. In practice, educators report that there is often little difference in the approaches to teaching values because of the secular nature of contemporary society (Ministry of Education and Science, 1986; Hooghoff, 1987). This pillarization of education may have alleviated some potential for tension over values education in the Netherlands, but clearly it has not eliminated concern. There is discussion over whether Judaism should be considered a new pillar with its own set of state-supported schools.

Furthermore, some Catholic and Protestant politicians in the Netherlands have been calling for a reassertion of denominational values as a way to attack societal problems of criminality, drug abuse, suicide and violence. Parents express a concern about declines in respect and politeness in children. There seems also to be renewed professional interest in values education. The Catholic Innovations Centre (FPC) has developed a new curriculum in values education which deals with the themes of the future, labour and sex. Specifically this programme adopts the theory of van der Ven at the University of Nimegen (Catholic) on "communication of values", which seeks a dialogue on values. This theoretical approach to values education is less individualistic than the work of Raths and others writing on "values clarification", however.

In the Netherlands, as with the other nations in our study, there are concerns among the public about values education as it relates to immigrants and refugees, to teaching the "basics" of national language and history and to political ideology. In some parts of Amsterdam and Rotterdam, 70 per cent of the population is not Dutch. New conservative political parties are reacting to increased immigration by calling for more attention to the national heritage in the school curriculum. Politicians and parents are reacting against the process view of education which was popular in the 1960s and 1970s. They want a return to an emphasis upon teaching the facts of history and geography, and basic subjects such as language and mathematics. There is another issue, similar to concerns in the UK; the anti-racist movement and related efforts are perceived by some Dutch conservatives as leftist. However, educators report that students of today are less concerned about joining social movements and are more concerned about getting jobs.

The political and public debate however does not tell the full story. While conservative views are heard outside of educational circles, more liberal statements are heard in professional discussions. For example, there has been considerable curriculum development and implementation in environmental education, intercultural education and the European dimension of studies.

In the Federal Republic of Germany, the political successes of conservative political parties have also coincided with increased interest in teaching traditional values. Here, as in the other countries, some groups have been disturbed by the permissiveness and shift to process education in the 1960s and 1970s. There are cries to return to an emphasis on the basics of German, mathematics and the facts of history and geography. Some want Latin restored to an important place in the curriculum. Some German educators in the 1980s incorporated world studies and peace and development education into their instruction, but have been met with increasing criticism. In Hessen, the topical contemporary problems course for 16–19-year-olds has been replaced by a course in chronological history. The influence which the leftist critical theorists had on some parts of the German social studies curriculum in the 1970s had, for the most part, disappeared by 1987.

In the FRG, as in the other four countries, there is concern about unemployment and immigrants. New programmes have been developed for vocational preparation. The Turkish "guest workers" who were brought in to meet labour shortages in the 1950s did not leave when unemployment rose in the 1980s. The children of these workers have been integrated into German society more successfully in some regions than in others. As increasing numbers of refugees enter the country through Berlin and the German Democratic Republic, anxieties grow.

The influence of the Green Party among young people and the protests against nuclear missiles have created further concern in some quarters about the values held by German youth, values acquired primarily from the youth culture or mass media rather than from schools and families. Yet at the same time, the numbers of German students selecting religious studies as an option in some upper secondary schools is greater than ever before.

Denmark also has experienced a resurgence of interest in values education in the 1980s which coincided with the coming to power of a conservative coalition in government. The Ministry of Education called for a return to the strengths of the past and those values related to "Danish pride". Recent school laws before Parliament emphasize a return to the "basics". Teachers report a re-emphasis on Danish language and history instruction in schools. They note that many parents and teachers have come to question the unstructured emphasis of the 1960s. Recently, pedagogical authorities in Denmark have been emphasizing that children need more structure. However, it is unlikely that there will be a substantial diminution in the emphasis on student participation in school decision-making or in the open discussion of controversial issues which characterizes the Danish classroom (Danish Ministry of Education, 1983).

In Sweden, after thirty years of uninterrupted rule by the Social Democrats, a coalition of more conservative parties came to power in 1976 and remained in power until 1982. There were no immediate calls for enhanced attention to value issues, especially since the Swedish tradition of consultation with all interested parties is a vitally important but time-consuming one. During the late 1970s concerns were expressed about school drop-outs and apathy, student fighting (mobbing) and vandalism, and the lessened emphasis on grading student performance in school. Some argued that the school reforms of the 1960s had gone too far. In 1978 a Study Group on the Formation and Transmission of Moral Standards in Schools was established and assigned the task by the Minister of Schools to prepare a report on how schools "transmit the fundamental standards of human relations which may be described as a . . . least common denominator of all upbringing" (Study Group on the Formation and Transmission of Moral Standards in School, 1979, p. 5). Representatives from organizations of parents, pupils, teachers, school administrators and the National Board of Education were appointed. The group defined its goals as fostering debate on the responsibility of adults for the upbringing of young people and explicitly denied that they wished to draw up moral rules on behalf of the state.

Papers were commissioned from experts, and a fifty-three-page booklet was published in 1979 under the title *Skolan Skall Fostra: En Debattskrift* (literally translated "Schools Shall Foster (or Upbring): A Book for Debate". The English translation bears the title *Schools and Upbringing*). The booklet is attractively presented and includes professionally prepared cartoons as illustrations. It was widely distributed in Sweden and discussed not only by parents and teachers but also by school personnel such as janitors and food-servers.

In this book a core list of values is endorsed as necessary in democracy: tolerance, equality of rights, respect for truth, justice and human dignity. The school must take responsibility for inculcating these values to justify its existence and ensure the survival of society:

> There are many important points concerning which we have consensus of values in this country. There are certain things which we can say are right and proper without infringing anybody's liberties . . . common to all party political codes and to all religious creeds and philosophies. It is the common duty of adults at home and in school to explain and demonstrate these values to young persons . . . Schools must endeavour to give pupils a moral capacity for perceiving and understanding other people and the determination to act with other people's best interests in mind . . . Schools must give their pupils upbringing (Study Group on the Formation and Transmission of Moral Standards in School, 1979, p. 10).

The report makes clear that although each student should be free to explore a plurality of values, relativism (the idea that all values are of equal worth) is not acceptable.

Some of the examples cited in the report relate specifically to immigrants, both their own problems in adjustment and problems that their divergent cultural traditions present to Swedish society.

> Some immigrants may have values . . . which are incompatible with one of the most funda-
> mental of our values, e.g. the equality of men and women. In this case, instruction must be
> dominated by our own view, even if this conflicts with the opinion of a certain pupil and his
> family (Study Group on the Formation and Transmission of Moral Standards, 1979, p. 10).

The report also argues that the schools "cannot accept" degrading views of immigrants on the part of pupils from Swedish families.

In order to further stimulate the incorporation of these ideas in the class-room, a series of workbooks was published by the Ministry of Education in 1980. Nearly ten years after the issuing of the report, few teachers remember the workbooks but some do recall the debate of these issues which took place in their schools. Other educators, however, speak with some disdain about what they believe was the authoritarian character of *Schools and Upbringing*, or believe that the report should be seen as a document respon-sive to a particular political context without much long-term effect.

Some of the ideas in the 1980 national curriculum in the section called Education and Development do resemble those presented in the report:

> Schools must provide upbringing . . . and develop within their pupils such values as are
> capable of sustaining and strengthening the democratic principles of tolerance, partnership,
> and equal rights . . . Schools must therefore work to promote the equality of men and
> women . . . Schools must endeavour to lay the foundations of solidarity with disadvantaged
> groups in this country and abroad . . . and a will to act in the best interests of other people
> as well as oneself . . . We are concerned here with the whole spirit characterizing a school,
> the expectations and demands of adults and their words and actions as examples (National
> Swedish Board of Education, 1980b, p. 10).

This comprehensive school curriculum was passed with the unanimous sup-port of all political parties and has an interesting blend of what might be thought of as liberal statements (such as those cited in an earlier section concerning the presentation of a conflict perspective on social issues) and somewhat more conservative ideas about an agreed-upon set of values which the school should inculcate. The incorporation of these diverse elements into a consensus is a hallmark of Swedish educational policy in general.

In summary, although most Swedish educators do not believe there was much renewed interest in values education from 1982 to 1987 (when such a resurgence of interest was taking place in some of the other countries stud-ied), there is a tradition of the school's involvement in promoting a common core list of values of democracy and solidarity which seemed to intensify somewhat during the conservative coalition government (1976–1982). Sweden's experience illustrates, however, that educational change is slow in the area of values education and that alterations in the political climate often have a relatively subtle rather than direct or immediate influence.

With respect to immigration and its influence upon schooling in the countries studied, some would argue that the schools had only begun to address the needs of immigrants when a counter movement set in. Some organizations which operate across national boundaries such as the Council of Europe, continue to emphasize the need to respect diverse subcultures and to plan educational programmes which are sensitive to the needs of immigrant children. Through publications and seminars interested educators receive substantial assistance. But it is doubtful that their message reaches the majority of teachers, who react primarily to pressure by communities to reinforce local values.[3] At the same time external global economic factors are causing many citizens in these five countries to worry about unemployment and competition for jobs from immigrants. The speed of change and increased pluralism in society has created insecurities so that many people seek a return to cohesion around accepted core values. Worldwide economic competition and shifts in the distribution of power and wealth on a global scale have further exacerbated insecurities. The target of criticism reflecting those insecurities and perceived threats has often been the schools and in particular their role in instilling values in the young.

These societies all place considerable importance on the next generation's support for the political, economic and religious values represented by existing systems and traditions. The school is seen as serving an essential system-maintenance function in maintaining the social values on which the system depends but as needing to conduct this role in a way which differs in some important aspects from the past.

Conclusions

Neither the discussion of the model, which makes distinctions between context, schools and families, nor the descriptions of similarities and differences fully convey the depth of interest in the values of the next generation existing in these five Northern European countries. The values which children adopt are of deep personal concern to parents, although most express considerable uncertainty about the specific values which will be adaptive for their children to hold as adults and about the best way to go about inculcating those values. To the extent that the model is a dynamic one, much of the energy or motive force comes from the investment and concern of parents. Most parents are aware of areas in which their children's values correspond relatively closely to their own, and others where the gap is large. Few parents in Northern Europe place much emphasis on their societal obligation to rear children with a basic set of social values, nor are parents

---

[3] For a discussion on the role of local values see the work of G. and L. Spindler, especially *Burgbach* (1974) and chapters in *Doing the Ethnography of Schooling* (1982).

much concerned with the contribution which the values education they give makes to the survival or health of society. Failures or gaps in values education which takes place at home are thought of primarily as an individual or family concern.

When policy-makers or educators discuss young people's values, however, their concerns focus more on the interests of society. The long-term impact of values education is difficult to measure. Statistics about increases in drug use or crime, or decreases in voting are often discussed. But the interpretations of these statistics are seldom unequivocal and often bear the imprint of a conservative or liberal ideology. Is there inadequate funding for family support and education by federal or state governments, or has society become too dependent on government funds? Should the blame be laid on mothers who work outside the home and devote less attention to children, or does the fault lie with a failure to fund exemplary schools or day-care centres where appropriate models of values are available?

The context-setting political institutions which were most visible in our review of Northern Europe and around which polarization most often took place were the political parties. Many of the arguments about education and its value component in countries such as the UK, for example, are mobilized through the political parties. It was during the government of a coalition of relatively conservative parties in Sweden that the debate on values education intensified. However, the extent to which an actual swing in the public mood is experienced may depend in part on whether there are two major parties which take well-defined positions or whether coalition governments are common.

In all the countries in the study, great concern was expressed about keeping partisan political discussion out of the classroom. But interpretations of values education issues both inside and outside the classroom were very frequently coloured by ideological factors. The polarization and vigour of these arguments in some countries appear to be partially the result of the time lag that exists between questions raised about young people's values, implementation of revisions in curriculum or educational practice, and evidence of change. It seems that no sooner have a majority of schools completed the curriculum preparation or training necessary to institute a new programme than questions are raised about whether schools should be concerned with student values. Weiler (1983) has argued that often experimental programmes are used to defuse arguments about the legitimacy of political education.

Economic values and institutions form a vital underlying context. The recent shift in the UK away from socialism and toward private enterprise has influenced education considerably. The degree of unionization of the work-force in general and of professional educators in particular is important, as Sweden demonstrates. Work-related values are of similar interest in countries with more and less mixed market economics. Parents and educators alike have a high level of investment in seeing young people find productive and satisfying work, which becomes of greater concern during periods of high unemployment.

A third important dimension of the context for values education depicted in the model was the power and image of the country in the world. None of these countries was actually nation-building, but all were grappling in their curricula with issues such as their nation's image and status in the world and how to transmit pride in their nation's cultural heritage. National patriotism receives relatively little explicit stress in school, perhaps because many educators see a thin line between patriotism and national chauvinism. In each country, however, there is a wish to transmit to young people a sense of pride in the country's image abroad; for example, Sweden and Denmark should be seen as presenting a model to developing countries of the "middle way" which characterizes Scandinavian politics and society.

The issue of national identity has been brought into focus in these countries by the recent influx of immigrants who have neither knowledge of the cultural heritage nor a sense of national identity. This concern has been associated with assertions about the need to transmit the nation's values to new immigrants. However, there is continuing ambivalence about whether Turkish children should actually be encouraged to think of themselves as German or whether young people from Muslim Pakistani families can fully take on a British identity, for example.

Religious institutions in these countries are a major source of the basis of values education. Religious education which takes place in schools is not usually related to a creed, and rote memorization of sacred texts is rare. Increased religious pluralism in society has in many cases reduced the correspondence of home and school values and increased concern about religious education. In some countries quite successful programmes of in-school religious education were developed within the context of a religiously homogeneous society. Particularly when these programmes have responded to recent increases in religious pluralism by developing mechanisms to respect others' rights of belief, acute polarization around religious education seems to have been avoided. In fact in some countries, the existence of religious education in the curriculum seems to impart a sense of control and assurance that the basic values necessary to human society are being transmitted.

In summary, the four contextual dimensions may be thought of as representing boundaries, more tightly drawn and constraining in some countries or at some times than in other countries or at other times. The implicit and explicit impact of these four contextual dimensions is of great importance to understanding values education in both families and schools.

Family

This was not an in-depth study of families, yet all five countries showed a strong investment by this primary group in the values acquired by children in and out of school. The research base concerning families and values in Western Europe is modest (see, for example, Jennings *et al.*, 1979). However, family power over schooling related to values is beginning to be of considerable interest in Western Europe as it has been in the United States. In Germany parent representatives serve on the school council, but their participation is curtailed by elaborate regulations and they do not perceive that they have much power. In Denmark, school councils have been retitled parents' councils. Only parents are voting members; student and teacher representatives have no vote. Recent proposals in the UK suggest that parents will be given more control over schooling by permitting schools to opt out of the local education authority upon a majority vote of parents of children in that school. It is not yet clear how many will take advantage of this or what the impact will be. In none of these countries do there appear to be many organized groups pressuring schools to teach—or not teach—particular values.

The role that second generation immigrant parents will play in the values education process in Northern Europe is not clear either. The demands on the schools from parents who have advanced educationally, economically and politically may differ in many ways from those of the previous generation.

Schools

Although the model does not make it explicit, countries in which there is a centralized curriculum which makes reference to specific values present a quite different situation from countries where value issues are dealt with on a decentralized basis. In both centralized and decentralized nations, however, the courses offered and their prescribed content or time in the schedule are explicit and relatively easy to change when compared with the difficulty of altering implicit assumptions which govern student–teacher interaction or increasing the frequency of open discussion about controversial issues or ethical dilemmas.

Northern European schools will continue to provide some form of values education for all students, taking it less for granted than was the case fifteen years ago but not making it as much a focus of attention as it has become in certain other countries. It is unlikely, for example, that specific moral education courses or examinations will be instituted.

Ideology will continue to have an important influence on education, as there will continue to be some polarization between liberal and conservative approaches to schooling and shifts in which is dominant, especially in countries where political coalition building is not common. There will continue to be vigilance about the expression of partisan political views. The inertia of schools will continue to guard against rapid changes in values education, however. In some countries these ideological factors will provide special difficulties in the preparation of teachers.

Some educational policy-makers are looking abroad for models of success in the inculcation of values through school programmes. They will tend to pay little attention to constraints of the political, economic or religious context. In contrast, others who feel greatly constrained by the context will claim there is little to be learned about promising educational practice from other countries. Some balance of these positions is probably the wisest.

Research questions relating to policy which deserve further attention abound. These include the following:

(1) Is heightened concern about instilling dominant cultural values the inevitable result of societies experiencing large migrations of families creating a pluralistic value situation in the society and the school? How does the flexibility of schools in absorbing new ideas or groups influence this process? To what extent is this primarily a local concern and to what extent a national one?

(2) Do democratic societies regularly swing from concern for instilling traditional values to greater permissiveness (and back again)? How are these swings associated with the ascendancy of political parties at different positions on the left-right continuum? How are such societal swings reflected in the way the social and political context influence schools and in the perceived legitimacy of the school's involvement in values education?

(3) Is there more concern about values education in countries that lack established institutional channels for it, such as courses in moral or religious education or separate school systems for those from different religious backgrounds, than in countries that have those provisions?

(4) What are the major differences between implementing a centralized curriculum which explicitly includes social values and implementing programmes originating at the local level or programmes in which values are implicit rather than explicit? Is teacher training of a different character or importance? What role does a broad or narrow choice of textbooks or curricular materials play in these differing situations?

(5) How is the climate of schools or classrooms as a dimension of schooling related to the more explicit curriculum? How is the transmission of a given content of values related to teaching ways of making value decisions in democratic societies?

(6) Are certain modes of values education which are suitable for primary schools likely to be less effective (or even counter-productive) at the secondary school level? What assumptions are appropriate about the needs or abilities of students of particular ages?

Future research should weave together the contextual and policy-related factors, the interests of parents and the three dimensions of schooling identified in the model. Peer group influence and the mass media also warrant attention. This research will be more valuable if it is multi-method in character. Large surveys of student attitudes provide benchmarks. Cross-national studies using classroom observations supplemented by the examination of policy statements, by interviews with educators and students and by the collection of survey information have much to recommend them. They present a fuller and more contextualized picture of values education than a single method alone.

References

Crick, B. and Lister, I. (1978) Political literacy: The centrality of the concept. *International Journal*.

Crick, B. and Porter, A. (1969) (Eds.), *Political education and political literacy*. London: Longman.

Danish Ministry of Education (1983) *Education in Denmark*. Copenhagen: Danish Ministry of Education.

Department of Education and Science (1977) *Education in schools: A consultative document*. London: Department of Education and Science.

Department of Education and Science (1979) *Aspects of secondary education in England*. London: Department of Education and Science.

Department of Education and Science (1980a) *A framework for the school curriculum*. London: Department of Education and Science.

Department of Education and Science (1980b) *A view of the curriculum*. London: Department of Education and Science.

Department of Education and Science (1981) *The school curriculum*. London: Department of Education and Science.

Elvin, L. (Ed.) (1981) *The educational systems in the European Community*. Windsor, UK: NFER–Nelson.

England, T. (1986) *Curriculum as a political problem: changing educational conceptions with special reference to citizenship education*. Stockholm: Almqvist &C Wiksell.

Heater, D. (1969) *The teaching of politics*. London: Methuen.

Heater, D. (1986) The politics of political education. *Westminster Studies in Education*, **9**, 33–44.

Her Majesty's Inspectorate (1977) *Curriculum 11–16*. London: Department of Education and Science.

Hooghoff, H. (1987) Curriculum development for political education in the Netherlands. Unpublished paper, National Institute for Curriculum Development, Enschede.

Jennings, M. K., Allerbeck, K. E., and Rosenmayr, L. (1979) Generations and families. In S. Barnes and E. M. Kaase (Eds.), *Political action: Mass participation in five Western democracies*. Beverly Hills, CA: Sage.

Kohlberg, L. and Higgens, A. (1987) School democracy and social interaction. Paper presented at the Society for Research in Child Development Meetings, Baltimore, MD.

Lindquist, A., Westhom, A. and Niemi, R. (1987) The effect of the social studies curriculum on Swedish students' knowledge of international organizations and events. Paper presented at Workshop on Political Socialization and Citizenship, Education in Democracy, Tel Aviv University, March.

Lister, I. (1986) Contemporary developments in political education: Global and international approaches. Unpublished paper, Department of Education, University of York.

Ministry of Education and Science (1986) *The Dutch education system*. Zoetermeer, the Netherlands: Ministry of Education and Science.

National Swedish Board of Education (1980a) *General subjects from the curriculum for the compulsory school*. Stockholm: National Swedish Board of Education.

National Swedish Board of Education (1980b). *The 1980 compulsory school curriculum*. Stockholm: National Swedish Board of Education.

Spindler, G. and L. (1974) *Burgbach: Urbanization and identity in a German village*. New York: Holt.

Spindler, G. and L. (1982) *Doing the ethnography of schooling*. New York: Holt.

Stradling, R. (1975) *The political awareness of the school leaver*. London: The Hansard Society.

Stradling, R. and Noctor, M. (1986) The provision of political education in schools: A national survey. Unpublished paper, Department of Education, University of York.

Study Group on the Formation and Transmission of Moral Standards in School (1979) *Schools and Upbringing*. Stockholm: Swedish Ministry of Education and Cultural Affairs.

Torney, J., Oppenheim, A. N. and Farnen, R. F. (1975) *Civic education in ten countries: An empirical study*. New York: John Wiley.

Torney-Purta, J. (1984) Political socialization and policy: The United States in a cross-national context. In H. Stevenson and E. A. Siegel (Eds.), *Child development research and social policy*. Chicago: University of Chicago Press.

Torney-Purta, J. and Schwille, J. (1986) Civic values learned in school: Policy and practice in industrialized nations. *Comparative Education Review*, **30**, 30–49.

Weiler, H. (1983) West Germany: Educational policy as compensatory legitimation. In R. M. Thomas (Ed.), *Politics and education*. Oxford: Pergamon Press.

CHAPTER 4

The Good Citizen—A Threatened Species?

MORRIS JANOWITZ

A citizen is a person who owes allegiance to a specific government and is entitled to protection from that government and to the enjoyment of certain rights. It is widely recognized that effective citizenship rests on a rigorous and viable system of civic education which informs the individual of his civic rights and obligations. The long-term trend, however, has been to enhance citizen rights without articulation of citizen obligations. To restore a meaningful balance between the two is, in my view, the core issue in citizenship and civic education.

The Decline of Civic Education

In Western political democracies, especially in the United States, there has emerged in recent decades widespread criticism of organized civic education—public and private. The scope and quality of civic education are matters of deep concern to public leaders, educators and parents.

I contend that there has been a decline in the vitality and clarity of civic education in the United States. It is not my purpose to glorify past achievements, since wide segments of the population were excluded from active citizenship. They were relatively untouched as well by organized civic education—public or private. Nevertheless, in the past, civic education operated to strengthen the political system and to deal with crucial problems of "nation-building". The United States was born in an armed political revolution, but the American Revolution was more than a military battle; it served as a powerful agency of civic education. It was one of those rare cases of the armed seizure of political power which resulted in strengthening democratic institutions. During the nineteenth century the public school system, in acculturating the continuous flow of European immigrants, operated as a significant institution of civic education appropriate for a society struggling to develop mass citizenship. The Great Depression weakened the system of civic education. Tension and strains of economic collapse undermined social and political consensus. Fragmentation in civic education started to develop during the New Deal and became the norm after 1945.

The main thrust of my analysis is that the decline in civic education after 1945 was fashioned to a considerable extent by "intellectuals" and teachers more concerned with immediate political issues than with an educational format for understanding the long-term trends in the American "experience". The result has been a decline in the vitality of the school system's contribution to the resolution of social and political conflict. Other agencies of civic education too have become fragmented. Indeed, the dilemmas faced by the United States as a political system reflect the well-recognized, fundamental cleavages of occupation, race, sex and age groupings. The United States must recognize alternative definitions of citizenship that have been created by professional educators of differing persuasion. We need to reconstruct a sense of patriotism—not in the traditional sense of civic citizenship but in a sense relevant for today. There is little reason to feel that a return to old formats of civic education are required, feasible or desirable. Yet much may be learned by an overview of the more than two hundred years of trial and experimentation.

Citizen Obligations

Citizenship is not a formal and abstract conception. On the contrary, it is an idea loaded with concrete, specific meanings which reflect the changing content of political conflict. The content of citizenship, as evolved since the Greek city-state, is a set of enduring political, economic and social problems which remain very much alive. In the last fifty years we have witnessed an expansion in the substance and procedure of citizen rights, including an elaboration of ideological justification. On the other hand, clarification of citizen rights and their implementation have lagged extensively.

Civic education limited to inculcation of traditional patriotism or conventional nationalist ideology is obviously inadequate for an advanced industrial society and a highly interdependent world. I find the words *national* and *patriotic* limiting, and offer the term *civic consciousness*. It refers to positive and meaningful attachments that a person develops to the nation-state. Civic consciousness is compatible with and required for both national and international responsibilities and obligations. It involves elements of reason and self-criticism as well as personal commitment. In particular, civic consciousness is the process by which national attachments and obligations are moulded into the search for supranational citizenship.

The Dual System of Civic Education

During the last two hundred years, the apparatus for civic education in the United States has grown into a complicated enterprise. But it has not become more effective or sensitive. On the contrary, the machinery of civic education as it expanded has produced less real consequences than earlier efforts.

From the American Revolution to the outbreak of World War II, the relative success of civic education in the United States resulted from two central efforts. First, a simple and rudimentary civic education was pursued in the schools. Second, the American armed forces followed to a considerable extent the pattern of the "citizen soldier" which came into being during the American Revolution. The United States is one of the very few nation-states where a revolution ultimately strengthened, rather than weakened, internal democracy. The citizen soldier concept helped both to win wars and to institutionalize democratic practices.

Until the outbreak of World War II, primary and secondary schools served as agencies of acculturation for immigrants. Although the constitution guaranteed separation of church and state, the impact of civic education rested in part on an uncomplicated religious ritual in the schools. The decline in religious orientation weakened the school system as a device for spreading a sense of nationalism. Civic education did not develop a model of the new American but, rather, generated cultural pluralism, which, until the years of the Great Depression, can be considered to have been relatively successful. The growth of the media, especially television, became a powerful factor after 1945 in shaping images of citizenship.

After World War II, there was considerable discussion of the need for new forms of civic education. It was claimed that "real-life" training in the form of political obligation was needed. To what extent and in what form could national service, or aspects of national service, assist the struggle for more effective civic education?

The school system and forms of military service contributed to a balance between individual rights and civic obligations. Civic education in the past implied that each able-bodied male had a series of military and non-military tasks to perform on behalf of the nation-state. It is for that reason that I stress the American Revolution as a form of civic education. In the conduct of that war, officers and enlisted personnel learned that sheer destruction of the "enemy" was less important than winning them over politically to the goals of the Revolution. They developed a strategy which stressed the need for restraining the use of military force. (Unfortunately, such a strategy did not dominate the Vietnam intervention.) The principle of civilian supremacy was established, together with a locally based national guard.

The relative balance between federal forces and local militia was beneficial to democratic forms of control of the military. Political pluralism was strengthened by the interplay of federal forces, which represented aspirations for a national state; on the other hand, pluralism was strengthened by the vitality of national guard units which represented local aspirations.

It is my observation that this dual system, even as it began to decline, continued to contribute to patriotism. Cross-national surveys show Americans very much more likely than citizens of other Western industrialized countries to report patriotic sentiments. Surveys conducted in the middle and later 1970s contain the question "What nation in the world do you have the most respect for?" ("None" was a possible response.) The percentages naming their own countries were: United States, 59; Canada, 35; United Kingdom, 33; France, 26; Italy, 15; and West Germany, 12 (figures taken from *Public Opinion,* **4**, June–July 1981, p. 27).

Yet, Americans are suspicious of institutional programs of civic education, especially those with overtones of manipulation. Wide segments of the American people would like to see stronger patriotic sentiment and greater emphasis on civic obligation. But Americans are sceptical about the ability of present-day public schools and agencies to mould civic consciousness.

Military service still contributes to a sense of patriotism, but the meaning of patriotism has become less and less clear. The public is resistant to any forms of civic education that gives the impression of partisanship. Nonetheless, in the period after 1945, the need for more civic education became apparent, although there is little agreement about the form, content and focus of efforts to strengthen patriotic attachment. The Korean War increased demands by public leaders for increased efforts in civic education to strengthen patriotism. The Vietnam War produced renewed debate about the strengths and weaknesses of patriotism in the United States.

Citizenship and Civic Consciousness

The result of my research effort has been to reinforce my belief that a simple-minded programme of increasing civic education to reinforce patriotism is of little import. Old-fashioned, uncritical patriotism is not effective in the current interdependent world. The more relevant term *civic consciousness* implies the persistence of love or attachment to a country—a territorially based political system. Civic education becomes a pressing issue when we realize that immigration into the United States is and will continue to be immense. Most immigrants are non-English-speakers. Moreover, the processes of acculturation have become more complex. In particular, for the broad range of Spanish-speaking immigrants, there is a powerful attachment to the home country which operates against the acculturation of immigrants into the larger society.

Democratic states are not particularly effective in civic education. However, at the risk of being misunderstood, I assert that civic education and youth socialization are more important in a multi-party state than in a single-party state. Single-party states make greater use of coercion; they operate with low conceptions of the meaning of persuasion.

Civic education means exposing students to central and political traditions of the nation, teaching essential knowledge about the organization and operation of modern governmental insititutions, and fashioning the identification and moral sentiments required for performance as effective citizens. It is clear that civic education remains deeply intertwined with patriotism and nationalism. To teach "civics" without encouraging students to explore their sense of nationalism is to render the subject tepid.

The Promise of National Service

Patriotism, as attachment and love of one's country, leads to various forms of belief and behaviour. While patriotism can result in performance which enhances the moral worth of a nation-state, it can also be a narrow-minded xenophobia. Given the extensive interdependence of the world community, an "update" in the form and content of patriotism is required to contribute both to national goals and to a more orderly world. As we analyse patriotism we repeatedly encounter the question whether some form of national service can operate to strengthen democratic practices and attitudes. In my view, there can be no reconstruction of patriotism without a system of national service.

I have sought to use a socio-political definition of citizenship. The result has been to highlight the conclusion that by legislation and judicial action the difference between citizen and noncitizen has lessened. The inherent advantages of citizenship are either not obvious or increasingly limited in consequence. These advantages in a democratic polity require repeated emphasis. As a result, classroom instruction in citizenship has grown even more important and, with increasing communalism and bilingualism, even more difficult. Some educators hold that the minimum cultural unity for democratic citizen rule in the United States has been eroded and has lost its self-generated effectiveness. I reject that view if only because of the potentials of the existing education system.

Education in the United States, despite weaknesses, produces a youth population with high levels of achievement and aspiration, especially among its very numerous college graduates. College and professional-level education remains impressive, even if cultural achievements are not effectively translated into a sounder set of political practices.

Moreover, the system of post-high-school education touches an immense number of students who attend junior college and community colleges. This junior college population includes large numbers of minority members who come from families with limited academic backgrounds.[1] Economic goals are very important to these students. Whether the essential balance between cultural pluralism and minimum common understandings can be achieved in the United States depends as much on the civic education of community college students as on the regular college graduate.

But it is clear to me that classroom instruction as presently organized is incapable of teaching the meaning of political obligations associated with citizenship. Economic goals appear paramount. Political obligation, especially in recent years, appears to be heavily derivative. Such an observation is incomplete for the United States. A tradition of political obligation is carried on by participation in voluntary organizations, many of which include various economic groups. Since classroom teaching is insufficient for civic education, the interesting question is whether the particular educational experience of national service with real-life content will strengthen popular understanding of civic obligations. Various types of national service are offered as a way of "teaching" citizens to perform the tasks which are part of civic obligation. National service should operate to balance the pursuit of economic self-interest against the collective civic obligation and thus should have long-term positive effects on the individual involved.

For more than thirty-five years I have advocated various forms of national service in order to improve and clarify one's sense of civic obligation. The early years of the 1980s have seen an intensification of the debate over the positive and negative consequences of national service. Can we think of national service as an institution that has a concern with the nation as a whole? Or must we plan for a disparate set of specialized agencies? I face an unsolved dilemma. The closer I examine the problems that must be solved in order to organize a meaningful service, the more complex those problems become. I have not abandoned the desirability of some form of national service. But I argue that the forms of national service are likely to be different from those currently recommended. We do not now know how to administer a system of national service, and learning to administer it by a series of experimental programmes is likely to alter its scope and content.

National service includes a military element, but of necessity the military and civic components will be separate. Moreover, it is doubtful whether various social and community elements could be extensively integrated. The outcome may be voluntary national service composed of decentralized units and diverse programmes. Even the term *decentralized* remains too bureaucratic: we are probably heading for a series of localized agencies.

---

[1] A considerable number of young men and women learn their "trade" at private vocational and trade schools. These schools are important institutions in the US economic system, but they hardly offer any civic education.

The Military Dimensions of National Service[2]

Young men and women who have enlisted in the all-volunteer army reveal strong patriotic moves as contributing to their decision to enlist. In data collected by military recruitment stations, patriotic reasons were given by 20 per cent of new recruits as either the first or second reason for joining. Attitudes manifested in these data reflected a much higher patriotic orientation among enlisted personnel than reported by the mass media. In fact, among new recruits 80 per cent included service to country as a reason for enlisting during the years 1971, 1977, 1979 and 1980. Other data demonstrate the stability of such attitudes. For the period 1974–1980, active duty personnel were asked whether "everyone should have to serve his or her country in some way". About 55 per cent of career personnel agreed. In essence, self-selection into the military and the impact of the military environment were at work. By contrast, first termers revealed a discernible rejection of the proposition that everyone should have to serve his or her country in some way. This negativism gradually dropped from 27 to 7 per cent. Clearly, without formal instruction or indoctrination, first-termers were internalizing values of the career armed forces. The character of patriotism expressed remains to be studied.

The social composition of ground combat arms and debate about performance of the all-volunteer military set the stage for proposals linking active duty force to a contemporary military option within national service. Under a national service military option, the armed forces might be able, if properly organized, to recruit between 100,000 and 150,000 persons annually. The rest would be recruited by present procedures, improved as feasible. The military option is designed to increase the social representativeness of the armed forces and to increase the educational qualifications of recruits. One obvious goal is to include more white middle-class Americans in the enlisted ranks. It is a programme designed to increase the outlet for patriotic motives and, in turn, to strengthen the civic education of new generations.

Let us examine a hypothetical set of proposals for the military option of national service. The term of service would be two years; national service personnel would be expected to have above-average academic achievement qualifications. They would be responding to national goals and values as well as to economic incentives. They would not be assigned to specialized training programmes but to run-of-the-mill assignments, especially those combat assignments that could be learned in a few weeks. A central element of such a programme is that, aside from nominal subsistence allocations and very limited cash payments, compensation would not come through

---

[2]There is an extensive body of writing on national service. For an overview see The Potomac Institute. Youth and the Needs of the Nation: Report of the Committee for the Study of National Service (Washington DC: The Potomac Institute, 1979). See also, especially, Sherraden and D. J. Eberly. National Service: Social, Economic and Military Impacts (New York: Pergamon, 1982).

monetary reward. Instead, educational benefits would be used. We would be dealing not with a mass GI education proposal but, rather, with a more limited programme. Experimental programmes of this variety have attracted superior personnel. For each year of military service, two years of college benefits (tuition plus a modest cost-of-living stipend, for a maximum of four years) would be offered. Such a programme could solve the man-power needs of the second half of the 1980s. The cost would be equal to or less than the current cash bonus. The programme would restore to the enlisted ranks important components of college-bound personnel, who would enrich educationally, technically and morally the climate of units to which they were assigned. Their presence would be a contribution to restor-ing the effectiveness and self-esteem of military units. A unit comprised of all or most recruits with limited educational background cannot have the morale and clarity of purpose of a unit with mixed educational achieve-ments. Soldiers with heterogeneous backgrounds supply broader linkage between the military and larger society. I would even offer the observation that mixed educational units will have higher standards of morality and personal conduct.

The Frontiers of National Service

There is a sharp difference between national service organized to supply military personnel and one orientated to civilian tasks. This distinction will persist and become greater if national service develops in the United States.

There is no shortage of plans for organizing a civilian component of national service. The list of tasks to be performed continues to grow. While national service could, in theory, be either voluntary or obligatory, it is my view that obligatory national service in the years ahead is not feasible. The political support for an obligatory programme does not now exist and is unlikely to develop in the next decade. Advocates of a comprehensive national service can aspire, over the short run, to the development of a series of experimental exercises. But in time, for example, a decade of effort could lead to a gradually growing number of participants that would involve at least half of the eligible youth—male and female.

Obligatory national service would mobilize a very small minority who are in blind opposition based on personal deviance or criminal-like personality. I would estimate that at least 5 per cent of youth would fall into this category. Neither the armed forces nor the civilian component would want to act as a reformatory for delinquents. It does not take many deviants to wreck or severely strain a programme. Administrative leaders would have to main-tain a system of rules which would allow for easy withdrawal of those who had an oppositionalist mentality. In fact, most current planning for national service is based on voluntary involvement. Milton Friedman's view that national service is a tax is widely accepted; the central issue is the size of the segment of society who are willing to pay the tax voluntarily.

Even limited experimental programmes of national service with civilian options are difficult to organize. Advocates of voluntary national service are sensitive to the complex administrative and organizational tasks. Many proposals for national service envisage a national, central organization. This reflects, in part, the ideology of energetic leaders concerned with social integration.

In my view, organization on a state-by-state basis or even by metropolitan centres would simplify administration. Many plans have called for national service to be run by public, non-profit national agencies. The effort is to separate the agency from the governmental structure. In fact, plans generally call for a national agency to direct the operation and a series of operating sub-agencies to oversee specific programmes. I am not impressed with the potential of such decentralization efforts.

Plans for national service that point to a single agency to oversee specific operational programmes are attempting to make up for existing institutional confusion. Such a direction does not excite me. Planners of national service are seeking to make up for defects in civilian society. I am more inclined towards a "loose" plan. To be effective, national service would have to be more of a youth movement than a youth organization. The youth movement would seek to fill in gaps and to be fluid in its approach and organizational structure.

A voluntary national service must develop a widely based strategy of recruitment. There has been considerable debate on this point. We are looking for a strong element of diversity in the youth groups recruited. At stake is the question, why are the work features of national service likely to produce more effective citizens? First, national service is committed to a heterogeneous population. The mixing and social interaction is designed to enhance the self-awareness of those who participate. Second, the work programme of national service should increase awareness of socio-economic realities. Third, and most important, cooperative endeavours should serve as forms of education that produce positive responses for a democratic society and lasting positive consequences for participants.

I am likely to be misunderstood when I emphasize that prospects for broad-scale national service opportunities are indeed limited and likely to remain so. The political support for a system of national service does not exist despite verbal support for particular programmes. Private groups can organize equivalent programmes, but they have failed to do so to any great extent.

My research leads me to the conclusion that national service can be defined as working at subsistence level after high school or later on one of the broad range of tasks such as conservation, health or old-age problems in order to participate in learning about the civic institutions of society. It is a device for teaching the student to balance rights against obligations. One cannot, of course, overlook the importance of prior classroom study in civic education. Because of routinized patterns of education one can afford to give a very broad content of national service. The goal is not the reinforcement of traditional patriotism but rather the development of an understanding of the tasks which must be performed in a democratic society.

We are a statistically minded nation; therefore, the suggestion has been made that we should tabulate annually the number of young people engaged in some form of national service. I am convinced that, even without governmental support, participation in some type of national service is certain to grow year by year. Such an observation, however, fails to confront the central issue of developing a national service programme—governmental or private sector—which will not be limited to the graduates of elite colleges but will include a broad pattern of participants. No national service system fills its objectives unless it includes all segments of the population.

Over the past fifty years, a variety of service programmes open to young people have been created and abandoned, a process which reflects an unstable commitment to service opportunities. During the Great Depression, hundreds of thousands of young people participated each year in the programmes of the Civilian Conservation Corps and the National Youth Administration. No federal programmes existed from World War II up to the 1950s, though small, CCC-like programmes were organized at the state level. In the modern era of youth service programmes, the Peace Corps began in 1961 and VISTA in 1964. The 1970s brought the revival of the conservation corps idea in the Youth Conservation Corps (1970–1983) and the Young Adult Conservation Corps (1978–1982). Major demonstrations of national service in urban areas occurred in Seattle (1973–1974) and in Syracuse (1978–1980).

However, as of 1982, the nation witnessed the decline of several youth service programmes and the abolition of several others. Among those eliminated as part of budgetary restrictions and retrenchment were the National Teacher Corps, the Youth Conservation Corps and the University of Action. Estimates for total number of participants in the remaining programmes for 1983 are as follows: at the federal level, the Peace Corps numbers approximately 6000, VISTA about 3000 and the National Health Service Corps about 3000. Of Peace Corps volunteers, about one-half are aged 18–24, the other half are 25 and older. The size of VISTA remains uncertain. In 1982 it entered a phase-out schedule, although Congress has been resisting its elimination. Altogether, one could say that federally sponsored service opportunities for teenagers and young adults in 1983 were estimated at approximately 10,000 (estimates from National Service Secretariat, Washington, DC).

At the state level, the conservation corps idea has been taken up by several states—most notably California, with about 1900 year-round partici-

pants in the California Conservation Corps in 1982. Much smaller programmes in Ohio and Minnesota add 300 more slots. Part-year and part-
time programmes in Illinois, Iowa, Kansas, Maine and other states might
add an additional 1000 positions, for a total of about 3200 (estimates from
Human Environment Center, Washington, DC). Other service programmes may exist at the local government level, but these are few and far
between and are not systematically tracked.

In addition, there are many purely voluntary efforts in which young
people participate in health, education, recreation, social welfare, religious,
political and other volunteer work. In a nationwide survey of volunteer
service in 1974, 22 per cent of 14–17-year-olds and 18 per cent of 18–24-
year-olds were engaged in part-time volunteer work of one kind or another
(Eberly, 1976, cites data from surveys by the Census Bureau).

In plans developed or implemented in the United States, most recent
national service programmes involve adding one year to public school
schooling. I prefer and am prepared to see the sixteen years required for
a college degree gradually and selectively reduced to fifteen years. The
"freedom" year would be devoted to some form of national service.
Advanced placement of high school students into college courses is an essential movement in this direction. The advantages of such a pattern would be
immense; especially the financial saving in expenditures for education. I
expect a gradual, long-term expansion in the productivity of the US economy. The current surplus of youthful labour will give way to increased
shortage, especially of trained young workers. Given that shortage, the
additional labour supply should, in the decade ahead, be of vital importance
to the US economy.

There is support for national service among both liberal and conservative
political leaders. Various bills have been introduced, but the drive for either
extensive programmes or even small experimental ones does not command
wide political support, in part because of restraints on the US federal
budget.

Public opinion findings must be carefully assessed. An overwhelming
majority of American parents want their children to receive civic education.
Only a very small portion have specific ideas. Moreover, there is a revival
of concern with a "sound" education programme in selected local communities. A "sound" local school programme means an attack on liberal trends
and parental rejection of programmes they believed to be excessively per-
missive. Such agitations receive extensive media coverage, but do not generate actual widespread parental participation. Nevertheless, it is striking that
the bulk of US parents—to judge by national surveys—support the idea that
young people should give one year of national service. There is a view that
a year of service would "be good" for their children. To some extent such
a reply is fashionable; but the replies also represent patriotic feelings and

the belief that national service will make their children more aware of their obligations as citizens.

The fundamental barrier to national service (including local programmes of community service) is the attitude of American youth. Again, public opinion surveys need to be read with great care. In the abstract, there is considerable support among young people for the idea of national service; almost one-half of youth in the early 1980s expressed favourable attitudes to and interest in serving. But many responses represented conventional expressions of what were considered appropriate attitudes. I do not doubt that there is considerable genuine desire among college students and selected young workers to demonstrate that they are "good citizens". I cannot make an effective estimate of the real support. Young people are caught in a bind generated by parents and the school system. They are attracted to the adventure and moral value of national service, but also feel obliged to get on with their careers. Many people believe—incorrectly in my view— that the economy will get worse. There is therefore considerable pressure to get on with education and the world of work. In addition, for some students, national service is no more than a possible alternative to service in the infantry and ground combat arms.

Nonetheless, there is clearly enough interest in and need for national service for a range of programmes to be launched. Priority should be accorded to conservation work and to meeting the needs of neglected senior citizens. Programmes for the elderly could be locally managed and organized, while resource conservation could be linked to national and state governmental agencies.

It is fortunate that the United States is not about to launch a large-scale national service programme including both military and civilian options. Existing restraints mean that when programmes are developed, they will be small and thus likely to develop slowly and adequately. We may be thus spared the typical American pattern of policy implementation which is one of shifting from extreme restraint to over-expansion. As the nation moves gradually to new forms of national service, the resultant programmes could be organizationally sound.

Most important, the forms of national or community service must be seen not as welfare programmes but as expressions of civic duty by those who actively participate. Those very conditions which can work to resocialize poor youth away from a dead-end existence depend upon national service not being defined as an employer of last resort, a definition that is hard to escape unless participation is relatively representative of all American youth. National service must be structured as part of a citizen's obligation.

One idea that has received lively discussion is to make federal aid to college students dependent on national service. This formulation, initially advanced by Moskos (1981), has attracted the attention of several political leaders. Most government loan and scholarship programmes have helped young people avoid military service through college deferments. In effect, we have created a GI bill without the GI. It is not politically possible to require *military* service as a condition for a government loan. But a programme requiring some community service for particular forms of governmental assistance to attend college is feasible and will most probably be introduced as legislation. Although this format does not encompass what I believe are the worthiest elements of national service, it does make sense today. Is it fully compatible with the previously discussed programme of education benefits in exchange for military service.

Linking government-guaranteed loans for higher education to service in the student's local community is a modified version of the old work/study idea. It involves national political incentives as well as economic ones. The nation appears increasingly prepared to accept such a work/study programme. As of 1982, more than six billion dollars annually are spent on student loans. A work/study programme would add little to those expenditures. On the contrary, by making a loan dependent on community service, federal costs would be reduced by the value of the work completed.

The vitality of democratic citizenship cannot be maintained by the existing range of political forms, such as voting and political participation. Historically, citizenship and patriotism have included various forms of local self-help currently associated with the idea of community or national service. Participation in these activities gives the idea of obligation concrete meaning. The need to make use of this tradition has grown, ironically, with the growth of the welfare state. The first step to make is voluntary national service available to all young men and women. But there is no reason why voluntary national service should not ultimately involve older people too, as they retire from regular work.

References

Eberly, D. J. (1976), Patterns of volunteer service by young people: 1965 and 1974. *Volunteer Administration*, **4**, 20–27.

Moskos, C. C. (1981), Making the all-volunteer force work: A national service approach. *Foreign Affairs*, **60**, 27–34.

The Potomac Institute (1979), *Youth and the Needs of the Nation*.

Sherraden and Eberly (Eds.) (1982) *National Service*.

PART 3

Asia

CHAPTER 5

Politics and Moral Education in Japan

YASUMASA TOMODA

Japan's ratio of problem children is less than that of other industralized countries, but, according to Japanese traditional moral principles, children should respect their parents and teachers, as well as go to school every day.

Recently, Japan's newspapers have been filled with stories of bullying among children (in several cases the victims have committed suicide), absenteeism from schools, children's violence to parents and teachers and teachers' beating of their pupils. These recent incidents of violence in the home and school have shocked the Japanese people.

Analysts point both to factors within the schools, and in the surrounding society to account for these developments. Factors within schools include the declining quality of teachers, the lack of teachers' organizational readiness to cope with deviancy, excess control and regulation of children's school life and the influence of excessive competition among children regarding extrance examinations. As regards the out-of-school environment, the lack of basic training of children at home, the disorganization of local communities, and the bad influences of the mass media on children are regarded as major causes.

Moral education was introduced as a means of strengthening the values of young people so they would not engage in the aforementioned anti-social behaviour. What is surprising then is the absence of reference by the analysts to moral education at school, especially moral education as a school subject, which was introduced into Japanese schools in 1958. In this chapter, I will examine the nature of moral education in Japanese schools, by first briefly turning to the historical origins of this subject and then examining its place in post-war Japanese schools. Finally, recent changes in the relation of young people to their schools, family and community will be considered in an effort to account for the recent shocking developments.

Pre-war Moral Education

At the time of the Meiji Restoration of 1868, Japanese leaders were divided into three groups, the Shintoist, Confucian and Western-oriented.

Initially, the Western-orientated group predominated over the other two groups, mainly due to the fact that the majority of Japanese leaders were deeply impressed by the high level of European science and technology, and believed that the independence and progress of Japan would be impossible without introducing European science and technology into Japan. This Western bias was embodied in the Fundamental Code of Education of 1872. As a result, the cognitive and technical side of education was emphasized, while the moral and affective side was neglected.

However, within a few years this newly introduced system of education was severely criticized by traditional leaders. Confucian education had long been a mainstream of education in Japan, and the national, Shintoist-orientated group had played an important role in the process of the Meiji Restoration. The level of compulsory education that had been proposed by the new government was more than could be realized at this early stage, and the education curriculum, consisting largely of direct translations of Western textbooks, was not based on the daily experiences of the great majority of the Japanese people.

A special concern of the traditionalists was the new system's inattention to moral guidance. In European countries, churches and religious groups played an important role in the people's moral education, but in Japan, the Buddhist and Shinto religions were not strong and active enough to independently promote the moral education of the Japanese. Thus, the traditionalists looked to the school system as a vehicle for improving the nation's morality. In fact, pre-Meiji Japanese schools, especially the elite schools, had a long history of moral education.

In 1879, the Fundamental Code was abolished, and a new Educational Ordinance was promulgated with moral education, *Shushin,* elevated to the top priority of all educational subjects. In 1890, the Imperial Rescript on Education was issued, and Japanese education moved from a liberal to a conservative orientation. The government thereafter enjoyed the authority to use the schools for systematic political and moral indoctrination. The Rescript continued to be the backbone of moral education in Japan until the end of World War II.

Until ultra-nationalism and militarism came to the fore, moral education in Japanese schools functioned fairly well. Historical biographies were used to exemplify moral principles, and among these were many great people from the West. For instance, the contributions of Florence Nightingale, Albert Schweitzer, Edward Jenner, Thomas Edison, Christopher Columbus, Marie Curie, Benjamin Franklin, George Washington, Galileo and Einstein were included in Japanese textbooks, to teach Japanese students the importance of effort, self-sacrifice, honesty, independence, humanism and so on. While it may be that the biographies of the Westerners were over-represented, these biographies offered an international perspective to students who were otherwise isolated in a Far Eastern island.

The approach of focusing on the deeds of great people to convey moral principles was occasionally criticized. Some people felt that this approach failed to cover all the main items of morality necessary for the maintenance and improvement of Japanese moral standards. Also, educators were not confident that young people would be moved by these stories or draw the intended inferences. Students sometimes merely memorized their lessons without reflecting on them. Despite these reservations, biographic presentations of great people continued to be one of the most important pedagogic methods relied on for moral education in pre-war Japanese schools. Reinforcing the separate moral education course was the inclusion of numerous stories of great people in the textbooks for Japanese literature.

The rise of ultra-nationalism and militarism in the 1930s led to the substitution of Japanese military heroes for great people from abroad. In this nationalistic period, other educational subjects were changed, especially history. At the beginning of the Meiji Era world history was emphasized, but gradually Japanese history took its place, and the objective of history was then redefined as a subject for inculcating students with the spirit of worship for the Imperial Family and patriotism. History came to include, for instance, descriptions of the great accomplishments of past emperors and factual assertions about the eternity of the Imperial Family. Even in the subject of geography the objective became "to make students understand how Japan stands in the world, and instill in their minds the love of their country". According to a content analysis of textbooks during this period, about one-third of the curriculum had a strongly nationalistic content (Brown, 1955).[1]

These changes of the curriculum were especially obvious in primary schools, which were expected by government to play a key role in instilling nationalism and militarism. As primary school students were not mature enough to criticize the content of textbooks, the changes certainly had a profound influence on Japanese public opinion.

Post-war Moral Education and Politics

One characteristic of post-war Japanese political parties is that the difference between right and left is quite large. Thus, it often becomes very difficult to compromise. The Liberal Democratic Party (LDP), the largest and most conservative party, regained power in the early post-war years and has not relinquished it since. The LDP is mainly supported by the business world and the old middle classes, such as farmers and merchants. Japan's business leaders are especially concerned with education, since they know that the quality of the future labour force depends on education. This might be an inevitable result if we consider the fact that Japan is a nation with few natural resources. Business leaders have presented various reports

[1] For a more detailed discussion of moral education in pre-war Japan see Passin (1965).

and proposals on education, and recommended many educational reforms. Their reform plans are presented to the Ministry of Education through the LDP, and are often realized, at least at the legal and financial level. But the Japan Teachers' Union (*Nikkyoso*) which affiliates with the progressive parties is strong, and through its influence on teachers has the veto-power to block the complete realization of those reforms at the classroom level.

The Post-war Moral Vacuum and Conservative Counter-reforms

After the war all militaristic and ultra-nationalistic influences were removed from the school curriculum under the directives of the Allied Occupation. The Japanese people initially concurred with this change, for in responding to the nation's military defeat they tended to regard pre-war moral principles as valueless and even harmful. But it proved difficult to find a new morality to replace the old. Terms such as "democracy", "equality" and "freedom" were introduced, but it was not easy for Japanese to understand the meaning of these terms.

Under the directives of the Allied Occupation, the pre-war moral education subject (*Shushin*) was abolished together with Japanese history and geography. In place of these subjects, the new subject of social studies was introduced. Although this subject was regarded as a symbol of "new education" for Japan's democratization, it was soon criticized on the grounds that it could not provide students with systematic knowledge. Social studies gradually tended to split into history, geography and civics. Furthermore, the lack of an independent subject dealing with moral education was also considered as a serious problem especially among the conservatives.

Partly as a result of pressure from the conservative sectors of society, and partly in order to counterbalance the leftist teachers, the Ministry of Education and the Central Council for Education prepared several reports and issued many recommendations.

In 1951, the Ministry of Education prepared *A Guide to Moral Education*, which encouraged teachers to include moral education in social studies as well as other subjects. In 1958, the special subject of morals was institutionalized as a formal school subject, in spite of the strong opposition of the teachers' union and other progressive groups. In 1968, the Central Council for Education prepared a report called *The Image of Ideal Japanese*, in an effort to influence the education goals of teachers.

The Teachers Union

The Japan Teachers' Union showed support for many of the Occupation's reforms, but has generally opposed the counter-reforms of the conservative government, including those on moral education.

Teachers reacted strongly to the role they played in pre-war ultra-nationalism and militarism. In fact, not a few teachers had inculcated their students with nationalistic and militaristic ideologies, and sent them into the battlefields. The remorse felt by teachers is considered one of the most important factors motivating their intense participation in out-of-school politics. The phrase "Never repeat the same mistake" became a slogan of teachers. One illustration of teacher sentiment was the idealistic Moral Code announced in 1961 by the Japan Teachers' Union.

The code outlines the following moral principles for teachers: (1) Teachers should protect youth by responding to the needs of our society, especially by keeping peace and building a democratic society. (2) Teachers should fight for equality of education. (3) Teachers should secure a lasting peace. (4) Teachers should act from a basis of scientific truth. (5) Teachers should defend educational freedom. (6) Teachers should seek righteous politics. (7) Teachers should try to create a new culture by struggling against cultural corruption concerning youth.

Peace, equality and democracy are still the union's major goals. At present, for instance, the integration of handicapped children into regular schools is being promoted by the teachers' union. Educational trips to Hiroshima for children are also promoted by the union.

Public Attitudes to Moral Education

The public was confused by these changes, especially during the early post-war period. Parents lost confidence in their own moral values, and thus could not teach children with confidence, but they expressed dissatisfaction with the performance of schools. While teachers tended to consider friendly relationships with students democratic, people of the older generation started to complain that youth disregarded their duties by insisting on their rights. A decrease in the scores on scholastic achievement tests by this new generation was also criticized. This negative attitude of the older generation toward "new education" encouraged the government to consider a new policy on moral education, despite the strong opposition of the teachers' union.

R. P. Dore, who conducted a questionnaire study in an urban Tokyo ward in 1951 before the official introduction of morals, found that 80 per cent of his sample wanted morals education in the schools. He described this situation as follows:

> The most frequently expressed reason was that the children are "badly behaved", "don't know how to be polite" and "have no respect for elders". The most common theme in justifying the need for an ethics course was that the children are no longer told the stories of famous men to inspire them—the old stories of Ninomiya Sontoku, Benjamin Franklin, Jenner or Noguchi . . . The necessity of teaching children to be filial to their parents is the next most common theme (Dore, 1958, p. 233).

In a rural area in the Kanto plain from 1962 to 1963, John Singleton made a field study, about four years after the establishment of morals as a distinct subject. He interviewed fifty-three parents of students in a junior high school and found that the majority of these parents wanted more moral education at school. He asked them what aspects of morals should be strengthened, and found that the traditional concepts of family and social heirachy were still strong elements of their thinking. For instance, twenty-seven parents agreed with the statement that one should have regard for one's parents, whereas two disagreed; twenty parents agreed with the statement that one should have patriotism and love of country whereas four disagreed; and thirty parents agreed with the statement that one should respect one's superiors, and no one disagreed (Singleton, 1967, pp. 43–44).

> Discipline (*Shitsuke*) was considered an important component of morals teaching. Though parents approved of, to a degree, friendly relations between teachers and pupils, there was an underlying assumption that teacher friendliness and student discipline were not compatible. Several comments were made that indicated distinctly different perceptions of teacher and parent roles. Parents are not expected to, and do not, severely discipline their own children, but they sometimes expect teachers to perform this function. It is assumed, therefore, that they cannot teach their own children. In traditional crafts like *tatami* mat-making, sons who will succeed their fathers in the business are sent to someone else for apprenticeship in the trade. After they learn the job, they come back home to work with their fathers (Singleton, 1967, p. 46).

The results obtained from both rural and urban areas in Japan show that educational reforms are often counterbalanced by traditional sectors, and that parents also have a strong influence in the politics of school reform. Furthermore, there seem to be deep-rooted reasons why Japanese parents expect schools to promote students' morality.

It should also be noted that the teachers' union and other progressive people tended to consider the post-war "new education" as an ideal education, and that this ideal education has gradually deteriorated through governmental reforms. So the union has tried to protect the educational goals and institutions established just after the war under the supervision of the American Occupation.

Ministry of Education Policy

The Ministry of Education has persisted in its efforts to respond to parental concerns. In 1971 the Central Council for Education presented a report entitled "Basic Policies for the Future Expansion of Public Education". In the first chapter of the Report, the following three goals were stressed: First, to have a deep understanding of the relationship between man and nature, and to live harmoniously with nature. Second, to participate in various social activities, and to learn how to collaborate with others in fulfilling one's duties in society. Third, to deepen the understanding of

Japanese tradition and history, and to contribute to future society through creative activities.

Due to rapid industrialization and urbanization, the natural environment has greatly deteriorated. The opportunities for children to participate in group and collective activities has become limited. And the younger generation's interest in Japanese tradition and culture has rapidly been declining. Effective ways have not yet been found to put these goals into educational practice, but the suggestion of the Council is important.

No one can deny the necessity of some kind of moral education in schools, but it is not easy to reach an agreement on the content and methods of moral education. As stated earlier, progressive political parties, conservative political parties, the Ministry of Education, the teachers' union, business leaders and parents are competing for a hegemony. Despite the constant antagonisms among these various groups, students are receiving moral education in school. Some moral education is formally and consciously promoted, some informally and unconsciously. In the following section, I will describe some of the characteristics of moral education in Japanese schools.

Moral Education at School

According to the School Education Law of 1947, still in effect, the aims of primary schools are described as follows:

Article XVIII

(1) To cultivate understanding of the spirit of cooperation and independence in connection with relationships between human beings on the basis of children's experience in social life both inside and outside the school.

(2) To develop a proper understanding of the traditions both of children's native communities and of the nation, and further, to cultivate a spirit of international cooperation.

(3) To cultivate basic knowledge regarding food, clothing, housing, etc., essential to everyday life.

(4) To cultivate the ability to understand and correctly manage the mathematical computations needed in everyday life.

(5) To cultivate the ability to observe and cope with the natural phenomena met with in everyday life in a scientific manner.

(6) To cultivate the habits needed for a sound, safe and happy life and to effect the harmonious development of mind and body.

(7) To cultivate basic understanding and skills in music, fine arts, literature, etc., in order to make one bright and rich.

The curriculum in primary and secondary schools covers the following three categories: (1) subject areas; (2) moral education; (3) special activities. Special activities include student council activities, homeroom activities, club activities, school events and classroom guidance. Regular school events, such as educational excursions, athletic and cultural meetings and entrance and graduation ceremonies, are expected to play an important role in moral education.

Here, I will briefly describe the following four aspects of moral education in Japanese schools: (1) objectives and practices of the independent subject of moral education; (2) the main characteristics of social topics as a foundation of moral education; (3) promotion of ethical behaviour through various group activities; (4) enforcement of detailed regulations concerning student conduct at secondary schools.

(1) *The Subject of Moral Education*

The number of school hours allotted to the subject of moral education is only thirty-four or thirty-five unit hours a year. This is based on the assumption that the goals of moral education cannot be accomplished through the special subject of moral education. Other subjects as well as special activities should contribute to the development of moral values. For instance, social studies and science might facilitate student understanding of the social and natural environment. Student council and club activities might promote student self-governing and leadership ability.

According to *The Guideline for Moral Education for Primary Schools (1958)*, edited by the Ministry of Education, the objective of moral education is described as follows:

> To nurture the student to develop a spirit of human dignity to apply to every aspect of social life and contribute to the enrichment of Japanese culture and the development of a democratic state and society, and work for a peaceful international society . . . This objective should be realized through all educational activities, as well as an independent subject of moral education.

An independent subject of moral education has been established in order to supplement, deepen and integrate all the other activities that might contribute directly or indirectly to the improvement of student morality. Most educational subjects such as history, mathematics, etc., might offer a broad foundation for moral education, and hence indirectly promote student morality. On the other hand, special activities, such as student councils, clubs, etc., might directly promote specific aspects of student morality.

The *Guideline for Moral Education* recommends that teachers draw up a comprehensive programme for moral education at the level of individual schools. All teachers are expected to participate in the process of this project. According to the *Guideline,* teachers are encouraged to investigate the most serious moral problems at their schools and to determine which means are most effective in settling those problems.

According to a national survey conducted by the Ministry of Education in 1983 on moral education, 72 per cent of the primary schools and 79 per cent of junior high schools were conducting school-wide, comprehensive programmes for moral education. About 90 per cent of both primary and junior high schools were offering moral education as an independent subject (Monbusho, 1983, pp. 72–79).

The great majority of teachers in primary and junior high schools are seriously trying to promote moral education. However, due both to a deep-rooted concern about the possibility of a revival of the pre-war type of moral education and to the inherent difficulty of efficiently teaching moral values, quite a few teachers are still at a loss about how to teach it.

Although some branches of the Teachers' Union are resisting governmental policies of moral education without presenting their own policies, some are active enough to take initiatives, and the problem of equality is often discussed. For instance, the problems of Japanese Koreans, *Buraku* minority people or handicapped people are often presented to students as serious problems to be solved.

On the whole, Japan's traditional values, such as filial piety, obedience to the old and loyalty to the state, are not popular themes today. Instead, more tangible problems in the school, family and community tend to become popular themes, as shown in the following ethnography of a moral education class in a primary school.

> I expected the worst when I went to my first moral education class: dull Confucian texts sermonizing on the need for patriotism or greater filial piety. Much to my surprise, they had no text. Rather, at the bell, one of the students turned on the television at the front of the classroom and for the next fifteen minutes we watched a short drama. Afterwards, the teacher and the students joined in a discussion to try to identify the moral lessons contained in the drama. From week to week the content varied, but never did I see programs concerned with political themes. Rather they emphasized fundamental matters such as the value of life, the foolishness of fighting, the importance of friendship, the problems of old people. Actually, no drama conveyed a specific message. The lesson was developed through the subsequent dialogue of the teacher and the students (Cummings, 1980, pp. 115–116).

This is an example of moral education at a primary school in Kyoto. As is shown in this description, audio-visual aids are in wide use, and free talking and discussion are often encouraged by teachers. According to a national survey conducted by the Ministry of Education, the most widely used materials are reading materials, which are used in most primary and junior high schools. TV and radio are popular among primary schools, but not in junior high schools; 83 per cent in the former and 25 per cent in the latter utilize TV and radio. In junior high schools, tapes, films and slides are popularly used in 50 per cent of junior high schools (Monbusho, 1983, p. 78).

Popular themes in moral education are no longer traditional values such as filial piety, nationalism, etc. Instead, daily problems facing students are presented and discussed.

As a reaction to the pre-war inculcation of abstract moral principles, it has been emphasized, since the war, to cultivate students to search out, analyse and solve problems facing them in collaboration with their class-mates. In this new moral education, therefore, students' own experiences at their school, home and community are emphasized. As a result, those moral values which students do not come into contact with in their daily lives tend to get neglected. In an increasing number of schools, the emotional aspect of moral education is emphasized. In these schools, teach-ers select carefully those materials that inspire students, and try to instil into the students some of the moral values that they cannot experience in their daily life.

(2) *Social Subjects*

As stated above, moral education was separated from social studies in 1958, and we can notice a trend toward a specialization in the subject of social studies. Students are still taught social studies as a broad subject in the primary schools, however in the junior high schools, there is no broad subject of social studies. Geography, history and civics are taught separately as independent subjects. These three subjects cover a wide range of knowledge; national as well as international information is offered to stu-dents through these subjects. In the subject of civics, students learn about modern society and democracy, organization and management of demo-cratic government, the economic and industrial structure of our society, etc.

It should be noted, however, that partly due to severe competition for senior high school entrance examinations and partly due to traditional teaching methods, junior high school students are generally forced to spend most of their time and energy in memorizing the content of textbooks. This might be a major defect of these subjects.

As William Cummings wrote, the content of Japanese textbooks is on the whole progressive, and teaching is carefully designed to promote students' understanding of their social and natural environment based on daily experi-ences both inside and outside of schools. Egalitarian values are especially emphasized in the primary school textbooks as well as in teaching in the classroom.

> All in all, these texts present a remarkably open-minded, even progressive, picture of Japanese society. Their strongest theme is the diversity of work performed by the Japanese people. Rather than picture some occupations as more worthy than others, the texts stress the interrelatedness of all occupations. Clearly, the hidden agenda is to cultivate a climate of mutual respect between students from diverse social backgrounds that will carry over into their adult lives. Many of Japan's social problems are openly recognized, as is the importance of the democratic governmental process in providing solutions (Cummings, 1980, pp. 123–4).

All the textbooks in Japan have to be approved by the Ministry of Educa-tion, and this Ministry is under the constant pressure of a strong conservative sector. If we take this fact into consideration, the existence of these progressive textbooks may seem miraculous. But there are many important factors which have contributed to the preservation of these progressive textbooks. Legally, even conservative parties cannot ignore the progressive spirit of the Fundamental Law of Education enacted according to the spirit of the Constitution based on democracy. Politically, various progressive groups, such as the teachers' union, peace movements, anti-public-nuisance movements, progressive journalism, and progressive intellectuals, have played an important role. Furthermore, the conservative government cannot ignore the protests from neighbouring countries against conservative content. People in these countries are deeply concerned about the revival of nationalism and militarism in Japan, and demand the correct description of the past foreign policies of Japan.

Social studies texts introduce first-year students in primary schools to various people whose work has some relation to the children's family or school. Next, people working in neighbouring factories or on farms are introduced. Through learning about the main functions of city hall, the health office, the police station, the post office, the telephone exchange office, and about the main transportation systems in their home town, students deepen their understanding of the main characteristics of their community. By the end of their sixth year, students learn about how farming and industry have developed, problems of natural resources, national history, economic relationships between Japan and other countries, and the political and governmental process in Japan. In other words, the social, economic and political environment surrounding the students extends gradually from their home to the world.

Moral education as an independent subject is also provided at junior high schools. In this transitional period, young people experience rapid physical and psychological growth, emotional instability, aspiration for independence, resistance against authority, cynicism, imbalances between thinking and experiences, and the influence of peer groups. One the whole, junior high school teachers tend to consider the independent subject of moral education as an extension of homeroom activities. Therefore, in moral education, students discuss and try to work out solutions to problems facing classmates, such as how to cope with problems of bullying in the class, how to promote the integration of handicapped students into their class, how to encourage classmates who are considering dropping out, or how to participate as a class in school events and student council activities, and so on.

In 1950, Japan's high school enrolment rate was only 43 per cent, but at present the enrolment rate is around 95 per cent. This means that senior high schools which started as "elite" institutions have become "universal" institutions in a short period of time. Due to this rapid expansion and transformation, social subjects in senior high schools have been repeatedly revised.

At the present time, senior high school students are offered the following six social subjects: politics and economics, ethics, geography, national history, world history, contemporary society. The subject of contemporary society, a required subject for first-year high school students, covers the basic problems of contemporary society, for example population growth, natural resources, energy, Japan's economic development and international relationships, social welfare, democracy, world peace, tradition and culture, and so on. Based on their background, students are asked to think about their own way of life.

After taking the subject of contemporary society, students are required to take two or three more courses from the group of social studies subjects. The subject of ethics was established in 1960 in order to promote students' morality. It consists of quite a wide range of philosophical and religious thought. It should be noted that ethics is included in the subjects tested by the unified college entrance examination whereas contemporary society is not. The latter subject has been excluded on the grounds that college entrance examinations promote cramming instead of facilitating students' understanding and thinking. This might also be true in ethics, but this subject was not excluded.

Many educationalists have discussed the objectives, content and teaching methods of social studies. Some have tried to promote the morality of students, whereas some have tried to offer "scientific" knowledge. Some have emphasized the "discovery method", while others have emphasized the "problem-solving approach". Politically, some have tried to promote "Marxism", while others have tried to promote nationalism. On the whole, however, Japanese students obtain a wide range of knowledge, providing a broad foundation in moral education.

(3) *Group Activities*

School is not only a place for learning but also forms an important part of the child's life. In order to teach students efficiently, teachers have to keep order in class. Students have to be trained to sit still, not to disturb others and to concentrate their attention on what the teacher says in class. In order to make life at school meaningful and significant, students are taught to contribute to the maintenance and improvement of the physical and social environment of the school, by doing such things as cleaning their classrooms and playground.

Schools consist of a large number of students from diverse family backgrounds. Students' abilities, background knowledge and personalities are also diverse. In order to keep order at school, students are disciplined to respect various school regulations. Students are also encouraged to work together with their classmates and learn from each other.

Therefore, it might be said that group activities have been especially emphasized in Japanese schools. On the other hand, self-assertion and questioning have been neglected.

In spite of the reform and encouragement of the American Occupation, "individualism" has not been promoted in Japanese schools. It would be difficult to try to promote individualism in such a country as Japan, which has had a long history as a densely populated agrarian society. Social criticism, self-assertion and independence have been considered contradictory to Japan's traditional values:

> American inspired education stressed individualism, social criticism, and personal development in a liberal atmosphere. The status quo was put in jeopardy, and this naturally appealed to the opposition camp. Pre-war schools had emphasized polite conduct, a sense of duty to society, and respect for authority. Older Japanese, witnessing rising juvenile crime, ethical confusion, motivational stagnation, and finally student protest readily laid the blame on the new school system (Rohlen, 1983, p. 212).

It is difficult to promote individualism in schools without parental support. Furthermore, orderly group activities have to be promoted within schools. In every class, teachers have to teach forty to forty-five students without any extra assistant teachers or specialists to help them. If the teachers were to allow students to do as they pleased, it would soon become impossible to teach students in overcrowded classes. In addition, it is considered natural for students to cooperate in various activities necessary for the maintenance and management of the school. For instance, students clean their classroom and playground every day. Student councils and clubs also contribute to the maintenance of schools by keeping the grounds in good condition, planting flowers, making necessary announcements through the school public address system or lending books at school libraries. The fact cannot be denied that these characteristics of Japanese schools have prevented the promotion of individualism.

Although it may be true that lack of individualism is a defect of Japanese schools, it is also true that the training of students through group and collective activities is a major advantage of Japanese schools. It is expected in Japan that students should learn to develop their individual characteristics through social relations with their peers.

In primary and secondary schools, all students are grouped into classes, each of which consists of about forty-five students. In the grouping of students, ability-based grouping has not been adopted. Thus, each class consists of a heterogeneous group of students. The enrolment of each class is fixed for a year or two, and each group of forty-five students continues to learn together in specified classrooms.

One teacher is appointed to each of the classes, and this teacher is in charge of the class members. S/he teaches almost all the subjects including music and physical education in primary schools. For this reason, not only the relationship between teacher and students, but also that between students tends to become very familiar.

Soon, a teacher becomes quite familiar with the characteristics of the students in her/his class. Once a year, s/he visits all the homes of the students in order to get to know their family backgrounds. Based on an understanding of individual students, the teacher tries to improve the quality of her/his class as a group.

Notes of students' opinions are often printed and distributed among classmates for the purpose of promoting communication. Various roles, such as representatives for the school council, library assistant, classroom cleaning student, message announcer or school lunch chief, are assigned to students. If a handicapped child is included in the class, students talk about what to do with the child. Each class member is expected to fulfil some kind of role for the maintenance and improvement of the class environment. Students develop their social abilities such as leadership and cooperation through these activities.

(4) *School Regulations*

Junior and senior high school students are generally bound by detailed school rules and regulations. For instance, only certain types of hair styles are allowed and the colours of the shoes and socks the students may wear are specified in detail. Even some out-of-school activities are strictly prohibited by school regulations. For instance, some schools have a rule that students are not allowed to go to the cinema without being accompanied by one of their parents. Some of the more liberal parents criticize these detailed school regulations, and have tried to abolish some of the extreme ones, but on the whole, they seldom succeed.

The sudden change from a liberal life in primary school to a restricted life in secondary school might have something to do with Japanese thinking on the handling of puberty; Japanese parents regard this period as "critical". At this stage, the "pure", naïve and pleasant period of childhood ends. Students grow rapidly, and soon become physically uncontrollable. They are awakened to sex and become unstable. In addition to this internal change, an important external change arises. The severe competition for entrance examinations is to start.

Japanese parents do not expect their children to be independent. Instead of giving them freedom, parents try to protect their children from the "evil" world outside. Parents generally expect them to concentrate their time and energy into something "healthy" rather than harmful—the best of which is to be absorbed in the preparation for entrance examinations. If this is not possible, students are expected to do their best in some kind of sports. It might be said that secondary school students are expected to lead a life that is simple and strict like Puritans.

Dark student uniforms, detailed school regulations and simple school facilities are the reflection of these parental expectations. In fact, no facility for air conditioning is available in most junior and senior high schools. In the simple school facilities, students compete for better marks. At the same time, the majority of secondary school students actively participate in a student club activity. Sports club are especially popular, and many students choose baseball, soccer, basketball, handball or volleyball.

> In Japan, the issue of sports is complicated by the examination syndrome. To become an "exam-pro" means devoting time to a painful regimen, not too different from hard sports training. The Japanese view the two as analogous in terms of sacrifice and discipline. Each is a modern version of an ascetic route to personal stature. Each is popularly said to enhance spiritual (*seishin*) strengths. Thus, sports and examination oriented study are really parallel practices in a cultural sense, and the two stand together in contrast to the laissez-faire ideals of schooling based on freedom and personal choice (Rohlen, 1983, p. 192).

The idea that sacrifice and discipline are an ascetic route to personal stature might be called the "hidden curriculum" of moral education in Japanese schools. There is no public description of this idea, but there seems to be a consensus about it among most parents as well as teachers.

Of course, it is impossible to control all aspects of student life. A large number of books and magazines are published and many of them are full of gossip, scandals and sexual matters. TV and radio programmes also provide students with a great number of bad influences, especially the late-night broadcasts. On the whole, however, the influences of the media does not seem to be as serious as is often asserted by some educationalists. Insofar as students are assured of leading a regular life at home, school and community, most of them can distinguish right from wrong.

Changes in Children's Out-of-School Life

More and more parents have become concerned about schooling and have been making their criticism heard. The following factors, however, must be taken into account.

First, especially in developing urban areas, a large number of new schools have been built one after another to absorb the increasing number of children. In these new schools, teachers have been extremely busy setting up new school regulations as well as organizing students. To catch up with the increase in students, a large number of teachers have had to be employed quickly, irrespective of their quality. It has not been an easy task training these new teachers. Furthermore, the average size of individual schools has greatly increased, which has made the management and administration of individual schools much more difficult. Antagonism between local boards of education and the teachers' union has also caused many problems in decision-making processes in schools.

Second, students have brought many new problems to schools. Since there are few stable community organizations to rely on, teachers have had to cope with these problems by themselves.

Third, with urbanization and the increasing nuclearization of family structure there are quite a few families with problems. In the majority of families the fathers go out to work and the mothers stay at home. As a result, the mother–child relationship has become dominant, and fathers tend to be indifferent to children's education. Furthermore, fewer children participate in family businesses, since self-employed occupations have decreased and the workplace has become separated from the household residence. Finally, in a growing number of families, both husband and wife work full-time and are not able to spend much time with their children; the children are given their own house-keys and the freedom to come and go as they wish. In all these cases, the human relationships that children experience at home have become simpler.

Fourth, children's play-groups have decreased. In traditional villages and towns, parents used to tell their children to be diligent, to be honest and not to trouble others. But parents in those settings had little time to be with children since they were too busy with farming or other work. Children spent most of their free time outdoors with their playmates. Children's play-groups were independent of parental control, and a rich "play culture" of children was transmitted from generation to generation. Through participating in these play-groups, children learned group behaviour. Therefore, it might be said that children's play-groups functioned as one of the major socialization agencies for children.

It has been frequently noted that children's natural and physical environments have significantly deteriorated. The government has established various public educational facilities for children in order to cope with these problems. Swimming pools, camping grounds, gymnasiums, playgrounds, parks, libraries and museums have been established by central and local governments. While it is true that children's lives have been enriched by these facilities, we should not forget the fact that opportunities to use these facilities are still very much limited to once or twice a year. In other words, these facilities are not available for children's daily use.

However, it is possible that today's children, even if they had abundant play facilities, would not make use of them. Many people have observed that children, even in rural areas, do not play outside, but remain at home, in spite of the access to rich natural environments and playing-fields in rural areas. Rural children apparently prefer in their spare time to listen to radio, watch TV and read cartoons. Recently, personal computers have become popular among children, which also encourages the preference of children to stay indoors.

Excessive competitiveness in the preparation for entrance examinations is an important factor behind the decline in children's play. In addition for formal schooling, the majority of children go to *Juku* every evening, others go every other evening. This makes it difficult for children to get together after school.

Being preoccupied with their children's preparation for entrance examinations, parents tend to disregard many important moral and social values that children should gain in their childhood. Parents are beginning to worry that their children will not adapt well to social values and will become "egoistic".

Conclusion

In contemporary Japan no one would deny that some kind of moral education is necessary at school. But the term "moral education" is ambiguous and has connotations of the special type of moral education prominent in pre-war Japan. On the other hand, moral education includes a wide range of activities which contribute to the development of children's character and personality.

The term moral education is controversial, since it was once exploited as a means to realize political goals. There still exists a deep-rooted distrust of pre-war moral education (*Shushin*), which was used for the indoctrination of ultranationalism and militarism. There also exists doubt of the effectiveness of teaching moral education as a special subject. It is often alleged that this subject can do no more than give children abstract and fragmentary knowledge, which has nothing to do with a child's personality development.

Furthermore, even if everyone agrees that moral education is necessary, it is not easy to get a consensus about what its content should be. In this diversified society, moral principles supported by one sector of society are not necessarily encouraged by other sectors of society. This kind of disagreement sometimes lead to deep-rooted antagonisms.

Therefore, moral education is not only a controversial matter for education, but also for politics and economics. Legally, of course, school education is independent from political control, but in reality, this is not necessarily so. Political parties creates images of their own ideal society, and may try to exploit school education as a means towards that realization.

References

Brown, D. M. *Nationalism in Japan*. Berkeley and Los Angeles: University of California Press.

Cummings, W. K. (1980) *Education and equality in Japan*. New York: Princeton University Press.

Dore, R. P. (1958) *City life in Japan*. Berkeley: University of California Press.

Monbusho (Ministry of Education) (1983) Koritsu Sho-Chugakko ni okeru Dotoku-kyoiku no Jisshi-jokyo no Chosa nitsuite (Results of a Survey on Moral Education in Public Primary and Junior High Schools). *Monbujiho*, August, 72–79.

Passin, H. (1965) *Society and education in Japan*. New York Bureau of Publication, Teachers College, Columbia University Press.

Rohlen, T. P. (1983) *Japan's high schools*. Berkeley: University of California Press.

Singleton, J. (1967) *NICHU—A Japanese school*. New York: Holt, Rinehart & Winston.

CHAPTER 6

Ideologies in Korea's Morals and Social Studies Texts: A Content Analysis

SOOYEON C. SUH

Confucian societies have always viewed education as a means of cultivating appropriate values and behaviour. In the traditional Korean Yi Dynasty (1392–1910) moral education was the most important subject in the educational institutions. Firm emphasis was placed on the "correct relations" between members of families, kinship groups and the broader kingdom. Among the correct relations, special attention was devoted to justifying the vertical relations between parents and children with the ideology of filial piety and between the king and his subjects with the ideology of heavenly mandate.

Even in the Japanese colonial period (1910–1945), moral education was continued through a course entitled "self-discipline" (or *shusin*). The only interruption in moral education occurred during the three years of US military government and the first years of Korean independence (1948–1955). During that time, morals courses were replaced by social studies courses in which civic virtues were emphasized. The Korean War (1950–1953) and subsequent national division brought about a decay in traditional morals and a crisis in national ideology. Therefore, in 1956, an "anti-communism and morals course" was adopted for the primary and middle schools, and a "national ethics course" was introduced into the high school.

Since 1956, the importance of values education has been progressively emphasized by the state. Critical of the state effort to promote values education, intellectuals have charged that the aim is to instil passive subordination to the dominant ideology rather than to cultivate personal autonomy. It thus seems important to explore which values and beliefs are featured in the school values education curriculum, whose values and belief systems are selected as legitimate moral themes, whose interests are served and why this bias occurs.

Historical Background

Immediately after Korean independence from Japanese colonial rule in 1945, Korea was split into two parts, and the two halves were absorbed into different world power blocs. South Korea suddenly emerged as a frontier country defending the capitalist bloc from the expansion of the world communist power, through military confrontation with North Korea. The US government, the core state, covertly and overtly supported the construction of a pro-American conservative regime destroying the nationalist party and communist party in the late 1940s, when after three years of US military administration, the government was turned over to the conservative party of Syngman Rhee (1984, pp. 79–80). The three years of the Korean War (1950–1953) proved even more precisely the strategic importance of South Korea for US military interests. Thereafter, South Korea has received a great deal of military aid from the US, and has had US military bases constructed at strategic points on Korean territory. The military alliance with the US, on the one hand, has convinced the South Korean people that they are protected from the risk of military attack from communist North Korea. However, on the other hand, South Korea has been subordinate to US interests economically, politically and militarily as well as ideologically. The state in South Korea has played the part of the periphery serving the interests of the core state.

Anti-communism is the typical ideology which is produced by the national division and "the implementation of peripheral role by the state in South Korea in the world system" (Sungkook Ko, 1985). In the 1950s, anti-communism became the first official ideology of the US government, as the US and USSR entered the cold war. The Rhee regime introduced anti-communism, and utilized it as a major device for political manipulation. (Sung Chul Yang, 1972, p. 30).

The military group which took over state power with a military coup in 1961 did not have any power base except the military coercive forces at the time of the coup. General Park rose to the fore of this group in 1963, and maintained leadership for the next eighteen years. The Third Republic regime (1963–1979) constructed legal edifices, such as the Anticommunist Law and National Security Law, and established the Korean CIA in 1961 for coercive control of radical political activities. These authoritarian tendencies steadily mounted in the late 1960s, and culminated in the Yushin Regime (1972–1979) (Althusser, 1972; Young-Whan Kirl, 1972; Han Sungjoo, 1977; Launius, 1983).

To gain legitimacy for holding state power, the ascending military group put forward democracy and economic development as the main policies of the new government. A democratic constitution was established, and economic development planning was launched by the military power group. In initiating economic development, the state elites played two roles: forming a capitalist class by providing economic supply, tax reduction, etc., and becoming capitalists themselves through monopolizing key industries such as the telephone service, railway transportation, and the electronics and tobacco industries (Hyun-jin Ym, 1984, p. 282). The main economic policy in the 1960s was to facilitate export with loans from abroad. In the implementation of that policy, the state elites sustained a low wage policy while repressing the organization of the working class, and also persisted in a low price policy on agricultural products to feed low wage workers (Lee Jaehee, 1984, p. 28).

As a corollary of this mode of domestic capital accumulation, the regime became not only self-sufficient and independent from the social classes, it also commanded overwhelming power over them, especially over the working class. Moreover, the regime allied with military power, which grew rapidly as a product of a high annual military budget as well as military aid from the US government. This situation permitted the state elites to wield their power for their own interests, prolonging their political power. Furthermore, the policy of promoting capitalists while exploiting the working class and peasants was finally accompanied by authoritarian control of workers' and other citizens' political activities. Under these circumstances, an authoritarian regime began to emerge in the late 1960s. The establishment of the Yushin Constitution in 1972 accelerated the authoritarianism.

An important difference between the Third Republic regime and the Yushin regime is the authority relation between the state elites and other citizens, and the degree of repression of the citizens' activities. In the Yushin regime, political power was concentrated in the political leader and other state elites, while interest representation of various social groups through party activities was extremely restricted. Moreover, the violent suppression of protest was prevalent. Indeed, authoritarianism escalated further in the process of interplay between opposition and suppression.

The differences between the two regimes are conspicuous in the following aspects of the constitution. First, the Yushin Constitution provided for an appointment by the President of one-third of the National Assembly members, whereas all the National Assembly members were directly elected by the people in the Third Republic government. Moreover, the legislature under the Yushin Regime no longer retained its previous authority to inspect the administration of the executive. Second, the Yushin Constitution allowed for the indirect election of the President by a locally elected "rubber stamp" group, called the National Conference of Unification, whereas the President was elected by a direct ballot of the people in the Third Republic regime. Third, the Yushin Constitution prescribed that the President could hold the office for an unrestricted number of six-year terms, whereas in the Third Republic the President could hold office for only two four-year terms. Fourth, in the Yushin regime the President was empowered to promulgate emergency measures and presidential decrees. During this regime, Emergency Measures 1–9 were decreed to severely punish the political activities of citizens, particularly students.

In summary, the Yushin regime was a repressive authoritarian regime where the authority to decide state affairs and to control citizens' behaviour was concentrated in the regime, particularly the President, while the Third Republic was a less authoritarian regime in that the authority was more or less distributed to the citizens based on a democratic constitution.

Regime Influence on the Curriculum and Textbooks

Durkheim long ago argued that commonly shared cultures are transmitted through educational institutions. Neo-Marxists, criticizing the consensus view of the school curriculum, argue that capitalist class ideologies representing their material interests are reflected in the school curriculum (Apple, 1979; Sharp, 1980). The neo-Marxist theory assumes that the capitalist class exercises overwhelming power over the state and ideological institutions, and that dominant ideologies are created by the ruling class without any influence from other power groups. But these assumptions do not fit the realities of South Korea, where the dominant group for the last two and a half decades has been the military authoritarian regime rather than the capitalist class, and where the state has occupied a peripheral position in the capitalist world-system since its independence from Japanese colonial rule in 1945. This dominant group has exercised control over the repressive and ideological apparatus, including the curriculum.

The traditional ethical system in Korea was relatively homogeneous. In terms of religion, Buddhism, Confucianism and Christianity influenced the behaviour of Koreans. Recently, the Christian population has been rapidly increasing. However, the school morals curriculum is totally under the central control of the state, and since the emergence of the recent authoritarian regimes these more traditional moral themes appear to have been supplanted by new emphases.

The Ministry of Education administers almost all educational affairs, including textbook compilation, entrance examinations and teacher recruitment (Bukwon Park, 1981, p. 76). The major vehicles of values education are the morals course and the national ethics course, the former in primary and middle schools, the latter in high schools and colleges. Under the Third Republic regime, morals textbooks were revised along with other textbooks in 1964. Under the Yushin regime (1972–1979), a second revision of the textbooks was carried out in 1973, immediately after the regime change. In both periods, the morals textbooks used in primary schools were entitled "Correct Life"; those in middle schools were entitled "Democratic Life"; and those used in high schools were entitled "National Ethics". In colleges, National ethics was introduced as a required course in 1970. Textbooks for primary to middle schools were compiled under the administration of the

Ministry of Education, while those for colleges were compiled by a research committee established by the Ministry of Education.

In the 1964 edition, morals textbooks dealt with four moral items: courteous life, individual life, social life and national life. In the 1973 edition, anti-communist life was added to the existing four dimensions. Courteous life involves cultivating a spirit of etiquette so as to be able to act in a suitable manner in one's daily life. Individual life aims to develop a sincere personality and healthy body. Social life builds a consciousness of oneself as a member of family, school and society, in order to be able to live a peaceful and healthy social life. National life encourages a love of and pride in the nation. Anti-communist life develops a correct understanding of the contradiction and fictions of communism, and an alertness to a possible military intrusion from communist North Korea. It is apparent from a review of these themes that the contents of morals textbooks are not drawn from particular religious value systems, nor from the values of a capitalist class culture.

National ethics textbooks, used in high schools and colleges, devote more attention to state ideologies than do the morals textbooks. According to the tentative plan formulated by the research committee, national ethics textbooks are supposed to contain at least four themes: Korean traditional culture, the ideal and reality of democracy, criticism of communism and the future of the nation.

Moral education in the 1970s was influenced by the National Education Charter, declared in the form of a presidential decree in 1968. The National Education Charter starts with "We are born into this land, charged with the historic mission of national revival. It is time for us to establish the attitude of self-reliance and independence". It ends with "Love of the country and the people, along with the firm belief in democracy against communism, is the way to survive and the basis of realizing the ideal of free world. We, as an industrious people with confidence and pride, pledge ourselves to create a new history with the untiring effort and collective wisdom of the people, looking forward to the future when we will have a unified nation to hand over to our posterity". This charter prescribes national goals and a required mode of behaviour for achieving those goals. It does not seem accidental that the promulgation of the charter coincided with the authoritarian shift of the political system.

The full text of the charter was given on the first pages of all textbooks used for primary and secondary education. Students were encouraged to memorize the whole charter and to practice the moral norms prescribed in the charter. Moreover, government authorities in the Yushin period were directed to reflect the spirit of the charter in the moral textbooks.

Content Analysis of Textbooks

The intervention of the respective regimes in curriculum revision and in the actual decision-making concerning curriculum content suggests that the regimes sought to project their ideologies in the school curriculum. Phrased in the form of hypotheses:

1. Regime ideologies will be reflected in the school values curriculum.

2. The peripheral position of South Korea in the world-system will be reflected in regime ideology and hence in the values curriculum.

3. The authoritarianization of the regime will be reflected in regime ideology and hence in the values curriculum.

To examine these hypotheses, a content analysis was carried out to determine the role of ideology in primary level textbooks for moral education and social studies. The primary level was selected as it is the only level in Korea that is compulsory, and these two subjects were selected as their texts had the strongest ideological emphasis. All the forty-six textbooks for the six grades used during the two periods were subject to the analysis without sampling. Categories of state ideologies were created through the process of going back and forth from conceptual definitions of ideologies to the textbook contents. Every page of a textbook was coded in terms of presence or absence of indicators of ideologies.

TABLE 6.1. *Percentages of Pages Containing Regime Ideologies Compared with Total Number of Pages of Textbooks by Period and Subject*

	1964–1972		1972–1982	
Subject	Pages containing ideology (%)	Total No. of pages	Pages containing ideology (%)	Total No. of pages
Social studies	22.2	1027	22.5	863
Morals	56.4	1345	56.7	1323
Total	41.6($N=982$)	2372	43.5($N=951$)	2186

The Prevalence of Regime Ideology

Table 6.1 indicates that the percentage of state ideology in the total contents of the textbooks is 42 per cent in the 1964 textbooks and approximately 44 per cent in the 1973 textbooks. Thus the proportion of state ideology is almost half the total textbook content in both periods. Morals textbooks have more than twice as much ideological content as social studies textbooks in both periods. Relative to morals textbooks, social studies textbooks contain more references to descriptions of facts than suggestion of values and norms. The modest increase in the proportion of state ideology in texts for the Yushin period is due to the increase in the time allocated for moral education and hence the increased length of the moral education textbooks.

TABLE 6.2. *Percentages of Pages Containing Regime Ideologies Compared with Total Number of Pages of Textbooks by Period and Grade*

| | 1964–1972 | | 1972–1982 | |
Grade	Pages containing ideology (%)	Total No. of pages	Pages Containing ideology (%)	Total No. of pages
1	24.2	231	28.0	236
2	26.9	276	32.3	300
3	29.3	355	32.8	366
4	36.2	467	43.6	473
5	48.1	541	49.1	399
6	64.3	502	64.6	412
Total	41.6(N=982)	2372	43.5(N=951)	2186

Differences by Grade Level

Table 6.2 shows that in both periods ideological content increases systematically with a higher grade. Textbooks of the 1970s have a little more ideological content than the textbooks of the 1960s. Table 6.2 thus suggests that the higher-grade students are exposed to more intensive ideological indoctrination than the lower-grade students for both periods. One reason is that the textbooks for lower grades contain more references to individual life, family life and school life than do the textbooks for higher grades.

TABLE 6.3. *Rate per Thousand Pages Containing Regime Ideologies by Subject by Period*

| | 1964–1972 | | | 1972–1982 | | |
	Social studies	Morals	Total	Social studies	Morals	Total
Anti-communism	35	385	234(554)	30	242	158(346)
Nationalism	49	120	89(212)	46	205	142(311)
Economic development	109	13	54(129)	114	86	97(212)
Militarism	7	75	46(108)	3	62	39(85)
Social stability	31	24	27(64)	35	48	43(94)
Democracy	40	3	19(45)	37	4	17(37)
Statism	13	1	6(15)	27	20	22(49)
Efficiency	0	2	1(3)	2	0	1(2)
Welfare state	0	0	0	2	0	1(2)
Total N*	1,027	1,345	2,372	863	1,323	2,186

*Total N in the bottom line indicates the total number of pages of textbooks from which the rate of each ideology is calulated.

Changes in Emphasis

Table 6.3 indicates the relative emphases on the state ideologies within each period and the changes of emphasis between the two periods. In both periods, anti-communism received the highest rank order of emphasis, and nationalism and economic development followed in descending order. After the top three themes, social stability, militarism, statism and democracy were ranked in a descending order in the 1973 texts, whereas in the 1964 editions the order was militarism, social stability, democracy and statism. A look at changes of rates for the three most prevalent themes shows that anti-communism decreased significantly while economic development and nationalism increased. Of the remaining themes, social stability and statism increased in the 1973 texts while militarism and democracy decreased.

(1) Anti-communism

Anti-communism has been emphasized the most over the two periods, although the emphasis is sharply diminished in the 1973 textbooks. In both periods, the specific indicators of communist attack and false propaganda, and defence against the destruction of communist attack account for more than half of the total references. Thus the actual content of anti-communism is much more focused on the crisis that a communist attack might bring about than on a criticism of the economic conditions of communist society. This suggests that primarily the authoritarian regime utilized the ideology to legitimize itself by invoking crisis-consciousness, although anti-communism inherently legitimizes capitalist economy.

Anti-communism has been the main ideology utilized by the regimes ever since the ideology was introduced by the Rhee regime (1948–1960). Anti-communism became an official ideology of the US government in the 1950s as the US and USSR gradually entered the cold war, establishing their respective international power blocs. The absolutist version of anti-communism—that communists are evil and liberalists are angels, so that communism should be destroyed on earth—became the prevailing ideology in the Western bloc (Hackjun Kim, 1983, p. 102). The state in South Korea introduced this ideology without adjustment and constructed a new world view, viewing North Korea as the number one enemy in the world and the US government as the number one friend.

The proclamation of anti-communism has always provided rationales for regimes to argue that the times do not permit the luxury of liberal democracy, and to repress radical movements. The Rhee regime, a conservative right wing regime, utilized anti-communism as a major device for political manipulation (Sun Chul Yang, 1972, p. 30). The Third Republic regime passed new laws, such as the Anti-communist Law and National Security Law, and established the Korean CIA in 1961, for coercive control of radical political activities. This supports Sungkook Ko's argument that anti-communism legitimized and reinforced not only political and military dependence on the core state but also the domestic authoritarian regime (Sungkook Ko, 1985, p. 155).

Anti-communism could be internalized into the people's consciousness as the first ethic of the state without any serious resistance, since older generations, who experienced the disastrous Korean War, and younger generations, who were still experiencing the precarious situation resulting from the war and the partition of the nation, commonly share the phobia of war. Also social groups are not preoccupied with other ideologies, such as bourgeoisie liberalism, since the bourgeoisie has not commanded either political or ideological hegemony in South Korea.

Therefore, the persistence of anti-communism as the first state ideology through the two regime periods can be explained primarily by the national division and the peripheral role of the state in the world-system. Less importantly, the domestic authoritarianization of the regime also contributed to the emphasis on anti-communism. The strong emphasis on anti-communist life as a moral value in the school moral curriculum can be explained by these intra-national and international contexts.

Anti-communism could not be emphasized in the Yushin authoritarian regime as much as in the Third Republic regime, although the ideology was still regarded as the most important. Taking advantage of the international climate of detente, the Park government proposed the national task of peaceful national unification. Anti-communism, with North Korea as the number one enemy, was toned down in the 1970s, since anti-communism is a contradictory value to nationalism and national unification.

(2) *Nationalism*

Nationalism is strongly accentuated in the 1973 textbooks. Nationalism is, by definition, the consciousness of collective national interests and confirmation of group solidarity as a unit of conflict with other nations. The elements of nationalism reflected in the textbooks are national unification, national independence and citizens' norms of behaviour—self-sacrifice, patriotism, loyalty, etc. In both periods, citizens' norms of behaviour received more attention than consciousness of national goals.

Since the nation was split regardless of national interests, the regimes holding political power have always tried to take advantage of the given situation rather than making an effort to change the national situation unilaterally. The intellectuals asserted the achievement of national unification to the exclusion of foreign countries' interests. However, the goals and methods of nationalism were not open to discussion in public (Sung Chul Yang, 1972). Therefore, the regimes have been criticized as anti-nationalist. The Yushin regime tried to make the best use of the ideological symbol of nationalism to legitimize its reinforcement of repression and authoritarianism. The proclamation of nationalism by a regime which accepts the dependency situation, could not but be illusive. No matter how sincere the intention, conservative nationalism that takes the international power order for granted, can only obscure the view of where the real national interests lie. Actually, the Yushin regime did not initiate any productive programme of action except the establishment of the Conference of National Unification in 1972, composed of members elected in all cities and towns of South Korea.

A notable difference is the perspective used for the compilation of the content. The 1973 text is organized to inspire national identity and pride as a Korean, by focusing on the economic, cultural and political lives of their ancestors, from the viewpoint of integration, while the 1964 text is much more focused on how the ancestors' state emerged and declined through attack by foreign countries or through internal conflicts. Another note-worthy item is that the front pages of all textbooks published since 1973 contain a picture of the national flag, showing how to put it up, a pledge to the national flag and a picture of the national flower. And, in the Yushin period, the words filial peity and loyalty were inscribed on the outside of all school buildings below college level.

The accentuation of nationalism throughout the school curriculum in the more authoritarian regime implies primarily the regime's efforts to legitim-ize the reinforced authoritarianism and partly the state's efforts at nation building under the given international order.

(3) *Economic Development*

The emphases on economic development is increased in the 1973 text-books. In the Third Republic, the ascending military group made an effort to enhance the legitimacy of the regime by the efficient achievement of economic development. Thus economic development was almost a political religion during the Third Republic. Economic development was still one of the main policies in the Yushin regime, since national prosperity and national unification were employed as major rationales of the Yushin auth-oritarian regime.

In contrast with the other ideologies, economic development has been accompanied by the state's action programmes. Consistently in both periods, the highest emphasis was placed on the role of the state for the capitalists, while the role of the state for the workers, which was de-empha-sized in the 1960s, has virtually disappeared in the 1970s. The role of the state for the peasants if emphasized slightly more in the 1970s, and the state ownership of enterprises is referred to with about the same frequency in the two periods. The consistently high emphasis on the role of the state for the capitalists and de-emphasis on its role for the workers in both regimes directly reflect state policies. As soon as the South Korean state was included in the capitalist world-system, the Rhee regime followed Western capitalism. However, as the Park regime was launched, the state began to intervene quite actively in domestic capital accumulation. Since the 1960s, the state has consistently supported capitalists for domestic capital accumulation mainly by initiating economic development planning. Just as consistently, the state has depressed the wages of industrial workers and helped to disorganize the working class. The authoritarian Yushin regime enacted an even more repressive labour law in 1972. The economic condition of peasants in Korea did not improve in the 1960s, partly because the state persisted in a low price policy for agricultural products and imported large quantities of agricultural products from foreign countries. Although the government initiated the New Village Movement in the late 1960s, the movement did not contribute to the improvement of the economic condition of peasants except superificially, by widening the roads and changing the style of houses.

The shift in the rates of ideological content related to the role of the state and the increased emphasis on the norms of citizens' behaviour may be due to the state's enhanced efforts at mobilization of citizens and more authoritarian control over social classes in the face of increased competition in the international commodity market, of financial crisis resulting from accumulated foriegn loans, and of the imbalance in the development of the industrial and the agricultural sectors. Economic independence seems to have constituted a substantial part of Korean nationalism in its conservative version throughout the two regime periods.

The indicators of economic development imply that state and capitalist interests are intertwined to a certain degree with regard to economic development when the state basically pursues a capitalist mode of production. The state has consistently played the role of supporting the capitalists. However, those state activities do not seem to be done just in the interests of capitalists, but for the state's own demand for domestic capital accumulation in the competitive world-system. I would argue that the creator of the dominant ideology was the regime which has been autonomous from the capitalists and acts as a representative agency of domestic social classes in the world-system. Moreover, the slight shift of emphasis from industrialization to the enhancement of the life of the people in the 1973 textbooks implies that national welfare is the product of the state rather than that of the capitalists.

(4) *Militarism*

The emphasis on militarism decreased slightly in the 1973 textbooks. Except for the references to military participation in the Vietnam War of 1965–1973, the rate of militarism is rather higher in the 1970s than in the 1960s. In both periods, the morals textbooks have many more references to militarism than the social studies textbooks. This implies that the military is pictured as a behavioural model for citizens in the morals textbooks.

The almost equivalent emphasis on militarism in both periods seems to reflect the occupational consciousness of the military group, which has held the political power throughout the two periods. The content of ideological references to militarism emphasizes that the army does good to communities as well as to the country, and that citizens should appreciate them. Stories describe the army building roads and schools and show schoolchildren writing letters of appreciation. One reason why a good image of the army is instilled from a low grade in the school is that three years of active duty in the army and participation in the army reserve until the age of 35 are required of all Korean men. The content of military participation in the Vietnam War, which contributes to raising the rate of militarism in the 1964 textbooks, appears to legitimize the political leaders' policy to send the Korean army to the Vietnam War (1965–1973).

(5) *Social Stability*

Social stablility was emphasized more in the 1973 textbooks than in the 1964 ones. Social stability references concern the basic attitudes and behaviours needed to maintain the social order, such as following social rules and state policy, etc. Therefore, those moral themes constitute the basic elements of political socialization in any regime. The data make clear that the more authoritarian regime demands of its citizens a higher conformity to the present social order.

(6) *Democracy*

The references to democracy decreased slightly in the 1973 textbooks, although the rates were not high in either period. The adjustment of democracy to the unique situation of Korea is not referred to at all in the 1964 textbooks, but invoked only in the 1973 textbooks. References to the realization of democracy also decreased slightly in the 1973 textbooks as compared to the 1964 ones.

The traditional political system in Korea was authoritarian, with the relationship between those who rule and those who are ruled maintained through strict command and obedience. The Japanese colonial rule (1910–1945) reinforced the political system which alienated those ruled from any participation in politics. Democracy suddenly appeared as the model of a political system during US military rule (1945–1948) in South Korea. The US military policy was reflected in educational policy too, so that the social studies subject entitled "citizen life" replaced the previous morals subject. The social studies subject emphasized the attitudes and skills necessary for building and maintaining a democracy. However, although democracy looked ideal, state power groups and citizens in those days did not really know what democracy was. Intellectuals, especially college students, were the most passionate advocates of democracy. Moreover, state power-holders disliked the idea of democratic rule, because it would sharply restrict the boundary of their authority and power. But still the regimes have tried to legitimize themselves under the name of democracy, since opposition groups have consistently advocated the ideal of democracy. The Third Republic regime put forward the democratic constitution to gain legitimacy. However, the Yushin regime tried to break through the attachment to Western democracy by invoking the unique political tradition in Korea and the necessity of the unique adjustment of Western democracy for the Korean situation. Yet the state elites in the 1970s did not totally discard the symbol of "democracy", as they wanted to convince the people that the regime was still a democratic regime, but a Korean version of democracy.

The overall low emphasis on democracy reflects the two regimes' reluctance to mobilize people for the realization of democracy. The decreased emphasis on democracy in the more authoritarian regime suggests that the state elites in the Yushin regime implicitly tried to legitimize authoritarianism by not talking about democracy.

(7) *Statism*

Statism is emphasized more in the 1973 textbooks than in the 1964 ones. An important feature of the Yushin authoritarian regime was the concentration of power in the President, combined with the repression of party activities and the function of the legislature.

Statist ideology emphasizes that the interests of the state precede the interests of individuals, and that the state exists as an agency of administration which does good for people. Statism is usually used as an ideology instrumental to nationalism. In other words, it asserts that the goal of a strong nation can be achieved only through strong state machinery. But when the real concern of the state power-holders is not with national goals, nationalism is used as an ideology instrumental to statism and authoritarianism. The increased emphasis on nationalism and statism had the function of justifying the establishment of the Conference of National Unification and the increased power of the President and the executive in the reinforced authoritarian regime.

Implementation of Values Education in Schools

Moral education in schools is intensively carried out through the morals course in primary and middle schools, and through the national ethics course in high schools and colleges. In high schools and colleges, the military training course was established in 1970 to train students in the military skills and military thought necessary for national defence. The time allocated to those courses in each school level has changed since that period, as Table 6.4 indicates.

TABLE 6.4. *Change of Time Allotment (Hours per Week)*

School	Course	1963–1972	1973–1982	1983–present
Primary	Morals	1	2	2
Middle	Morals	1	2	2
High	National ethics	1	1	1
	Military training	2	1	2
College	National ethics	2	1	2
	Military training	1	1	1

Notes: (1) The military training course in high schools and the national ethics and military training courses in colleges were imposed in 1970.
(2) The national ethics course at college level was imposed as a one semester course only.

Time allocated to the morals course in primary and middle schools increased in 1973. The national ethics course was introduced into colleges, and the military training course into high schools and colleges in 1970. Besides the given courses, moral education was implemented throughout the whole curriculum, including the social studies and national language courses. Teaching–learning activities in the classroom are mainly textbook-centred instructions. Extracurricular activities directed by the government are also practised: examples include the anti-communism oratory contest, the anti-communism poster contest and the anti-communism composition contest, which are offered to the students below college level. The Principal of the school, from primary to high school, delivers an instructive speech at least once a week in the morning meeting of all students and teachers.

Evaluation of moral achievement is mainly carried out through a written test in terms of moral judgement rather than moral activities. The Yushin regime introduced a new evaluation system into monthly tests and entrance examinations, in which moral subject scores were given a priority not only as a criterion for selection in high school and college entrance examinations, but also as a criterion for determining the order of academic achievement of those having the same number total points in their monthly tests in the middle and high schools.

In sum, the practice of moral education in schools of below college level tends to be thoroughly controlled by the state, by means of directions, standardized textbooks, time allocation and centralized education mechanisms.

Moral education in colleges was relatively autonomous until 1970 when national ethics was established as a commonly required course. Students and concerned professors have raised the question of whether the national ethics course was necessary in universities. Some opponents argued that a unified transmission of official state ideology to college students is dissonant with the nature of a university, with its ideals of autonomy and pluralism. Proponents argue that the national ethics course teaches ethical norms from which people can contribute to national development in the unique situation of South Korea.

An the controversy implies, national ethics is one of those courses which professors try to avoid teaching and students dislike taking. Therefore, the national ethics course does not seem to be practised in colleges as perfectly as the government expected.

Recruitment of Teachers

Primary school teachers are mostly graduates of junior teachers' college. In the primary school, one teacher teaches all subjects to a given class. Therefore, the morals course is taught by general teachers who do not specialize in moral education. However, in the teachers' college, students get two credits for national ethics and three credits for moral education. Teachers also take an in-service training programme in which state ideologies are reflected throughout.

A qualification for middle and high school teachers is earned by those who graduate from a college of education or those who take courses for the teaching profession. Those who specialized in education, philosophy or religion were qualified to be morals course teachers until 1982. From 1979, Departments of National Ethics were established in the national universities in accordance with government policy. Since 1982 when the Departments produced their first graduates, the Ministry of Education has restricted the qualification for morals teachers only to those who specialize in national ethics. The graduate programmes of the Departments of National Ethics will provide more and more teachers for national ethics courses and national ethic departments in colleges as time goes on.

Conclusions

Moral education in contemporary South Korea is very much determined by the authoritarian state's particular way of survival under the situation of national division, the military–political intervention of a foreign power and economic competition in the world-system. These conditions were embodied in the centralized system of moral education.

Moral education seems most effective in the primary schools and least effective in the colleges. Although the strong emphasis on the "pecularity of the situation" and collective values brought about resistance from college professors and students, moral education is a very important vehicle by means of which students are socialized into the authoritarian and peripheral society.

It is expected that the content and method of moral education will change as Korea's international power strengthens and as the political system becomes more democratic.

References

Althusser, L. (1972) Ideology: ideological state apparatuses. In B. R. Cosin (Ed.), *Education and structure and society*. Harmondsworth, Middx: Penguin.

Apple, M. (1979), *Ideology and curriculum*. London: Routledge & Kegan Paul.

Park, (1981) A sociological analysis of the decision-making in the process of textbook compilation. Unpublished MA thesis. Seoul: Department of Education, Seoul National University.

Hackjun Kim, (1983) Political culture under the independence and division of country. In Research Association of Sociology in Seoul National University (Eds.), *Tradition and culture of Korea*. Seoul: Bummoonsa.

Han Sungjoo (1977) Power, dependency and representation in South Korea. Report of the Annual Meeting of American Political Science Association.

Hyun-jin Ym, (1984) Dependent development and the transformation of the state. In Park, *New Understanding of Korean Society*. Seoul: Han Wool.

Kirl Young-whan (1972) Korea's fifth republic: domestic political trends. *Journal of Northeast Asian Studies*, Vol 6.

Launius, M. (1983) The state's corporatization of labor in South Korea. Unpublished paper.

Lee Hunchang (1984) Socio-economic aspects of national liberation in the theory of Korean capitalism. In H. Lee (ed.), *Korean capitalism*. Seoul: Kachibang. (1985).

Lee Jachee (1984) Capital accumulation and the role of the state. In Daegen Lee *et al. Korean capitalism*. Seoul: Kacachibang.

Sharp, R. (1980), Knowledge, ideology and politics of school. London: Routledge & Regan Paul.

Sung Chul Yang, Political ideology in Korean politics: its elements and roles. Se-jin Kim and Chang-hyun Cho (Eds.), *Government and politics of Korea*. Seoul: Research Institute on Korean affairs.

Sungkook Ko, A research on political change in 1970s. In Choi Jangjip (Ed.), *Capitalism and the state in Korea*. Seoul: Han Wool.

CHAPTER 7

A Subtle and Silent Transformation: Moral Education in Taiwan and the People's Republic of China

JEFFREY F. MEYER

Since 1949, when the nationalist government moved to Taiwan from the mainland, political authorities have considered the Republic of China as the conservator of all that was best in traditional China. Paramount among traditional values was the stress on morality in education, which has therefore received the continued practical support of national authorities as a central educational task. Drawing on a millenia-old Confucian moral system which has influenced most of East Asia, the Republic of China has now had some five decades of experience in trying to harmonize this ancient outlook with the exigencies of the modern world. I will first look at the current status of this effort, then give a general assessment of moral education in the People's Republic of China since 1949.

The Structure of Moral Education in Taiwan

Moral education in Taiwan has both a formal and an informal structure within the nine years of compulsory (and free) education. Formally and directly, morality is taught in specific classes, *Sheng-huo yu lun-li* (life and human relationships) for the six years of primary school and *Kung-min yu tao-te* (citizenship and morality) for the three years of junior middle school.[1] But indirectly, a concern for morality is evident in the entire curriculum, especially the language, literature and social studies courses.[2] It also has an important place in various kinds of extracurricular activity—periodic convocations, contests, displays, exhibitions, sports activities, Boy and Girl Scouts, celebrations of national holidays and other times dedicated to some

---

[1] Life and human relationships presents the more traditional moral tradition, based on the Five Relationships of Confucianism. Citizenship and morality is more oriented to the contemporary political situation.

[2] A good overview of the whole education system in Taiwan may be found in the *Educational Statistics of the Republic of China* published each year by the Ministry of Education.

particular virtue, such as filial piety. Thus, in numerous direct and indirect ways, the schools play their part in effecting the subtle and silent transformation which makes a Chinese person in Taiwan.

What the Textbooks Say

From the first to third grades of elementary school, there are lessons in morality for two hours each week, but no textbooks are used, although instructional syllabi and manuals are available for the teachers. Textbooks are provided for years 4–6 (*Sheng-huo yu lun-li*), organized around eighteen traditional virtues which are presented over the course of each year.

First semester	*Second semester*
Diligent study	Love/friendship
Courtesy	Courage
Patriotism	Filial piety
Forgiveness	Neighbourly harmony
Civic virtue	Frugality
Trustworthiness	Sense of shame
Cooperation	Responsibility
Law-abidingness	Perserverance
Justice	Peace

Most of these virtues are rooted in the Confucian tradition, while some, like patriotism and civic virtue, are a response to more modern conditions.

The civics and morality textbooks are organized according to the traditional Confucian pattern laid out in the *Ta Hsueh* (*The Great Learning*, a Confucian classic), beginning with the individual and expanding in ever wider social circles. There are again six volumes, one for each semester of junior middle school:

1. The Healthy and Virtuous Individual
2. The Full and Beautiful Family
3. A Perfect School—How to Be a Good Student
4. A Progressive Society
5. A Prosperous and Strong Nation
6. How to Be a Good Citizen of the World

The Civics emphasis becomes stronger as the child gets older and is the almost exclusive interest of the last three semesters' work. As one can see, this is a comprehensive programme of instruction, the main concerns being shared by most of the nations of Asia. And while the content has some specifically Chinese and Asian features, such as the extreme emphasis on filial piety, most of the virtues would also be prized by nations everywhere.

Indirect moral education is pervasive in other textbooks, particularly those of the language (*Kuo-yu*) classes of primary school and the literature

(*Kuo-wen*) classes of junior middle school. A thematic analysis of the language and literature textbooks reveals that the point of almost all the lessons is either moral or aesthetic (see Table 7.1). A Chinese educator has written that, unlike Western cultures which emphasize knowledge, religion or law, Chinese culture has stressed morality and art, and these two concerns have accordingly been the foci of traditional education (Wu Sen, 1979, p. 14). An analysis of the textbooks mentioned confirms this assertion. Cognitional or informational aims are relegated to other textbooks—history, geography, natural science, etc.—while the cognitional aims of language and literature classes are presented in exercises and application sections of the textbooks, not in the lessons themselves.

TABLE 7.1. *General Thematic Analysis of Textbook Lessons*

	Moral	Aesthetic	Cognitional
Language (12 vols.)			
Grade 1	7	9	
Grade 2	17	13	
Grade 3	23	17	
Grade 4	31	13	
Grade 5	29	11	
Grade 6	29	13	
Literature (6 vols.)			
Grade 7	22	18	6
Grade 8	26	17	4
Grade 9	32	6	1

The surprising frequency of aesthetic themes is certainly one of the unique characteristics of Chinese education. By "aesthetic" I mean those lessons which promote a love of the beauties of nature, the land, the sea, of animals, flowers and vegetation, the changing seasons, night and day, rain and sun, etc. (Less frequently it means some sort of art appreciation.) Yet in the Chinese context, even the aesthetic has an indirect moral aim. This connection of the aesthetic and moral has a long history, beginning at least with Confucius, who saw music (*yueh*) as a civilizing agent and an impetus to societal morality, which, together with ritual (*li*) could create a harmonious and orderly society. In the textbooks, the same connection is drawn with the appreciation of beauty. A good example would be the story of the flower sent to an unkempt and lazy man whose house and yard are a mess. The flower is so beautiful that he feels compelled to clean a table to accommodate it. Soon he is cleaning the room in which the table stands, then the entire house, inside and out, and finally his own person. A moral transformation has taken place. This story is found in the sixth-grade language text as well as in the eighth-grade literature textbook (*Kuo Yu* 11, pp. 13–14; *Kuo Wen* 4, pp. 51–52).

Let me offer another example of how the indirect approach to values instruction is used in these textbooks. Perhaps the chief aim of the civics/ morality textbooks for junior middle school (grades 7–9) is to stimulate patriotism in the students. Frequently the method is merely hortatory or moralistic. Sometimes the textbooks recount stories of military heroism set off against Japanese aggression or communist treachery.

While some of the stories of heroism are no doubt inspiring, the indirect method of the language and literature texts can be equally or more effectively used. One lesson describes how a man finds the remnant of an artillery shell on the site of a wartime battle in north-east China. The discovery brings to mind the suffering and tragedy of the war, yet he perceives a certain beauty in the now corroded shell fragment. It has a strange resemblance to one of the highly prized rocks resembling mountain ranges which the Chinese often place on wooden pedestals and keep in their homes. They are *yang* symbols with cosmic significance. The author decides to mount the shell fragment in the same way, to remind him of the sufferings and heroism of the past (*Kuo Wen* 3, pp. 42–43). Not all lessons are this skilfully done, but the indirect method certainly makes most of them more effective than mere exhortation.

A careful study of the textbooks makes clear that the morality taught in the schools is traditional Confucianism modified in a few areas to harmonize with modern needs. This conclusion was clearly confirmed in a survey questionnaire answered for me by eighty teachers in the Taiwan school system. (Meyer, 1988) Like most Chinese, they do not regard Confucianism as a religion, but as a system of moral, social and political philosophy. Therefore it is not seen as contravening the principle of separation of religion and state, nor as interfering with anyone's freedom of religion. Their conviction is that all people in Taiwan, whether Buddhist, Christian, Muslim, or Taoist, can accept Confucian moral principles. I have never heard or read any strenuous objection to this viewpoint, so Taiwan has a consensus here which many more pluralistic nations might well envy. Their problem is not trying to find a commonly agreed upon set of moral principles, but how to effectively teach the already accepted Confucian values. I should point out that I am speaking of the views of educational authorities here. There may well be some resistance to Confucianism among the young, especially as they get to senior middle school and higher education. Occasional reports of demonstrations among Taiwan college students would suggest this.

As for the nature of Confucian morality, it can be subtle and complex if one studies the early classics, but as far as today's schools are concerned, it is quite simple. My respondents showed a great unanimity in describing it. Of the eighty answers to the question of the essence of Confucian morality, fifty-nine mentioned the *Pa Te*, the Eight Moral Virtues: loyalty to ruler or nation/filial piety; benevolence/love; trustworthiness/love; harmony/peace. (The virtues can be considered separately, but are often paired.) Fifty-two mentioned the *Ssu Wei*, or Four Cardinal Virtues: ritual or etiquette [difficult to translate, it implies the whole host of external expressions which indicate, as one relates to another, one's place in the total hierarchy of society], righteousness, integrity and a sense of shame. Two other groupings of virtue were mentioned, mostly repeating those above, but adding wisdom and courage. Some respondents tried to summarize Confucian morality in a single central virtue. Filial piety was mentioned most frequently, twenty-nine times, benevolence twenty-eight times and loyalty sixteen times.

Now if we look at the textbooks, we find an apparent inconsistency with the teachers' views. An analysis of the language (grades 1–6) and literature (grades 7–9) textbooks reveals a somewhat different scale of values. The following list does not simply refer to the number of times that a virtue is *mentioned* in a lesson. I recorded it only if that virtue is a *major focus* of the chapter.

Patriotism	78	Hard work	11
Filial piety	45	Sincerity/honesty	10
Diligent study	24	Brains over brawn	8
Neighbourliness	23	Justice	8
Deference, obedience	22	Frugality	8
Scientific spirit	21	Integrity	7
Service to others	21	Sense of shame	7
Right ambition	20	Friendship	7
Civic virtue	20	Trustworthiness	5
Benevolence/love	16	Peace	5
Courage	16	Perseverance	4
		Respect for others	4

All other moral qualities are a focus in two or fewer chapters. Filial piety is a distant second to patriotism, which is subsumed under the traditional value of loyalty (*chung*).[3] The reasons for this are probably twofold. First, there has been a keen awareness in modern times that traditional Chinese morality has been too family centred, too clannish. The emphasis on civic virtue, on service to others, and especially loyalty to the national entity are meant to counteract that problem. Second, and more important is the embattled state in which Taiwan has found itself since the communist victory in 1949. The government of Taiwan continues to stress a strong national defence to resist any possible attack from the PRC, as well as to give credence to their incessantly reiterated intent to be a springboard to restore the mainland. The emphasis on patriotism is meant to support these goals. I am sure that

---

[3] The emphasis on filial piety is stronger in elementary school, as Martin (1975), p. 244ff.) has pointed out.

the teachers do not see this as inconsistent with Confucianism but their responses simply reflect the more traditional viewpoint. Of course, they also see filial piety as the root virtue out of which patriotism, and all other virtues, grow, and so in that sense it does have a certain priority.

"Scientific spirit" may also require explanation. It is obvious that the Chinese credit science as the source of Western superiority in modern times. To its lack they attribute China's weakness in the nineteenth century, and to it they look today for a better life for the people and a stronger nation among the nations of the world. Often the lives of famous scientists such as Einstein, Edison, Curie (as well as Chinese "scientists" like Ts'ai Lun, the inventor of paper) are used to show the achievements of science as well as the benefits it confers on humanity at large.

Looking over the list of virtues promoted in the textbooks, one immediately sees the overwhelming emphasis on the group over the individual. Even the virtues one would normally consider individualistic, such as integrity, honesty, trustworthiness, wisdom, courage, etc., are, as explained in the textbooks, really directed toward the welfare of the group. The lessons are clear and adamant about this point, seeing it as a fundamental difference between Chinese and Western morality. They point out that the *hsiao wo* ("little self" = the individual) must be sacrificed to the greater interests of the *ta wo* ("greater self" = society). "If there is a conflict between the individual and society, we ought to consider the good of society to be more important, ought to sacrifice the 'little self' to complete the spirit of the 'greater self.' " (*Kio-min yu tao-te* 4, p. 2). This is the leitmotif repeated again and again in the textbooks. It is a conscious rejection of what is considered the extreme individualism of the West.

In conclusion we may say that the textbooks present us with a consistent picture of moral education in Taiwan: the nature of morality, its content, and priorities among the various virtues taught. We must remember however that the texts tell us nothing about the actual moral situation among Chinese youth. They represent an ideal to which education authorities subscribe, a goal toward which they hope to lead the next generation.

The Role of Teachers

The teachers of morality in Taiwan, like teachers everywhere, have their problems, and I will consider these in a moment, but first let us look at some uniquely positive factors which they enjoy. As mentioned earlier, they are heirs to a long and continuous tradition which has stressed the importance of their subject. "In 1924, Dr. Sun Yat-sen clearly revealed that what the Chinese had to learn from the West was not political philosophy or morality, but science . . . This principle remains valid at the present time and has been an important guide for educational planners in the republic of China since 1949" (Lin Ching-jian, 1983, p. 107). In a recent speech to high school administrators, Taiwan President Chiang Ching-kuo reaffirmed the same view: "Today, although our education has of course absorbed modern Western scientific knowledge, we still want to proclaim the spirit of our Chinese traditional education . . . which is a blend of educating the mind, moral education, character building and education for living . . ." (Chiang Ching-kuo, 1983, p. 6).

I wondered whether such statements of official support were more than just rhetoric, and in a discussion (a classroom situation) with about thirty teachers of morality, I asked whether these were just "official statements" or if moral education was truly important to national authorities. Nearly every hand in the room shot up, without a moment's hesitation, which indicated to me that this group of teachers felt that the importance of their work was sincerely affirmed by the authorities.

Generally speaking, teachers hold an honoured place in Chinese society, and parents teach their children to respect teachers (though, as in other societies, this esteem is not sufficiently recognized in terms of salary). A study by a Chinese scholar comparing children in Taiwan and Great Britain has confirmed this (Hwang Chien-hou, 1974, pp. 52–53, 135). What discipline problems there are in the classroom are trivial compared to the situation in the US, for example.

Another way in which teachers of morality feel government support for their job is that they are provided with comprehensive teachers' manuals for teaching the subject. While the manuals present extensive and useful supplementary materials for the teacher (additional stories, suggestions for visual materials, sayings, discussion questions, etc.), one can see that they promote a very traditional teaching method. The so-called "discussion questions" in the textbooks are not really that, they are simply questions to produce correct answers, and the teachers' manual offers no help in aiding the teacher to encourage a real discussion.[4]

Do the teachers believe they are successful in their task of moral education? Turning again to my survey, I asked two questions to get at their feelings about this issue.

1. What kinds of results are today's schools getting as they try to promote traditional moral culture?
2. What are the reasons that some students in modern society are not inclined to accept traditional moral culture?

The first of my two questions gets at the very difficult issue of assessing the results of moral education. To do justice to this question would require an extensive and sophisticated sociological analysis. I give here only a brief summary of the view of my eighty respondents. The following is my judge-

---

[4] See for example the teachers' manual *Sheng-huo yu lun-li chiao-hsueh chih-yin* 6, pp. 42–51, as typical. The corresponding textbook lesson is *Sheng-huo lun-li* 6, pp. 24-31.

ment of the number who believed the results of moral education were excellent to disappointing:

Excellent	5
Generally positive	19
Middling	29
Disappointing	15

Twelve respondents answered vaguely or said that the results were difficult to assess. None judged results as a complete failure. Obviously, the great majority fell into a middle range of opinion. Placed in the "excellent" category were statements such as the following: "Good results. Citizens love their country, the way of filial piety is deeply rooted in society." "The effects are very good. The Principal leads, other teachers follow along, all is well coordinated."

For the remaining three categories, answers weighted toward the positive were placed in the second category (e.g. "Not bad", "Mostly satisfactory", etc.), those weighted toward the negative were placed in the fourth category (e.g. "Not very good", "Only superficially successful", "Only external compliance", etc.), and the rest were placed in category three. In summary therefore, we have the bell-shaped curve, with the majority inclined toward the positive. But more valuable than these approximations, I think, are the reasons given by many of my respondents for the partial failures noted. Twenty-six respondents complain that there is too much emphasis on intellectual knowledge and not enough on practical application. Fifteen others mention related aspects of the same problem: too much stress on texts, qualifying exams, memorization and "promotionism" (*sheng hsueh chu-i*).

Awareness of the gap between knowledge and practice was often coupled in the responses with a criticism of current teaching methods. Sixteen respondents complained that teachers of morality are too doctrinaire and dogmatic, approaches which encourage externalism, formalism and external compliance. Finally, nineteen respondents said that home and society in general do not support the morality that children learn in school. Therefore, even for those who judged the success of moral education to be relatively good, there is the feeling that it is underminded when the students leave school. As one respondent said, "Because family and society don't support us, the older the students get, the more their standards are lacking. When they leave school, we lose all hope!" Another said, in the same vein, "the schools can't oppose the pollution of society". Most respondents, however, were more positive in their assessments of results.

In responding to the second of these questions, the teachers gave the following reasons why students might not accept traditional morality:

1. The bad influence of Western culture (thirty-three times).
2. Factors inherent in modern society (such as, for example, urban anonymity, break-up of extended family) (twenty-one times).
3. Chinese traditional moral culture is not taught effectively (twenty times).
4. Defects in traditional moral culture itself (fifteen times).
5. The students are at fault—they are lazy, distracted, superficial, etc (twelve times).

One can see that the great majority of the teachers feel that extrinsic factors are to blame for the students' reluctance to accept traditional morality. Less than 20 per cent feel that the problem is intrinsic, which is an impressive reaffirmation of the value of traditional morality in the modern world.

Problems and Issues for the Future

Moral education in Taiwan is blessed with some very real strengths. It is based on a long tradition, its nature and content is a matter of essential agreement, it is supported by government authorities and parents, it has an honoured place in the primary and middle school curriculum, it is taught by competent teachers who are trained in their subjects and backed by extensive material in teachers' manuals. It is therefore free of some of the serious disagreements which beset the subject of moral education in the United States and other more pluralistic countries. Yet its problems are very real, and I would like to conclude this brief assessment by mentioning some of the issues which I think moral education in Taiwan must confront if it is to meet the needs of the future.

(1) *Traditional Morality, Modern Society*

This is a problem shared by every nation that wishes to pass on its moral heritage, and for Taiwan includes the changing notion of filial piety as it applies to what is more and more the nuclear family instead of the traditional ideal of the extended family. And because the moral principles were formulated in a basically rural/agricultural society, some of those principles seem quaint and antiquated in an increasingly urban society. Ancient China was thoroughly hierarchical in its structure, but now professes to be democratic and egalitarian. It was in times past totally patriarchal, but is now aware of the first glimmerings of a new women's consciousness. These issues have begun to be addressed, but will require further thinking and implementation by textbook editors as well as the teachers themselves.

(2) *Teaching Methodology*

Even if informal moral education is more effective than having specific classes devoted to moral instruction, the current system is not likely to be changed in the near future. Realistically then it is important that a new, more discussion-based and inductive method be developed for the classroom, and that teachers be given training in the new methodology. I have seen in the textbooks and heard in classrooms a supposed "discussion" in which students are merely questioned until they come up with the desired conclusions. As noted above, the "discussion questions" of the textbooks are not true discussion questions at all. The teachers' responses to my questionnaire also indicate that a doctrine and "preachy" method is one of the reasons why students resist traditional morality. They seem ready for a new method but will need training in how to implement it.

(3) *How to Assess Results*

The first problem is to get beyond assessing results on the basis of test grades, to get beyond the cognitional to the volitional. Yet observation of moral behaviour in students is not sufficient either. Teachers cannot observe the students once they have left the school grounds, and even if they could, there is the problem of external compliance without internal assent. This is what Ch'en Ying-hao, basing his assessment of Taiwan students on the Kohlberg model of moral development, calls the "good boy" level of morality. Dr Ch'en worries about the failure to develop moral cognition in the students, and looks to a more inductive, discussion-based classroom methodology (Ch'en Ying-hao, 1978). His research is moving in the right direction, but I believe it would be a mistake to uncritically accept Kohlberg's model. Just as Carol Gilligan has shown that it is not sufficiently universal to apply to young girls, so I believe that it fails to allow for certain unique Chinese cultural characteristics. Further refinement of the stages of moral development must be made before it can be usefully applied in Taiwan.

(4) *High Ideals, Impossible Goals?*

A substantial number of teachers in my survey felt that the morality presented in the classroom was too idealistic and was discouraging to most students who were unable to live up to it. I have found the same problem in the textbooks, both in the content and illustrations. Families always consist of father, mother and two children, ever smiling and living in tidy surroundings and perfect contentment. Society is progressive, cities clean, the countryside beautiful, children always perfectly obedient, helpful and respectful. In all the textbooks I studied, I found only a single example of a child who was "bad", a little boy who was watching TV instead of studying

(*Kyo-yu* **11**, pp. 65–70). The textbooks and classroom would be considerably improved with a sizeable dose of reality, some candid discussion of problems which do exist in Taiwanese society.

(5) *Cooperation or competition?*

One final problem which ought to be addressed arises directly out of the exam system currently used in Taiwan. One author has called the exam system "the fuel which drives the system", indicating how dominant a concern it has become in the educational process (Grambs, 1986). While not as stressful as the Japanese system, it is nevertheless beset by the same problem. Success in the exams determines whether a student will be able to go to the better senior high schools and, more important, who will be able to go on to college and university, which is the key to success in finding good employment. There is fierce competition for the limited number of places available in higher education. Fortunately, morality classes are not directly included in the battery of exams (although morality is, through the literature exams). The problem lies in the fact that the exams, an overwhelming concern in the experience of most students, are ignored in morality classes. There is a great emphasis on education as a cooperative enterprise, a harmonious situation in which students help one another in the process of learning. That is an admirable ideal, but again, it completely ignores the pressures and anxieties of the exam system, which are a very real part of the students' experience and therefore ought to be directly addressed.

Moral Education in the People's Republic of China

An assessment of moral education in the People's Republic is a far more complex undertaking. First of all there is the size of the country and its regional diversity. The provinces of the north-west are thinly populated, undeveloped and have large ethnic minorities. The provinces of the heartland and east coast are more urban, developed and culturally uniform. The schools of the rural and borderland areas lag far behind those of the latter regions.

Second, there is the huge population of the PRC. Educational policies cannot be implemented rapidly, so there is sometimes a long time lag between the proclamation of a policy and its actual implementation. In fact, some policies are more ideological calls to action than actually enforceable strategies (Cheng Kai Ming, 1986).

Third, there is the gap between cities and countryside. Because of some degree of local autonomy, city schools are far more advanced than their country cousins. In the recent drive towards a universal nine-year compulsory education, allowance is made for rural areas where implementation is assumed to be a long-range goal only. Whereas a full curriculum is prescribed for full-time city schools, the "simpler primary school provision in some rural areas, only Chinese language (with some literature) and arithmetic is enjoined" (Zhao Bao-heng, 1984).

Finally, there is the fact that drastic changes have occured over the thirty-eight years since the PRC was founded, and what were considered the essential moral teachings about 1970 are not the same today.

What I would like to do here is to briefly summarize the nature of moral education in the three major periods through which the PRC has passed since the Revolution. Since I have not done any personal research in the PRC, I will be summarizing publications and documents and the research of others, in order to provide some contrast to the situation in Taiwan and other nations of Asia. It can be useful to see where the various Asian countries' experience of implementing moral education is diverse and how in some respects it is the same.

From 1949 to the Cultural Revolution

In the earliest years after the founding of the PRC, moral education had to emancipate itself from the American and European models which had been used during the nationalist period. The reforms were chiefly based on Mao's seminal essay "On New Democracy", which called for an education which was "democratic, national and scientific", that is, which served the masses, upheld the dignity and independence of China against imperialist aggression and replaced feudal superstitions with scientific and historical truth. The Central Ministry of Education initiated a curricular reform which stressed the following: (1) reinforcement of political-ideological education; (2) the importance of productive labour; (3) development of specialized technical fields needed for national construction; (4) Marxist-Leninist thought and theory; (5) uniformity and centralization (Shi Ming Hu and Seifman, 1976, pp. 4–5).

From the very beginning of the PRC, Mao followed the traditional Chinese emphasis on moral/political education as the ultimate aim of schooling. "What is strikingly new in the writings of Mao is the repeated moral exhortation . . . Mao Ze-dong remains to some extent within the Chinese tradition which has always regarded moral instruction as its first duty" (Price, 1970, p. 17). This emphasis has never been abandoned, although there have been some changes in its content. During this early period, the Ministry of Education promulgated a set of "Rules of Conduct" for primary school and middle school students, whose purpose was to carry on communist morality, raise the political consciousness of the students, develop the spirit of collectivism, and cultivate good habits and character in students (Shi Ming Hu and Seifman, 1976, p. 43). Factors which later affected Chinese educational policy generally, such as the Soviet influence (1953–1957) and the Great Leap Forward (1958–1959), did not have a profound effect on the content of moral/political education.

Generally speaking, the PRC has not favoured specific classes in morality, but has sought to diffuse moral education throughout the curriculum. Much moral/political education took place outside the classroom, although some schools did have classes in Marxist thought. Within the primary school curriculum, it was in the language and literature classes that moral education took place. As Zhang Bi-lai said in discussing the aim of teaching literature, its purpose was to "cultivate ethics and behaviour of a high calibre through subtle and silent transformation" (quoted in Price, 1970, p. 132). Therefore it seems best to look to the language texts of primary school as the best indicators of the authorities' total programme for moral development. I would accept the judgement that "the elementary school *Readers . . .* reflect the basic or core values in which the Chinese leadership wishes to inculcate its citizens" (Ridley *et al.,* 1971, p. 3).

For this first period these core values were summarized in the "Five Loves" education: love of country, love of labour, love of science, love of the people and protection of public property. Hu Yen-li's book on the "Five Loves" indicates the desire to go beyond the pre-revolutionary methods of moral education: "It cannot be considered sufficient for *Five Loves* education to consist merely of obtaining a few dogmatic items of knowledge about the so-called *Five Loves* as happened in the former ethics and citizenship courses . . . Consequently, the implementation of *Five Loves* education is not the responsibility of the political information teacher only, but is the common task of the entire body of teachers" (Ridley *et al.,* 1971, p. 39).

Analysing the ten readers used in the five years of elementary education, Ridley *et al.* pinpoint three basic themes or aims of the lessons: informational, political and behavioural. The first is of the least importance (Ridley *et al.,* 1971, pp. 87ff.) The readers concentrate on political and behavioural goals, both of which are expressions of moral education. In order of frequency of occurrence, the following sub-themes are the ten most frequent to appear in the textbooks, either as a central theme or an auxiliary theme in a lesson: (1) Devotion and allegiance to the new society; (2) Benevolence of the new society; (3) Glorification of Mao; (4) Evils of Kuomintang China; (5) Military conflicts (against Japan, the KMT, etc.); (6) Social conflict (against reactionary elements); (7) Deception. (The students are alerted to being vigilant for subversives in society, although sometimes the category glorifies cleverness for a good end, e.g. a child outwitting a Japanese officer); (8) Love for the people; (9) Learning from the masses; (10) Inherent virtues of the labouring people.

Under behavioural sub-themes, the authors find the following to be the most important (again listed in order of frequency): (1) Social and personal responsibility (including such things as devotion to duty, obedience, thrift, hygenic behaviour, honesty, neatness, etc); (2) Achievement; (3) Altruistic

behaviour (self-sacrifice); (4) Collective behaviour (cooperation, solidarity); (5) Prosocial aggression (aggressive behaviour in the right cause);
(6) Conquest of natural environment; (7) Role acceptance; (8) Starting from
reality (implies a scientific approach and conflict resolutions which begins
with the study of an actual situation); (9) Aesthetic aspects of nature and/or
farm life; (10) Willingness to accept advice and criticism.

Clearly, this analysis of themes for the earliest period leaves no doubt as
to the dominance of group over individual values, an emphasis continuing
during the two later periods and which we also saw in our analysis of the
Taiwan textbooks. It is the definitions of the collectivity which change. The
traditional emphasis on family has been replaced in both cultures by a call
to a new national loyalty, whether the PRC under Mao and Marxism, or
the ROC under Sun Yat-sen's *san-min chu-i* (the "Three Principles of the
People", the basis of the Republic of China's political ideology). Among
the value conflicts which inhere in the PRC textbooks of this era, that
between achievement and self-sacrifice stands out particularly. Ridley *et al.*
see this as one possible factor in the frustration which burst forth so violently
in the actions of the Red Guards during the Cultural Revolution. Though
called to achievement, the vast majority were destined to sink into the
mass of farmer–worker–soldiers, i.e. into the collective. The same value
contradiction was found in the Taiwan textbooks, but there individual
achievement was always carefully described as having as its purpose the
benefit of the group.

The Great Proletarian Cultural Revolution

This period goes from 1966 when the Cultural Revolution was announced
to the death of Mao and arrest of the Gang of Four in 1976. In a real sense
the Cultural Revolution was a dramatic and aggressive attempt to educate
the whole of China and its results dwarfed by comparison in-school efforts.
Mao attempted to make the whole nation into a kind of classroom-theatre
as he tried to revitalize the revolutionary spirit of the people, especially the
young. For a time, all formal education was interrupted. When the schools
reopened, they were to be guided by a very different ideology, and a new
moral agenda. Some of the changes which have definite implications for
moral education are:

(1) Opposition to elitism. Education was to be open to all, not just those
who came from intellectual families or had attended the "key schools".
(These were schools which had been set up previously in 1966 to train the
best and brightest, so that China could quickly fulfil its goals of development
in industry, science and technology. The "key schools" were reintroduced
with the same purpose after the fall of the Gang of Four.)

(2) The concept of knowledge, art and literature for their own sake was

discredited. Education should be practical, at the service of economics and especially politics.

(3) Exams, grading and competition should be eliminated. The goal should be to learn a practical skill which would be useful in serving the socialist state. Climbing the educational ladder as the way to success was to be eliminated.

(4) The value of manual worker was reaffirmed. Ordinary labourers were glorified, effete intellectuals vilified. Students at all levels should divide their time between study and manual labour. The ambitious rustication programmes were undertaken, sending students for long periods of time to the countryside (see Bernstein, 1977).

(5) Workers and peasants were to be educated to become a new force of the proletarian intellegentsia. Admission to the better schools and to the colleges and universities was to be on the basis of political correctness rather than success in passing qualifying exams. The perennial "Red v. expert" debate was decided during this period more decisively in favour of "Red" than ever previously. Susan Shirk (1982) in her study of urban high schools calls this the period of "virtuocracy", when moral correctness determined one's education opportunities and career success. Let us look at how these radical changes in outlook are reflected in the textbooks of the period.

Politics, mathematics and Chinese language textbooks are the only ones continuously available through the decade of the 1970s. Physics, biology, history and geography were eliminated from many schools during the Cultural Revolution as being irrelevant to current social needs. Politics is the study of Marxism, so the best indicator again for measuring moral education is the language textbooks. Two articles have been published which give us a glimpse of these readers during and immediately following the cultural Revolution (Price, 1980; Kwong, 1985).

The Cultural Revolution attacked certain authorities who were labelled elitist, reactionary or bourgeois. Lin Biao and Liu Shao-ji were notable casualties. But Mao himself received even more adulation as a godlike leader, the Great Helmsman of the Chinese people. A second-grade text says: "The words of Chairman Mao have the highest standards, the highest prestige, and the greatest power. His every word is truth. A single word from him is superior to a thousand words by others" (Kwong, 1985, p. 199). Other CCP leaders are held up as models insofar as they are Mao's best students, disciples, lieutenants.

The highest purpose and noblest goal proposed by the textbooks in the early 1970s was to preserve the purity of China's Marxian socialism against the threat of an insidious capitalism, elitism and bureaucratic hierarchies. (I ignore the problem here of distinguishing between socialism and communism. As Price has pointed out, there is no way of clearly distinguishing the two on the basis of what appears in the texts.) The textbooks call upon the children to serve the state, to help realize the vision of a prosperous egalitarian society. They must resist the blandishments of evil elements, "former landlords stealing collective grain, ex-capitalists bribing the workers and government officials, or a corrupt bourgeoisie discouraging the young from working in farms and factories". The many stories about unregenerate capitalists show how much revolutionary zeal had waned in the twenty years since 1949. Education should serve production, the children should dedicate themselves to their given roles as farmers and workers. It was no doubt wise to glorify these occupations, since the vast majority of China's students were destined to work in them when they left school.

There was also some change in behavioural attitudes promoted by the textbooks. Besides the predictable exhortations to honesty, truthfulness, diligence, selflessness, etc., there was a tendency to connect "good" behaviour with the political category of socialism, while "evil" was exemplified as inherent in typical capitalist society. A third-grade textbook lesson illustrates this point. A truck-driver's children asked their father why he did not give grandmother a ride even though he was going in the same direction. He explained, "If we take advantage of public utilities and the amenities of the state, we are revisionists." Kwong points out that the children learned their lesson. When a bus-driver friend of theirs offers them a free ride, they insist on paying because "if we do it that way, how different will we be from the capitalist?" Generally speaking, the children portrayed in the textbooks are deadly earnest, noble, "austere little heroes catching a rich peasant stealing grain or fighting armed poachers with their bare hands". They are single-minded in their pursuit of revolutionary ideals, and the language texts from which their stories come are more ideological than informative (Kwong, 1985, pp. 204–205).

From 1977 to the Present

Immediately after the fall of the Gang of Four, some attempts were made to purge the textbooks of what are now seen as egregious errors. Already in 1977, a third-grade textbook had a lesson entitled "Ferociously criticize the Gang of Four as Suitable Successors", and they are described within it as "ferocious wolves" and "devious snakes" who discouraged learning. In September of 1979, a statement was made by the CCP Central Committee, almost breathtaking in its simplicity, which stated that "China's principal contradiction was between its people's expectations and China's ability to satisfy them" (quoted in *Beijing Review*, no. 45, 10 November 1986, p. 17). Mao's constant theme that the basic contradiction among the people was class conflict was thus swept away in one stroke. In the same year a new set of textbooks was made available throughout China. Kwong compares these texts with those of the early 1970s and I will summarize her conclusions as they bear on moral education.

In terms of authority, Mao remains the central personage (see also Price,

1980, p. 539). However, he is no longer the godlike figure of the early 1970s. He is more humanized, described as a man of the people, frugal, willing to do manual labour, and he shares his authority with other leaders, like Zhou En-lai, Zhu De, etc. From the current perspective we know these were early indications of the rejection of the "cult of personality" and that may be the reason that the new leaders like Deng Xiaoping have not loomed larger in the textbooks.

The new goal is no longer ideological purity, but to bring China up to the standards of the First World countries by 2049. The tolerance for private economic initiatives which has now become so prevalent was already suggested in the 1979 textbooks. In one essay, the author recounts how his parents bred silkworms, in addition to their regular jobs, to save extra money for their children's education. In a fourth-grade text there is a lively description of a free vendors' market. The items are abundant and the text comments: "Four years ago, the market would not have carried all these supplies" (Kwong, 1985, p. 201). To achieve its developmental goals, China must have engineers and scientists, so the children are encouraged to study science and technology, to help society reach the high goals (called the Four Modernizations: in agriculture, science/technology, education, industry) set by its leaders. Studying hard is important again. The days are gone when the Gang of Four praised a student named Zhang Tieshang for handing in a blank paper to his teacher. Manual work is not downgraded, but it is no longer lauded as the highest goal.

As to behavioural attitudes, much has remained the same, though the previous encouragements to criticize teachers has been eliminated, and all young students are urged to study hard to further the Four Modernizations. The capitalist road is still evil, but the heroes presented in the textbooks are now more varied and less stereotyped. In one story a monk, a figure of ridicule during the Cultural Revolution era, becomes the hero of a story in which he uses a scientific approach to bring up six iron oxen which were mired in a river bed (Kwong, 1985, p. 204). Newton and Edison are held up as heroes, their intellectual and scientific achievements presented for emulation. And generally, the children presented in the 1979 textbooks are more natural, relaxed and playful than the grim little heroes of the earlier textbooks.

The changes initially indicated in these readers have proven to be accurate indicators of the directions taken in post-Mao China. Lacking information about any more recent textbooks I would like to survey changes in educational policy over the years since 1979, particularly those which have direct implications for moral education. These changes have been most generally described as moving towards hierarchical and developmental values rather than the more egalitarian and redistributive values of the earlier period of the Cultural Revolution (Rosen, 1982; see also Pepper, 1980, p. 1ff.).

It is clear from numerous official statements that the current Chinese leaders socialist modernization cannot be achieved at the price of abandoning Marxist ideals, so in recent years there has been an effort to strengthen ideological and moral education along with the renewed emphasis on academic performance. In other words, the leaders perceived the danger of too much emphasis on "expert" and are trying to balance that with a corresponding stress on "Red". At a forum sponsored by the CCP Central Propaganda Department, Wang Renzhong emphasized the need for improvement in moral education. "Now we are working hard for socialism and are engaged in socialist construction. We are working for the goal of communism." He particularly called for teacher training programmes and development of textbooks and teaching materials, suggesting that teachers already known as effective could be brought together to form a textbook, and direct two-week crash courses in the summer to help their colleagues (FBIS—Federal Broadcast Information Service, 20 July 1982, K-10).

Striking educational changes took place in China during 1985–1986. In May 1985 the CCP Central Committee published a document in *Renmin Ribao* announcing a thorough reform and overhaul of the educational system in China (Cheng Kai Ming, 1986, p. 255). The central feature of the reform was the institution of nine years of free and compulsory education. Although it seems chiefly geared to the needs of the new push for economic reform, the moral/ideological component has not been neglected. The document states: "The development of culture and ethics is an important characteristic of socialism, which finds expression in advanced education, science, and the people's political consciousness and moral character" (*Beijing Review*) no. 50, 16 December 1985, p. 16).

In explaining the new policy at a national educational conference the same month, Vice-Premier Wan Li laid great stress on the moral dimension. He said that new people for a new period in Chinese history were needed:

> People needed by the new period should have lofty ideals, moral integrity, education and a sense of discipline. They should love the socialist motherland and the socialist cause, be ready to dedicate themselves to and work hard for the prosperity of the country and the people, continuously seek new knowledge, have the spirit of seeking truth from facts and be bold in making innovations . . . those who lack such new qualities—that is, lack lofty ideals, a sense of discipline and the enterprising spirit—cannot be considered as people needed by the new period, no matter how much knowledge they have (quoted in *Beijing Review* no. 24, 17 June 1985, p. 19).

In the following year Chairman of the State Education Commission Li Peng made an official explanation of the draft of the Compulsory Education Law to the Sixth National People's Congress on 2 April, 1986, quoting the document to underscore the importance of moral education: "Efforts must be exerted to improve the quality of education so that children and youngsters can have a comprehensive moral, intellectual and physical development, and so that a foundation will be laid for improving the quality of the nation through training ethical, educated and disciplined builders of socialism having lofty ideals" (FBIS, 24 April 1986 K-13). There has also been some indication that a specific course in both political and moral education may be in the works. It was reported on 12 June 1986, that the State Education Commission had issued a circular calling on primary schools to offer a course on communist ideology and morality. The course is to teach school children to "form a correct attitude toward labour, to be hard working, thrifty, self-managed and willing to help others, and to have the ability to distinguish clearly between right and wrong" (FBIS, 11 September 1985, K-5; see also Lo, 1984, p. 158).

These recent developments make it clear that there is currently, as there has always been, a keen interest in moral education. Unfortunately, such documents as we have quoted do not get down to details. They are grand statements of purpose only, and we must wait to see what changes may occur in the methods and content of moral education as the recent reforms get implemented.

Problems for the Future

I would like to conclude by briefly setting forth what appear to me to be major problems for moral education in the PRC. The organs of moral formation in the PRC are many and varied—the Young Pioneers, the Communist Youth League, CCP committees, various people's organizations such as labour and women's federations, literary and art circles, radio and TV, etc. While these may be in the end more important than classroom practice, still I think that the following are important issues which must be faced in planning for formal moral education.

(1) Teacher status. Traditionally high in China, the prestige of the teaching profession suffered a terrible blow during the Cultural Revolution, when the intellectual class were portrayed as the enemies of the people. Teachers were criticized, physically abused and driven from their professions. An editorial in *Renmin Jibao* admits: "The 'leftist' mistakes and errors in our work caused the vast numbers of teachers to suffer a great deal" (FBIS, 9 July 1982, K-9). Today there is a teacher shortage in the PRC, and the previous derogatory treatment is partly to blame. This problem is widely recognized and steps have been taken to rectify it. Two approaches have been followed: raising teachers' salaries and exhortation of students by national and local authorities to respect their teachers. In 1985, a Teachers' Day was instituted, and Zhao Ziyang and other national leaders attended the ceremonies and gave laudatory speeches. *Xinhua* reported: "He [Zhao] said that the undertaking teachers are engaged in is a sacred one, and added that they are the transmitters and builders of human civilization" (FBIS, 11 September 1985, K-1). The Compulsory Education Law, approved by the Sixth National People's Congress on 12 April 1986, states: "The whole society should respect teachers. The state shall protect teachers' legitimate

rights and interests, take measures to raise their social status and improve their material benefits, and commend outstanding teachers" (FBIS, 22 April 1986, K-9). Li Peng's remarks, quoted above, contain the same message. Yet the scars of the Cultural Revolution remain and it will probably be years before there is an adequate supply of teachers available.

(2) Once there are enough teachers the PRC will have to work toward changing a rather traditional teaching methodology which has persisted through the decades even since the Revolution, despite the radical change in ideology. It may be described as the teacher-orientated classroom. In it the teacher as authority figure dispenses knowledge while the students passively absorb it. This doctrinaire, dogmatic approach has been recognized as a problem for a number of years (see Unger, 1982, p. 67ff.; Hawkins, 1983, pp. 168–169). Vice Premier Wan Li put it forcefully in the speech already quoted: "China's traditional educational thinking and ossified teaching methods have a long history and are deep rooted. For several thousand years, people trained by the feudal ruling class needed only to be obedient and docile; they thus did not pay attention to increasing their ability of independent thinking." He adds later: "Traditional educational thinking, which only pays attention to passing on knowledge, and the cramming method of teaching are incompatible with training a new breed of qualified people . . . Students should not be force fed" (quoted in *Beijing Review,* 24 June 1985, p. 20). In addressing this problem, authorities will be at the same time dealing with the conflict noted by Ridley *et al.* (1971, p. 197) in their analysis of textbooks: although they seek initiative and independence in solving problems, they advocate obedience to rules and deference to authority.

(3) Moral standards are almost always presented as though they were eternal verities. Part of their ability to convince lies in the belief that they are stable and will not change. It is problem enough that the PRC has had to orchestrate a fundamental change in moral values as it sought to eliminate earlier attachments to capitalism, to family sanctity and other traditional authority structures. It is hard to assess the extent to which these traditional values persist in the Marxist state, but for moral education a graver problem than merely supplanting the old values lies in the contradictory versions of Marxian socialism/communism which have been presented to the people before, during and after the Cultural Revolution. Scepticism increases as young people watch the "eternal verities" change. Intellectuals were at first honoured, then denigrated, and now honoured again. The assessment of the importance of academic achievement has followed the same pattern. Even the teacher's traditional model, Confucius, was honoured, then totally defamed as an upholder of the feudal order, and now again honoured (Kam Louie, 1984). Peasant-farmers are no longer the country's greatest heroes. Cadres and their children whose political correctness once won them admission to colleges and universities are now told that success in examinations

is again the criterion. Perhaps only a fairly long period of political stability marked by stable values will be able to heal the inevitable cynicism which many feel today.

(4) The last issue I will mention is one that any institution faces when it passes from the period of struggle and heroism in the face of adversity to a time when material conditions improve, giving rise to ever higher expectations. In some developing countries it would be felt as the conflict of traditional religious values with the materialism which seems to be the inevitable accompaniment of "progress". In the PRC, it is the conflict of the old revolutionary zeal of Yenan and the Long March with improving economic and material conditions of more recent times. It is part of what Mao saw happening and which so distressed him that he launched his Cultural Revolution. Insofar as Deng Xiaoping and the current leadership are able to move toward their goal of catching up with the First World nations in the twenty-first century, to that very extent the problem will get worse. This is the problem of the traditional and modern and is now found almost everywhere. In acknowledging this problem, I am sure educational authorities in the PRC would gladly echo the words of one of my respondents in Taiwan: "These students simply haven't had the experience of real suffering." While no one has a ready solution, this problem must still be faced if moral education is to effect the subtle and silent transformation to which it aspires.

References

Bernstein, T.P. (1977), *Up to the mountains and down to the villages: The transfer of youth from urban to rural China.* New Haven: Yale University Press.

Ch'en Ying-hao (1978), *Wo kuo ch'ing-shao-nien tao-te pan-tuan ti fa-chan chi ying-hsiang ti yin-su* (The development of moral judgement among Taiwan adolescents). Kaohsiung Teachers College Report, January.

Cheng Kai Ming (1986), China's recent educational reform: The beginnings of an overhaul. *Comparative Education,* **22** 267–268.

Chiang Ching-kuo (1983), Tui tang-ch'ien kuo-min chiao-yu ti chi-tien k'an-fa (Views on certain aspects of contemporary national education). *Kao-shih wen-chiao,* **13**, October.

Grambs, J.D. (1986), Entrance examinations in Taiwan: The power that drives the system. Paper presented at the Comparative International Education Society Meeting, Toronto.

Hawkins, J.N. (1983), The People's Republic of China (Mainland China). In R.M. Thomas and T.N. Postlethwaite (Eds.), *Schooling in East Asia: Forces of Change.* Oxford: Pergamon Press. Unger, J. (1982), *Education under Mao: Class and competition in Canton schools, 1960–1980.* New York: Columbia University Press.

Hwang Chien-hou (1974), *A comparative study of social attitudes in Glasgow and Taipei.* Taipei: Orient Cultural Service.

Kam Louie (1984), Salvaging Confucian education (1949–1983). *Comparative Education,* **20**, pp. 27–38.

Kwong, J. (1985), Changing political culture and changing curriculum: an analysis of language textbooks in the People's Republic of China. *Comparative Education,* **21**, pp. 197–209.

Lin Ching-jiang (1983), The Republic of China (Taiwan). In R.M. Thomas and T.N. Postlethwaite (Eds.), *Schooling in East Asia: Forces of change.* Oxford: Pergamon Press.

Lo, B. (1984), Primary education: A two-track system for dual tasks. In Ruth Hayhoe (Ed.), *Contemporary Chinese Education.* Armonk, New York: M.E. Sharpe.

Martin, R. (1975), The socialization of children in China and on Taiwan. *China Quarterly*, **62**, June, pp. 242–262.

Meyer, J.F. Feb (1988), Moral education in Taiwan, *Comparative Education Review*.

Pepper, S. (1980), Chinese Education after Mao: Two steps forward, two steps back and begin again? *China Quarterly*, no. 81, March. pp. 1–65.

Price, R.F. (1970), *Education in communist China*. New York: Praeger.

Price, R.F. (1980), Chinese textbooks, fourteen years on, *China Quarterly*, no. **83**, pp. 535–550.

Ridley, C.P., Goodwin, P.H.B., Doolin, D.J. (1971), *The making of a model citizen in communist China*. Stanford: Hoover Institution Press.

Rosen, S. (1982), Obstacles to Educational Reform in China. *Modern China*, **8**, pp. 3–4.

Shi Ming Hu and Seifman, E. (Eds.) (1976), *Toward a new world outlook: A documentary history of education in the People's Republic of China, 1949–1976*. New York: AMS Press.

Shirk, S.L. (1982), *Competitive comrades: Career incentives and student strategies in China*. Berkeley: University of California Press.

Wu Sen (1979), *Pi-chiao che-hsueh yu wen-hua* (Comparative philosophy and culture). Taipei: Tung-ta tu-shu yu hsien kung-ssu.

Zhao Bao-heng (1984), Education in the countryside today. *Comparative Education*, **20**, p. 104.

CHAPTER 8

Being and Becoming: Education for Values in Singapore

S. GOPINATHAN

Singapore's programmes for moral and religious education are best understood in the context of an evolving political and social framework, for while
the list of virtues to be inculcated—respect, tolerance, patriotism, respect
for law and order and the like—are no different from those to be found in
similar programmes elsewhere, the issues and dilemmas are unique. Singapore has wrestled with the issues of moral instruction for two decades with
shifts in emphasis and rationales. It would appear that the view taken of
values education in Singapore is that the problem is essentially one of bring-
ing about social integration and consensus, of establishing a set of core
values, drawn preferably from the traditions of the ethnic groups represented in Singapore. No less than the survival of the nation is seen as
riding on the success of the moral education programme. There would be
broad agreement in Singapore with the Durkheiman view that the schools
are the guardians of national character and should be used for the inculcation of common moral sentiments on the basis of a secular rather than a
religious inspired morality (Benjamin, 1976; Hassan, 1976).

The Socio-Political Framework for Values Education in Singapore

In Singapore, rapid urbanization and a bilingual school policy have erased
ethnic enclaves and the mutual linguistic ignorance that characterized pre-
war Singapore. The dramatic transformation of an entrepôt economy to one
based on manufacturing, service and financial services has largely removed
the link between economic specialization and race. Nevertheless, Singapore
continues to be a society in which racial, linguistic and religious attributes
are important. Singapore has an ethnic Chinese majority, a unique feature
in South-east Asia. In 1985 the Chinese made up 76.4 per cent of the population, the Malays 14.9 per cent, the Indians 6.4 per cent and others 2.3 per
cent. Singapore has four official languages, English, Chinese, Tamil and
Malay, the last named being also the national language. The 1980 Census

reported the following for religious affiliation: Taoism 29.3 per cent, Buddhism 26.7 per·cent, Islam 16.3 per cent, Christianity 10.3 per cent, Hinduism 3.6 per cent, other religions, 0.6 per cent and no religious preference 13.2 per cent.

The major thrust of government policy since 1965 when Singapore became independent has been, while affirming the value of multicultural-ism, to build bonds between the various ethnic groups. Traditional linkages, such as mixed marriages and shared religion, especially Christianity, have been supplemented by the popularity of English-medium education which has resulted in English emerging as the lingua franca. The school system, once heavily segregated in terms of language and race, is now largely de-segregated and English is the main medium of instruction in all schools, though all pupils must learn a second "ethnic" language.

In many other ways, too, Singapore is atypical of South-east Asia. It is an island nation, of high population density (3787 persons per square kilometre), heavily urbanized and with no backward or rural sector. It has not quite lost its migrant mentality since a part of the adult population was born outside Singapore and this group's social institutions, such as clan associations and cultural and linguistic preferences not to mention a strong commercial morality that valued strong government as essential for business activity, still exert influence. In this scheme of values, individual preferences and responsibility were quite willingly subordinated to government leader-ship. It is also a global city, for it is a major tourist and communication centre, open to and indeed positively receptive to "valuable" modernizing influences.

It is unique also in the type of government it has. It has a cohesive and committed political leadership, extremely articulate and willing and capable of taking unpopular decisions and sticking to them. While the trappings of Western-style democracy remain, the population has been largely de-politicized in the belief that political argument, debate and opposition are destabilizing and detract from more pressing issues of economic growth and national unity (Chan Heng Chee, 1976, pp. 30–31). In the view of Mr S. Rajaratnam (1977, p. 100), a senior cabinet minister, "if Third World societies are not to relapse into anarchy as modernization gathers pace, more and not less authority and discipline are necessary". Constant refer-ence is made to several developing societies in Asia—"broken-backed states" which are contrasted with states like Korea, Japan and Taiwan, the latter obviously seen as worthy of emulation for their political stability, cohesiveness and dedication to economic growth.

It is this combination of strong government with economic growth and societal stability as a prime national goal that drives the moral education programme. It is not accidental that on several occasions government leaders have noted that, like Singapore, Taiwan, Hong Kong and South Korea, all with good records of economic growth, have a shared heritage in

Confucianism. The Confucian ethic is seen as doing for these societies what the Protestant ethic did for the development of early Western capitalism (*New Nation*, 13 June 1982). This notion was in fact taken a step further by one of the consultants to the Confucian Ethics (school curriculum) project who saw the Eastern societies' use of Confucianism as offering "very rich spiritual resources to people, especially overseas Chinese to become successful entrepreneurs" (*Straits Times*, 5 August 1986), and a profound challenge to the Western mode of social and economic organization (*Straits Times*, 1 July 1983). At a convocation ceremony the chairman of the Housing and Development Board was moved to remind graduates in business administration of the relevance of Confucianism for chairmen and chief executives of corporations in Singapore (*Straits Times*, 17 November 1984).

Given the nature and goals of the political leadership and the type of society aimed at, the values that are prescribed to help achieve this fit logically enough. The government is emphatic that not only should Singapore avoid the model of poorly run, corrupt, developing societies in Asia and Africa, but that it should also avoid the excesses of the industrial West— which are seen as hedonistic, weak-willed societies where the rights of the individual have been favoured to such an extent that they threaten social and political cohesion. The goal is a distinctive Singapore society, worth the preserving. In a seminal analysis of the Singapore society-to-be, the Prime Minister in 1972 said "It is basic we understand ourselves; what we are, where we came from, what life is or should be about and what we want to do . . . Only when we first know our traditional values can we be quite clear that the Western world is a different system, a different voltage, structured for purposes different from ours" (Lee Kuan Yew, 1972, p. 1). The metaphor is modern and industrial but the appeal, especially to the majority Chinese population, is based on more traditional memories.

In his 1972 speech the Prime Minister had sketched the values Singaporeans should adopt. Indeed, he explained Singapore's successes as being due "to the hard framework of basic cultural values and the tightly-knit Asian family system". Over the years such words and phrases as hard-working, disciplined, confident and self-reliant, collective will and character, qualities of industry, perseverance and resilience, thrift, honesty, self-sacrifice and regard for others, have collectively come to stand for a set of desirable values, uniquely Asian in origin, which needed preservation and strengthening in Singapore society. The family came to be regarded as a core unit of a stable society and the government took administrative measures (income tax relief, for instance, for supporting parents) to strengthen family cohesiveness. As one newspaper editorial put it, these values would give the Singaporean roots, "to hold him steady as his life travels the paths of the English language, American technology, Swiss expertise and Japanese business acumen". In characterizing these values as Asian, the government, perhaps in an effort to simplify the choices for its citizens, was following the types of contrast it had offered between various types of societies. It is also not unreasonable to suppose that it was using the ethnic variable, pride in indigenous culture and language, as a means of mobilization in support of government policy. What is noteworthy in the Singapore context is the use of other countries both as positive and as negative examples, a strategy that has often enough annoyed the countries specified!

In the mid-1970s the government found an easy symbol of what was going wrong with Western societies and what must not be allowed to take root in Singapore, in the ubiquitous longhaired hippie. There was genuine fear that this youth subculture of alienation, hedonistic self-expression fed by drugs and the rock music revolution was attractive and therefore potentially corruptive of Singapore youth: in the words of one official, "the philosophy of patched-up jeans and patched-up souls" was not the model to emulate. Official characterization then of the attitudes of Singapore's youths— materialistic, unwilling to sacrifice, to put nation before self, even unfilial— implied that corruption had already taken root. Later, in a 1980 survey of life values of 1878 youths in secondary schools it was reported what characterized these youths were their selfishness, a value vacuum and the possession of a "self-interested morality".

The freedom given to discussion of religious matters has now resulted in a more explicit identification of the role of religion in character building. In papers presented at the Islamic Missionary Convention held in Singapore in September 1986, several speakers spoke about "a moral crisis in the Malay community" pointing to increased incidence of drug-taking and other criminal offences, and of broken marriages (*Straits Times*, 8 September 1986). The solution to these problems was seen to lie in the "more vigorous teaching of Islamic values". However, there was also concern expressed that the Malay Muslim community was facing the threat of evangelism from other religious groups, especially Christian groups, and the teaching of Islamic values was seen as necessary to counter this as well.

The School Environment

While it has been sometimes fashionable to decry the significance of schooling in Western industrial societies, and indeed to be sceptical about the possible roles schools can play in inculcating values, there are few such doubts in Singapore. Both at the government and the individual level there is almost complete faith in the value of education and its ability to do almost everything. This is perhaps understandable in a new nation-state with poorly developed social institutions and civic traditions; education in these circumstances is the instrument for making citizens and a high degree of centralization is often evident. This is especially the case in nations such as Singapore where the "migrant mentality" is seen as a barrier to adequate socialization of the young into the "national culture". Over the last three decades the education system has been in Singapore the chosen instrument for "social engineering" and has benefited enormously in terms of resources made available to this sector. The school is thus clearly seen and deliberately used as an instrument for the inculcation of core values.

Even a brief examination of the features of the Singapore school system will reveal quickly many features relevant to an examination of moral education in Singapore schools today. As with many other British colonies, English-medium education was begun largely through the efforts of Christian missions. Early grants-in-aid were given to the London Missionary Society, and the Roman Catholic Mission for educational purposes. The Protestant missionaries were the pioneers of the Western type of education in Singapore (Doraisamy, 1969). The schools that were then founded were attractive not only because they offered instruction in English, the colonial language, then as now the language of opportunity, but also because they imported religious instruction; ironically, this was the very reason that the Malays, whom the British authorities favoured as deserving of government-supported education, shunned these schools. Today, mission schools such as St Andrews, St Joseph's Institution, the Methodist Girls' School and the Anglo-Chinese School are in great demand not only for the general excellence of their academic programme but because they are seen to be providing valuable character education through the religious basis of their school ethos.

As with the Christian community, so with the others. The Malays, whose social and cultural structure is dominated by adherence to Islam, provided for religious instruction outside the formal school system; even today there are more than ten *madrasahs*, or schools whose curriculum and school ethos is religion-based. In much smaller and informal ways the Hindus and Sikhs have continued to provide religious instruction for their communities. Thus religious plurality, a fact of life in a multi-ethnic society and, more importantly, a clearly acceptable and important source of traditional values and mores, continued to be maintained by the various communities in the education sphere.

When we view Chinese-medium schools, a different perspective appears. It must be noted that British education policy generally left the migrant groups, the Chinese and the Indians, to provide education for themselves. The Chinese, with commercial wealth and numbers, responded by providing a system complete with a university and technical college. Feelings of discrimination by the British authorities fuelled Chinese pride in their school system, with the latter further strengthened by the traditional feelings of Middle Kingdom cultural superiority over the barbaric West. Thus there prevailed a notion in pre-war Chinese schools of the cultural and educational superiority of the type of education provided. The school ethos, the respect for scholarship exemplified by respect for teachers/elders, the teaching style which emphasized the teachers' authority and in which difficult and painstaking mastery of script and text were virtues, and finally the very language of instruction, seen as uniquely rich in proverb and idiom, at every turn illustrating and providing insight into a cohesive and culturally rich society, these features were seen as valuable, even indispensable, in being Chinese. This view was given prominence and respectability by the Prime Minister. In keeping with his view of different types of societies and the value of certain languages for certain purposes, he has characterized some of the products of English-medium schooling as individualistic, irresponsible, materialistic, with weak social commitment, decadent and with poor qualities of self-discipline and endurance. The government has supported nine special schools to be attended by ethnic Chinese pupils in an effort to retain the "valuable" traditional character of Chinese schools, a decision that checked the movement towards the final elimination of schools segregated on the basis of race and language.

Two other points need to be made about the place of the education system within the larger society. Although a case was made earlier for the importance of schooling as a mechanism for inculcating values, Singapore's small size and mass media saturation suggest important roles for other societal institutions. The government itself is the "great educator". For more than two decades government leaders have used the mass media extensively to hector, cajole, persuade and inform. Singapore has seen numerous national campaigns. The present commitment to greater openness, the institutionalization of feedback on government policies, extensive grass-roots involvement in the framing of a national agenda indicate continued education outside the school. Illustrative of this is the recent discussion of a new education reform report which involved widely publicized discussions, including the seeking of student views. Just how much a student's notions of national identity and loyalty for instance are due to school learning and how much to other institutions has not been empirically examined.

The other major sources of values are the peer groups and service in the armed forces. There is accumulating evidence of the importance of peer group sub-cultures in the lives of many young Singaporeans. This should not be surprising in a rapidly changing society with a high emphasis on work, effort and intellectual merit. A percentage of youths find school life alienating and their preference for other values is visible on Singapore's streets, shopping centres and fast-food restaurants. Their penchant for wearing black has recently come in for criticism by no less a person than the president of the Chinese Chamber of Commerce. The values of the military barracks, of national service as enculturation into the symbols and substance of national identity have yet to be explored. But since all Singaporean males must serve in the armed forces, and the Singapore Armed Forces is a potent, public symbol and the nation's pride it would be reasonable to assume that it is significant. What other values are engendered or sustained in the routines of barrack life are also worthy of investigation.

Curriculum Initiatives

Singapore education has seen several efforts to develop a values educa-tion programme adequate to the needs as defined by the political establish-ment. Before we begin with the specific curriculum initiatives we need to look at Singapore's language policies within the context of efforts to incul-cate value consensus. Singapore is perhaps unique in the way in which the educational authorities have explicated and implemented moral education policies at the same time that they were implementing language policies.

The roots of this situation lie in the ways the language policy evolved. An early political need to placate the Chinese-educated was subsequently elaborated into a formula for cultural authentication, of language as the embodiment of culture. In 1960 the government made the learning of a second language compulsory at the elementary level and in 1966 at the secondary level. In 1966 and 1969 it became a compulsory examination subject. Even today, when the trend has shifted decisively towards ever wider use of English, the government continues to emphasize the value of the ethnic language.

The defence of language as culture-carrier has two interrelated aspects. One is the notion that language and culture or, more specifically, "tradi-tional values", as the government labels it, are inextricably linked. The failure to learn and thus preserve the language was *ipso facto* to give up on the culture and thus "become completely deculturalized and lost . . . [and thus not] a society or nation worth the building, let alone defending" (Lee Kuan Yew, 1972, p. 4). A second notion closely related is that of language not as vehicle but as the embodiment of culture. Thus Lee says: "It is not just learning the language. With the language goes the fables and proverbs. It is the learning of a whole value system, a whole philosophy of life" (Lee Kuan Yew, 1971, p. 5). There is a suggestion here that the essence of lan-guage learning was the embodiment of a cultural and ethnic personality, a theme taken up in the annual Speak Mandarin campaigns; last year's slogan was "Mandarin is Chinese".

In terms of policy implementation these notions have resulted in the bifurcation of roles for the mother tongues and for English. The mother tongues were to be learnt for the maintenance of group ethnic identity, and at one stage subjects with large cultural content—social studies, civics, art and music—had to be taught in the mother tongue. The continuance of English was justified on the grounds that it provided for continuity in admin-istration, was a neutral link language and, most interestingly, was touted as admirably suited to the communication of scientific and technical knowledge. What Singapore wanted was Western knowledge and tech-nology but not the values. The evolution of the bilingual policy and its rationalizations can thus be seen as an early attempt to grapple with educa-tion and values.

The most notable early effort to provide for values education was the introduction of the Education For Living (EFL) programme in 1974. This replaced a syllabus for civics which had been taught since 1967. The aims of EFL were stated to be to help pupils understand the purpose and importance of nation-building, to help pupils to understand and appreciate the desirable elements of Eastern and Western traditions and live under the changing national and societal conditions. EFL was meant to be both moral and social education and for the latter purpose the syllabus included history and geography.

When Dr Goh Keng Swee, second in power and authority only to the Prime Minister, was asked to prepare a report on educational reform he established as well a committee to review moral education, headed by Mr Ong Teng Cheong, the Acting Minister for Culture. The *Report on Moral Education 1979* (Ong Report) criticized the way in which values were taught because instruction in civics was seen as inadequate for moral instruction and because teachers and pupils were not seen as being serious about moral education. The Ong Report recommended a specific programme of moral education in the primary schools with an emphasis on personal behaviour, social responsibility and loyalty to country. It quoted with approval the Prime Minister's specification for a good Singaporean as one "who can live, work, content and co-operate in a civilized way". In line with previous policy it recommended the teaching of values in the mother tongue: "children will be able to understand the moral concept better if they are taught in the mother tongue which is closely linked with the dialects which most of them speak at home".

The proposals in the Ong Report resulted in the rapid development of a moral education syllabus and curriculum materials for the elementary and lower secondary schools. In 1981 the *Being and Becoming* moral education programme developed by Dr (Rev.) R. P. Balhetchet, a Singaporean Jesuit rector, was pilot tested. The major focus of the *Being and Becoming* programme adheres closely to the recommendations of the Ong Report, namely *Personal Behaviour*, *Social Responsibility* and *Loyalty to Country*. In terms of preferred methodology this programme leans towards a values clarification approach. At the same time a programme with Chinese-language materials named *Good Citizen* was introduced. Unlike *Being and Becoming* this course grew out of earlier civics syllabi and drew heavily for illustrative material from Chinese myths and legends. In keeping with the more prescriptive approach preferred by Chinese teachers *Good Citizen* is relatively more teacher-centred. It is estimated that more than 80 per cent of primary schools are using the *Good Citizen* programme. However, at the lower secondary levels only *Being and Becoming* is available.

It was, however, in religious education that the most radical changes were made. A government that had previously restricted religious instruction to non-curriculum time in the aided mission-run schools has now acknowledged the value of such instruction. It had been hinted at by Dr Goh's comment earlier on the Ong Report that moral beliefs needed an intellectual basis and a consistent system of thought if they were to be sustained in later life. The government had in 1979 accepted Bible knowledge and Islamic religious knowledge as examination subjects. In 1982 Dr Goh announced that at the upper secondary level students (ages 14–16) would be offered a more extensive religious knowledge curriculum. The original offerings were Bible knowledge, Buddhist studies, Hindu studies, Islamic religious knowledge and world religions; later Confucian ethics was introduced at the request of the Prime Minister and Sikh studies at the request of the Sikh community. Parents were to be allowed to make the choice for their children and all schools including mission schools were to offer the option if twenty students requested instruction in the subject. The programme is compulsory for all pupils and the options may be offered as an examination subject. The Curriculum Development Institute of Singapore was given the responsibility for the development of curriculum materials.

Subsequent elaborations of the rationale provided insights into the way the government viewed religious education. First, it made clear the distinction between a religious knowledge curriculum and a religious instruction one; what was intended for Singapore schools was the former. Religious knowledge was to be studied "like studying Shakespeare", i.e. as a classroom subject, and there were to be "no prayers, meditation, preaching, worship and mass conversion. The aim was to help students appreciate the origins and precepts of the religions which have influenced Singapore's cultures and thus give an understanding of the moral principles that have shaped society" (*Straits Times*, 6 and 7 December 1983).

The introduction of the moral, and especially religious knowledge, curriculum differs from other curricular developments in Singapore in significant ways. In the first instance, the development of curriculum materials was coordinated not by theologians but by academic specialists, many of them, as in the case of Buddhist studies, Hindu studies and Confucian ethics, from outside Singapore. Though Singapore has knowledgeable Buddhist authorities, the consultant for Buddhist studies was a professor from the University of California. The Hindu studies consultant is a professor of English and Indian Literature at the Sri Aurobindo International Centre for Education. The Confucian ethics programme was launched with the assistance of eight scholars from overseas. This paradox of calling upon expatriate expertise in a curriculum area both heavily cultural and sensitive is seldom noted. Perhaps the explanation for their use lies in the desire to have some non-Singapore reference point as a way of managing internal differences. It is known, for instance, that there were some sharp differences of opinion regarding curriculum material in Hindu studies but the expatriate consultant who clearly had official backing was able to mediate the differences.

The contestation over content selection and legitimation will only be briefly touched upon here but it is an important issue. The complexities of selecting content can be illustrated by reference to the Confucian ethics project. When the government first proposed the idea there was considerable public reaction, most of it unfavourable, if letters to the English-language press are any guide. Opposition to the project centred in its relevance to a rapidly industrializing and plural society, what was perceived as its authoritarian character and fears that Confucian ethics would provide the government with rationales for continued social strictness, and its generally negative attitudes to women. The government for its part argued that the Confucian tradition was capable, through careful selection, of being made relevant, and that the economic prosperity and stability of Taiwan, South Korea and Japan could be attributed to their Confucian roots.

Equally interesting was the manner in which the programme was sold! A team of overseas Chinese academics from prestigious US universities was assembled to provide intellectual support for the decision. A key figure was Professor Tu Wei Ming from Harvard University, who was subsequently appointed as consultant to the curriculum materials writing project and later still appointed as a member of the board of directors of the Institute of East Asian Philosophies founded (and endowed with more than US $7 million) to encourage research into East Asian philosophies and in particular Confucianism. Professor Tu is now a familiar figure and an unflagging promoter of Confucian ethics, serving on panels, and giving talks and has become a visible symbol of overseas Chinese interest in the Confucian ethics programme. The media campaign to promote Confucian ethics continues unabated.

A second feature, again unusual in Singapore's curriculum history, is the drawing upon from the religious establishment to conduct some RK classes. In addition to selecting and training serving teachers the government has had to make up for the teacher shortage by encouraging "authorized religious associations", such as the Singapore Buddhist Federation for Buddhist Studies and the Majlis Ugama Islam Singapore to both train and provide teachers to man religious knowledge classes. The recently established Institute of East Asian Philosophies could in the future be a major source of expertise for teacher training and development of curriculum materials and methodology, especially in Confucian ethics, but for now its influence is limited. Notwithstanding the openers noted above, the Ministry remains firmly in control of the moral and religious knowledge curriculum.

A third feature that needs noting is the breakdown, as far as the religious knowledge curriculum is concerned, of the language-culture formulae for the government has stipulated that the following languages can be used: Bible knowledge in English; Buddhist studies in English and Chinese; Confucian ethics in English or Chinese, Hindu studies in English, Islamic religious knowledge in Malay and English; Sikh studies in English. A request by the Tamil Teachers Association for Hindu studies to be taught in Tamil, making use of the government's earlier rationale, was denied. It has also been reported that Chinese-medium teachers already worried about declining standards of competence in Chinese are now worried that the option to study Confucian ethics in English will mean further pressure on the Chinese language. This view is supported by the Head of the Department of Chinese Studies at the National University of Singapore, who said that the declining standards had led to a "worsening crisis" in the transmission of cultural values (*Straits Times*, 27 August 1986). What seems to have occurred is that the concern for mastery and adequate performance at examinations and the availability of teachers to teach the subject has pushed the government to agree to the language variation noted above.

Towards an Assessment

The *Report on Moral Education, 1979*, significant in that it was written by a group of parliamentarians and endorsed by Dr Goh, is however problematic. Its principal shortcoming—and this it shares with various official statements on the Singapore society-to-be, of the cultural and political personality that will characterize the Singaporean—is that it fails to provide a sufficiently comprehensive analysis of Singapore's multicultural society and the implications of various in-school and out-of-school policies. The committee takes for granted the various generalizations made about Singapore society and fails to push the analysis any further. Indeed, it may be claimed that, at least in part, the Report was overtaken by events such as the decision on the religious knowledge programme.

Three further recommendations made by the Report need to be critically reviewed. The committee, while making the valuable observation that moral instruction may be effected in a variety of ways, and while encouraging the use for moral instruction of clubs such as civic clubs, Rotary and Interact, inexplicably wants these, which are useful because they are informally structured and allow for cooperation and leadership away from the competitive atmosphere of the classroom, to be conducted in a more formal manner. Indeed, it makes the further extreme suggestion that feedback on the effectiveness of the moral education programme be tested by including questions related to moral issues in language examination papers. The irony of a moral education programme based on respect for others, and group solidarity being tested in a competitive examination environment is lost on the reformers. As for teachers, it recommends that a specially selected group of moral education teachers should be trained to teach only the moral education syllabus. It fails to examine the difficulties in selection of individuals deemed worthy of teaching the subject, or the consequences of such selection on other teachers in the school. Indeed it appears to see moral instruction not as something involving the whole school but as a subject, formally taught and examined.

More important is the problem of national and Asian values. Many of the government's views on culture and society, predicated on the values it propounds as being necessary and useful, have to be inferred from an examination of its cultural policies. It would appear that the government seeks the retention, encouragement and further development of ethnic identities and cultures; cultural norms are seen as inherent in the expression of identity and while there is an occasional suggestion that there are values common to Chinese, Indian and Malay cultures, this notion has not been fully developed. Often it appears that it is the values of the Chinese community that are most important—as in the action taken to preserve Chinese schools and the argument that one could not be Chinese if one could not speak Mandarin. In the development of the religious knowledge curriculum, for example, it is the Confucian ethics project that has attracted and continues to attract the most attention. In contrast to this emphasis on Asian values there appears also to be a belief that common school experiences, service in the armed forces, the spread of urbanization and industrialization, the spread of a common non-native language like English and its cultural concomitants of rationality, scientific spirit, etc., will provide another set of values—"meritocracy" is often used to sum up this set of values—which it is hoped will be commonly shared and co-exist with ethnic values. (Gopinathan, 1979).

It has been pointed out that the sharp contrasts (in the government's view) between Eastern and Western values are grossly overstated (Clammer, 1979). While it is certainly possible that cultural tradition and historical circumstances might have accentuated some values and dampened others, such values as filial piety, group spirit, cohesive family life, effort and discipline are certainly not unknown in Western societies. The propagation of the view of a decadent, declining West while at the same time importing Western technology, sending Singapore's brightest students overseas, creating a consumer-oriented society and preaching the virtues of a free-enterprise system is, to say the least, inconsistent. There has been a failure to make a distinction between the values of modernization and those of Westernization: such concepts as meritocracy are not uniquely Western, any more than love of parents is Eastern.

A third observation may be made about the effort to derive Asian values from the traditions of the ethnic groups represented in Singapore. No one who has been in Singapore can fail to be struck by the modern character of the city and patterns of work and leisure. The social engineering of Singapore towards modernization has in a real sense emptied the ethnic cultures of their essential substance. The older dialect and clan associations have been replaced by social clubs; patterns of economic organization—production, consumption, value bear little resemblance to older patterns of status and alignments. Thus even within Singapore it would appear that only an abstract form of traditional values is possible.

The notion of an Asian cultural tradition, and how such a tradition may be used in an acceptable manner in the schools, needs close and careful analysis that has not so far been forthcoming. In choosing to use the ethnic variable and to draw upon the considerable potential of ethnic pride as a mobilizing and motivating factor, it is necessary to be mindful of the context in which such energies are being released. The insistence on teaching the moral education programme in the mother tongue has led to the segregation of classrooms on a language/race basis, unacceptable when the objective is the teaching of a set of core values.

The decision to prevent the phasing out of schools that served the majority Chinese community is another example. There is a real danger that the drive towards a cohesive society sharing a supra-ethnic set of values is being hindered by the emphasis on cultural heritage unique to the various communities. There was even a suggestion that schools teach the distinctive cultural histories of each of the major groups in the language of the respective groups. This could lead to unwarranted cultural assertiveness and a lack of empathy for other cultures. A case can be made out for diluting and blurring the edges and differences between the various groups, particularly when the sizes of Malay and Indian minorities are such as to create worry and apprehension.

There is need for more systematic research as well both about policy rationales and about the implementation processes. At the policy level certain questions may be posed. One major question would be the rationale for offering such a wide range of religious knowledge options. In part the issue is similar to the one that was raised with regard to the choice of official languages and languages of instruction. In that instance the government choose Tamil over other languages, such as Hindi and Malayalam, on the basis that the other languages had few speakers. Why was it then felt necessary to agree to religious knowledge options for minority groups? The necessity for the introduction of Confucian ethics needs also to be researched. That decision and the public debate over materials development had the government for a while on the defensive, especially over charges that Confucian ethics would make authoritarian government easier; it now appears that only a small percentage of ethnic Chinese pupils have opted for Confucian ethics.

At the level of classroom processes several important questions need researching. Most observers of the Singapore education system see the system as excessively competitive and examination-oriented. Indeed, one reason for making religious knowledge an examination subject is to ensure that students take it seriously. Also the school system, as with most systems elsewhere, is hierarchically organized and it is seldom possible to question the authority of the principles and senior teachers. It needs to be asked how well such a system of school organization, with its emphasis on cognitive skills and examination grades, can provide the context for the development of responsibility, shared concerns and an integrative orientation. Next, there needs to be research on the tension between a prescriptive and a non-prescriptive approach in terms of teaching method. Already there has been some disagreement on an appropriate moral education methodology at the elementary level. There was an expressed preference among Chinese-educated teachers for a more prescriptive methodology. Though the preference among teacher trainers involved in the *Being and Becoming* project is likely to be on the side of pupil reasoning it is not clear what the actual school situations are like.

Finally, within the area of methodology, and keeping in mind the earlier injunction against prayers and meditation, the special relationship between religious bodies and the RK curriculum needs to be studied. The origin of the Christian mission schools was a desire to spread the gospel while providing education and by all accounts they performed their educational mission well; well enough for the government to encourage their expansion. And yet these schools, or, more accurately the religious organizations behind them, are in a dilemma. Their preference in the present policy context is both to have Bible knowledge taught at all levels of the secondary school system, and if possible to offer only Bible knowledge in keeping with their special religious character. This poses problems for the government which wishes to keep access to these schools open to all who qualify academically, and that means offering other religious knowledge options, and to ensure that these schools' natural desire to propagate the faith is not reflected in syllabi which are slanted towards conversion and are consistent with the earlier syllabi such as *Being and Becoming* and *Good Citizen*. Having to play the role of arbiters of doctrine cannot be an easy one for a Ministry of Education.

A third area for fruitful research is the area of materials production and teacher training. More so than in the other areas, devising a variety of religious knowledge curriculum materials in a multi-religious society is fraught with difficulties; religions are by no means unitary in dogma and practice even if state prescriptions imply otherwise. Yet it would appear that Singapore's curriculum-makers have pulled off a difficult task with a reasonable degree of success. It would be useful to document this process for it might offer valuable insights into the content selection process for moral education. The anticipated roles of the teacher, especially in terms of the religious knowledge curriculum, would also be worth exploring. The position is likely to be that many teachers teaching religious knowledge subjects would not be very well acquainted with the religion while a small minority may be very knowledgeable and committed. In these circumstances how is the issue of teacher neutrality and expertise likely to be played out, and what impact is this likely to have on pupil knowledge and attitudes to religious knowledge?

When one looks at the discussion of values education issues in Singapore today, one cannot fail to be struck by the urgency and earnestness which characterize the debate. In common with many other Asian nations aiming at stability and growth without losing "national character", Singapore too places great faith in the education system. Unlike other countries, however, which are fortunate in having a homogeneous cultural tradition, the complexities of managing values education in a plural context bedevil Singapore's educators. The very richness of the cultural tradition here imposes the task of selection, and subsequent justification, of the core values to be taught: both the values and the manner of teaching, touching as the latter does upon the school's relationships with the home and, in particular, religious institutions, come under close scrutiny. In addition there is the need to win the benefits of modernization and to implant notions of loyalty and sacrifice while retaining the best virtues of the migrant mentality.

The challenges, then, are formidable, and current efforts praiseworthy. The authorities are seeking to utilize the potential of a rich and varied cultural tradition to enrich moral education in the nation's schools. The overriding concern to ensure political stability, and the need to be sensitive to ethnic sensibilities, have produced a cautious reliance on generalities. Hopefully, greater clarity in the analysis of Singapore culture and its goals will lead to a more assured programme for values education in Singapore.

References

Benjamin, G. (1976) The cultural logic of Singapore's "multi-racialism". In R. Hassan (Ed.), *Singapore: Society in transition*. Singapore: Oxford University Press.

Chan Heng Chee (1976) The political system and social change. In R. Hassan (Ed.), *Singapore: Society in transition*. Singapore: Oxford University Press.

Clammer, J. (1979) Asian values in a changing world (book review). *Contemporary Southeast Asia*, **1**, 109–113.

Doraisamy, T. R. (Ed.) (1969) *150 Years of Education in Singapore*. Singapore: TC Publications Board.

Gopinathan, S. (1974) Towards a national system of education in Singapore, 1945–1973. In R. Hassan (Ed.), *Singapore: Society in transition*. Singapore: Oxford University Press.

Gopinathan, S. (1979) Singapore's language policies: strategies for a plural society. *Southeast Asian affairs 1979*. Singapore: Heinemann Educational Books (Asia) for Institute of Southeast-Asian Studies.

Lee Kuan Yew (1972) Traditional values and national identity. *The Mirror*, **8**.

Rajaratnam, S. (1977) Asian values and modernization. In Seah Chee-Meow (Ed.), *Asian values and modernization*. Singapore: Singapore University Press.

CHAPTER 9

Moral Education in a Developing Society: The Malaysian Case

HENA MUKHERJEE

Stretching over some 340,000 square kilometres, Malaysia comprises the Malay Peninsula and the states of Sabah and Sarawak located on the island of Borneo across the South China Sea. It has a multi-ethnic population of approximately 15 million, 85 per cent of whom live on the Malay Peninsula or *Semenanjung*, as it is locally referred to. Malays and other indigenous peoples (or *Bumiputras*, sons of the soil) make up about 55 per cent of the population; Chinese 33 per cent; Indians 8.5 per cent; while the rest including Eurasians are labelled as "others".

Islam is the official, state religion co-existing with a spectrum of other religious and spiritual practices. While all Malays are Muslims (by definition in the Constitution), Buddhists make up 17 per cent of the population, Christians 7 per cent, and Hindus 7 per cent. There are smaller religious groupings such as the Bahai and Sikh as well as those who practise animism and ancestor worship. Bahasa Malaysia, the national language and the language of government and instruction, is the language of the Malays. Other spoken languages include Mandarin and several Chinese dialects; Tamil and several Indian regional languages; and the languages and dialects of the indigenous population of Sabah and Sarawak. Malaysia, a federation of thirteen states, is governed on the pattern of Western-style parliamentary democracy and the bureaucracy that manages the administration is fashioned on the British model.

About 42 per cent of the gainfully employed population live in the rural areas, involved largely in agriculture, fishing and forestry. Malays and other indigenous groups are prominent in the rural population. The Chinese comprise the largest single group in the urban areas, although on the Peninsula the average annual urban growth rate is highest among the Malays at about 7 per cent. In terms of race, language, religion, culture and ecomomic involvement, Malaya was a complex plural society at the time it gained its

147

independence from the United Kingdom in 1957. The formation of Malaysia in 1963 with Sabah, Sarawak and Singapore (which left the alliance in 1965) served to deepen the complexities.

Development of Education

During the British period (1786–1957) before World War II the social, political and economic changes brought into existence a modern bureaucratic government that needed the support of clerical and administrative officers trained in Western-type schools. At the same time the population of Malaysia took on its present multi-ethnic character. The tin and rubber industries expanded with the aid of a significant flow of immigrants from China and the Indian sub-continent. This influx of a population different in religion, language and culture from the indigenous Malay population changed Malaya from a monolingual Malay society to a plural society with nearly half the population comprising Chinese and Indians who had very definite ideas about the preservation of their languages and cultures. While each of the foreign influences in Malaysia contributed to educational ideology as well as educational practice, the educational system as we know it, expecially its structure and mode of organization, is the outcome largely of the British period in Malaysia.

The education system which independent Malaya inherited was the outcome of the efforts of the British colonial government, missionaries and the immigrant communities to organize a system of schooling that would meet their individual, social, political and economic needs. A system of diverse strands marked the educational landscape, a situation which almost all commentators perceive as the prime source of issues and problems dominating Malaysian educational changes in the post-independent period, (Wong Hoy Kee and Ee Tiang Hong, 1971; Loh Fook Seng, 1975). In attempting to effect a transition from the colonial to the nationalist education system, the existing ad hoc but entrenched educational structures created by the British obviously could not be changed immediately. Rather, energy was directed to modifying the system, orienting it to nationalist ideologies, aspirations and political realities, especially in relation to the multi-ethnic population which became a permanent feature of Malayan society in the war years (Ho Seng Ong, 1952; Chai Hon Chan, 1977). The nationalist phase (1946–1956) established long-term objectives and targets for national development, seeing in the education system an instrument essential for achieving national goals.

The National Education System

The pattern for post-independence education in Malaysia was set by the *Report of the Education Committee* (1957) whose most outstanding paragraph states that the multi-stranded structure of the education system would be reshaped to bring about

> a national system of education acceptable to the people of the Federation (of Malaya) as a whole which will satisfy their needs and promote their cultural, social, economic and political development as a nation, having regard to the intention of making Malay the national language of the country whilst preserving and sustaining the growth of the language and culture of other communities living in the country. (*Report of the Education Committee*, 1957, p.1).

Prior to independence, Malaya (as Malaysia was then known) had four distinct, exclusive strands in her school system. The Koranic (Islamic religious) schools of the pre-colonial period formed the basis of the Malay vernacular school system and were located largely in the rural areas with no provision for secondary education. Also limited to the primary level were the Tamil (South Indian) schools, confined chiefly to the rubber plantations where the Tamils worked. Chinese schools located in the urban areas provided both primary and secondary education. Both Tamil and Chinese schools looked overseas, the former to South India and the latter to mainland China, for values, curricular content and teachers. The British colonial government, not recognizing education as its responsibility, did not initiate the establishment of English-medium schools. These were established by Christian missions and other bodies which were later given government aid. Up to independence, then, the four distinct types of school helped to reinforce the separate racial, social, linguistic and cultural groupings in the country apart from the cleavages already existing in the occupational and administrative sectors.

After World War II, events made it clear that radical changes were in the air. The Chinese and Indians no longer saw their sojourn in Malaya as temporary and community leaders demanded that educational provision be seen as a government responsibility. As in other developing countries, formal education was seen as the chief instrument of social, economic and political development by all the ethnic groups. The demands of the various communities led to the Education Ordinance of 1957 which was based on the 1957 Education Committee Report's blueprint for a national education system.

The "national" aspect of the system was to be effectively seen in the restructuring and expansion of the school system, changing the ad hoc nature of multimedia streams into a formalized, planned system; the ultimate use of a common medium of instruction—Bahasa Malaysia; and the creation of a common curriculum with approved instructional materials that would foster a common Malyasian outlook and identity leading to common public examinations. A fundamental part of this centralized planning and control of the curriculum was the training of teachers in colleges throughout the country who in turn followed a common syllabus.

The term "national" as a description of the state-sponsored education system needs elaboration. It does not imply uniformity in that all schools are replications of each other. Until 1969, for instance, instruction in English continued in the English-medium primary and secondary schools, and Malay in parallel Malay-medium schools were supported by state funds. Chinese secondary schools however, by 1961, were directed either to be self-supporting or change to English or Malay medium while both Chinese and Tamil vernacular education remained available at the primary level as part of the state system. Malay and English were taught in all schools and all races were prepared to accept the primacy of the Malay language while English-medium education still continued. In this context, then, "national" connotes an attempt to organize and centrally plan the education system in response to the perceived needs of the country.

After the traumatic race riots in 1969, the process of schooling was subjected to scrutiny by the government and found to be wanting in relation to "Malaysian" national characteristics. Bahasa Malaysia began to be phased in as the medium of instruction in all English-medium schools and by 1983 all former English-medium schools had converted to Bahasa Malaysia. The Chinese- and Tamil-medium primary schools remained. Controversy arises from time to time regarding the continued support of these vernacular schools, seen by many as dead-end institutions, especially the Tamil schools, which are largely situated on the rubber and oil-palm estates, are in poor condition and have high drop-out rates. But the Malaysian constitution and the 1957 Education Ordinance which upholds the preservation of the various ethnic cultures provide politicians with visible legal reasons for maintaining the status quo.

As in other nations engaged in mapping policies designed to inculcate a sense of national identity, education in Malaysia is seen as an instrument that is indispensable to its socio-political cohesion. We are told that

> This search for national identity and unity involves the whole range of economic, social and political activities: the formulation of educational policies designed to encourage common values and loyalties among all communities and in all regions (*Second Malaysia Plan 1971–1975*, 1971, p.3).

The *Third Malaysia Plan* reiterates the fact that education must assume a major responsibility in the effort "to nurture the evolution of a truly Malaysian identity and way of life" (*Third Malaysian Plan 1976–1980*, 1976, p.12). That the notion of "a truly Malaysian identity" has never been clearly elucidated, if it is possible to do so, will not be taken up here. We need to note, however, that some form of unity of cohesion is signalled as of overriding concern and should be manifest in the educational enterprise. To add substance to the search for social cohesion and a common framework of values for all sectors of society the *Rukunegara* was drawn up. This is a set of five ideological principles or "pillars of the nation" that are expected to guide deed and action in Malaysian society and the school curriculum should reflect them. They are: Belief in God; Loyalty to King and Country;

Upholding the Constitution; Rule of Law; Good Conduct and Morality. Teaching activities in Malaysian schools are not expected to conflict with the *Rukunegara*.

Towards the Moral Education (ME) Syllabus

Prior to the formulation of the common curriculum, a large number of Christian mission schools had a weekly slot on "ethics" for their non-Christian pupils. These lessons were based on Christian teachings with liberal extracts from the Bible accompanied by frequent exhortations to "be good". In the post–1957 common curriculum, however, only the Islamic religion (referred to as Agama in the school timetable) can be taught in the approved curriculum, a major section of which is *Akhlak* or Islamic ethics. The *Akhlak* syllabus is heavily content-based and includes prescriptions and rituals as stipulated in the Koran. The orientation of the syllabus and teaching strategies is generally highly authoritarian, depending on rote-learning and memorization skills and not focused on affective outcomes. The fact that it is a subject examined in all public examinations reinforces the cognitive focus. If Christian mission schools today wish to teach their religion then time has to be sought outside of the school day and in most cases it is the church that has taken over this as a parochial responsibility.

In the early 1970s, directly on the heels of the 1969 race riots, civics as a compulsory, non-examinable subject was introduced, but a 1974 programme evaluation indicated that as the only non-examinable subject in a heavily examination-oriented system it was not being seriously regarded in most schools. At about this time, the wave of student unrest in the West, drug abuse and growing street violence caught up with Malaysia and concern was expressed in parliament about the need for some form of moral guidance that schools should be responsible for. These concerns were taken up by the local press which reflected the growing feeling that school learning should be intertwined with the business of living outside the school; that formal learning in the school should be continuous with the world outside the school; and that the school has the responsibility for developing not only marketable knowledge and skills but also those skills that would assist the growth of morally mature and responsible members of society.

One consequence of these discussions was that the Cabinet Committee on Education asked the Ministry of Education to set up the machinery for the formulation of a moral education programme to be directed to non-Muslim pupils as, it was pointed out, Muslim children had *Akhlak*. The moral education class was to be conducted during the periods Muslim children attended Agama classes and since the Agama syllabus was an examinable subject, so should the moral education syllabus also be examined (*Cabinet Committee Report*, 1979, para. 127.1).

The Curriculum Development Centre (CDC) then appointed a Moral

Education Committee comprising Ministry of Education officials, representatives of various religious and voluntary groups, colleges of education,
universities and heads of schools. From this large committee a smaller,
eight-member syllabus committee was drawn whose task it was to produce
a draft syllabus for discussion. The findings of this committee were periodically submitted to the main committee for discussion and amendment, consensus being the major working principle. At about this time Malaysia
became involved in a series of workshops on moral education in Asian
countries sponsored by UNESCO and organized by the National Institute
of Educational Research (NIER) in Tokyo, Japan (NIER, 1981). One of
the objectives of these workshops was the attempt to identify "universal
moral values" that participants might want to adopt and use as part of the
core content of moral education programmes in their respective countries.
The notion of the core values as an integral part of the Malaysian moral
education syllabus, as described below, was triggered off by this exercise.

The Moral Education (ME) Syllabus

The term "syllabus" is preferred here to "programme" as referring to the
exact content of the written and officially approved curriculum to be taught
to Malaysian, non-Muslim children. Several exhortations are made, however, to view the practice aspect of the syllabus as part of the total school
programme. After several fits and starts the Central Curriculum Committee
(the highest level of curriculum decision-making in the Ministry of Education without whose approval new curricula cannot be introduced in schools)
accepted the syllabus presented by the CDC.

The preamble to the ME syllabus expresses concern for the "observed
instances of indiscipline in schools, disrespect for elders, vandalism and
increase in crime, destructive demonstrations, drug abuse and violations of
individual and societal rights". It goes on to say that as in many other
developing societies, life-styles in Malaysia are moving swiftly from those
based on a rural, agrarian economy to an urban-based one. Due to the
rapidity of these changes, "various influences compete and conflict with
traditional norms, principles and values of society". The function of the
moral education programme of the school is seen "as a means of maintaining
and improving the moral consciousness of society. Such a strengthening of
the moral fibre of the nation can form the basis for political, economic and
social stability as well as unity within the context of a plural . . . democratic
society". The moral education programme is thus conceived as:

> a planned sequence of experiences and activities, both formal and informal . . . [in order]
> to assist pupils to identify, clarify and internalize values which will be based on the religions,
> traditions and values of multiracial Malaysian society as well as universal moral values that
> are in accordance with the principles of the Rukunegara (Moral Education Syllabus, 1982,
> p. 1).

The overall objective is the development of an individual who recognizes and accepts his role as a moral decision-maker "in a democratic society such that his actions are governed by moral principles". The long-term objectives in terms of pupil outcomes at the end of the eleven-year curriculum (primary 1 to form 5 in a 6+3+2+2 education system) are stated as follows:

— To be aware of existing norms and values of Malaysian society and their influence on the conduct of the individual, community and society in general.
— To develop moral attributes and principles as a basis for developing the moral maturity of the individual.
— To make moral judgements based on acquired moral principles.
— To be able to give reasons for making a moral decision.
— To bring rational thinking to bear upon the interaction among different moral values and principles.
— To translate moral judgements into moral action (Moral Education Syllabus, 1982, p. 4).

The primary content of the syllabus centres around a core of sixteen values that are introduced into the various levels over the total eleven-year period. How were these values identified and selected? As mentioned in the previous section, the list of values emerging from the UNESCO-NIER workshops were used as a starting point. This list was dispatched by the CDC to the thirteen states in Malaysia with a request to State Curriculum Officers that it be circulated among a wide spectrum of people. Respondents represented voluntary welfare and youth groups, religious bodies, school heads and teachers, parent–teacher groups and teacher training colleges, all of whom were asked, firstly, to identify those values they considered to be cherished by Malaysians and, secondly, to add to the list values they perceived as relevant in Malaysian and universal terms but had not been included. CDC committees studied these listings, pondered on meanings and overlaps, and finally agreed on the following sixteen core values:

cleanliness of body and mind	honesty/integrity
compassion/empathy	humility/modesty
cooperation	justice
courage	rationality
moderation	self-reliance
diligence	love
freedom	respect
gratitude	public-spiritedness

Handbooks prepared for teachers at every class level attempt to indicate the concepts these values or "labels" are intended to encapsulate by breaking them down into specific objectives accompanied by suggested content and activities for the class. In principle, these various sets of objectives are expected to be seen as intermeshing and not exclusive. Intermeshing of concepts is seen not only in lateral but also in vertical terms. Perhaps the

[1] All quotations from official documents are translated versions of the original in Bahasa Malaysia.

notion of the spiral curriculum clarifies the kinds of connection and association both teacher and pupil are expected to make over the entire programme. For instance, activities planned for the unit on cooperation will have meaning for the unit on public-spiritedness at the same class level. In terms of vertical or spiral development of the curriculum, cooperation and public-spiritedness may be seen in terms of the immediate family and neighbourhood at the lower primary level, expanding to include the country and its immediate neighbours at the upper primary level, and moving out to embrace consideration of the world in terms of mankind in general.

Curriculum Implementation

In 1983 a new primary school curriculum was launched at the first level of primary schooling and this included ME as a compulsory subject for all non-Muslim pupils while Malay pupils attended Agama classes. The year of writing, 1986, sees the curriculum in its fourth year of national implementation. By 1989 the syllabus is expected to be implemented at the secondary school level.

Teachers in general seem unhappy with the syllabus for various reasons. There is a general level of dissatisfaction about the new primary school curriculum as a whole which had as one of its aims the intent of reducing the textbook dependency of teachers by not providing texts at the initial stages except for mathematics and Agama. Initially, CDC provided all teachers with prototype curriculum materials as no textbooks were planned. Curriculum officers were not able to keep up the momentum of supplying materials as a consequence of which workbooks and textbooks have mushroomed, with teachers and pupils frantically grabbing them as they are churned out. Teachers were expected to prepare their own materials following the guidelines given in the CDC's Teacher Guides and prototype materials. This encroachment into their "free" time created a great deal of resentment and antagonism towards the new curriculum. Malaysian teachers tend to be heavily dependent on the "set" text and the common curriculum and the examinations system supports this dependency. More importantly, the majority of teachers throughout the country was inadequately or not at all trained for ME. Those who have attended in-service sessions organized by CDC might have had anything between two and ten hours of exposure to the ME curriculum. At pre-service level of teacher training the situation is equally depressing. In 1981 a ninety-hour ME syllabus was introduced, spread over the three years of the college-level programme. To date, there are only three or four lecturers among the twenty-eight teacher training colleges who have had any formal training in the relevant content and methodology of ME.

ME as a Single Subject in the School Curriculum

When first implemented, ME teachers were of the opinion that value orientations indicated in the syllabus were being done anyway. A series of interviews conducted by the writer of this paper in Brookline, Massachusetts (USA) schools in 1974 had brought forth similar responses from teachers trialling Kohlberg's cognitive-developmental approach to ME. They declared that a separate subject was not required. Besides, in terms of developing an individual's "moral point of view" the values dimension should be integral to subject areas across the curriculum and not limited to a single slot in the timetable (Baier, 1958). Information from CDC reveals that initially this was the organizational approach selected when ME was first mooted. Insiders state that the "Me-across-the-curriculum/approach" would have been selected if some powerful religious groups, particularly from the Islamic community, had not lobbied against it. The explanation given to this writer was that values taught to the non-Muslim community should not be systematically presented to Muslim pupils. Such is the delicacy of the ethnic situation in Malaysian politics that even if this explanation were a rumour, it would be more than sufficient to make the government change horses midstream. One wonders, however, if anyone in the corridors of power had pointed out that the final set of core values was the result of consensus among representatives of all religious groups and given the composition of the government machinery, the Muslim component had been the largest in number during the decision-making meetings.

There are those who argue, however, for the single-subject organization on the grounds that unless ME is visible in the curriculum it is not taken seriously. It needs to appear formally in budget allocation requests for the various activities that accompany any one school subject. Moreover, given the current climate of Islamic religious fervour, it is difficult enough to garner allocations at all for any activity that smacks, however remotely, of ways of life other than Islam. Rejecting the ME programme at the present moment would imply not having it at all. To let ME merge with other subject areas, moreover, would be tantamount to having its inherent concerns fade away.

Curriculum materials

In early 1982 when prototype materials prepared by CDC personnel were trialled in national schools which include schools using as their medium of instruction Bahasa Malaysia, Mandarin and Tamil respectively, there was a considerable reaction from representatives of the Chinese and Indian communities. Their examination of materials being used by first-graders seemed to confirm earlier apprehensions of a generation on the brink of being indoctrinated by the powerful, majority ethnic community to the extent that they would lose their own identifies and cultures.

What was being objected to was the dominance of Malay culture in the stories, folk-legends, songs and pictorial illustrations used. Since all schools share a common curriculum the ME materials, predominantly Malay in ethos, were perceived to be part of an elaborate master plan. Embarrassed curriculum officers took fresh stock of their materials and indeed many discovered for the first time how biased the content of the materials was. It is the opinion of this writer that habitual myopia concerning ethnic issues *vis-à-vis* school curricular materials was responsible for the fiasco rather than a Machiavellian plan of indoctrination (Mukherjee *et al.*, 1984). Recruitment into Malaysia public sector occupations is based on a 4:1 quota principle in favour of the indigenous, generally Malay, population. As a consequence, taking the ME curriculum debacle as illustration, the chain which includes decision-makers, curriculum writers, illustrators, evaluators, publishers, etc., is overwhelmingly from the Malay community. In addition almost none of them had had at the time any formal experience or training in ME except as participants/observers in short-term international and local workshops/seminars. Given the fragile ethnic situation in the country and the fact that the overall national education goal calls for unity among the various ethnic groups, one would have expected that such gross oversights would be avoided by a group of professionals involved in a crucial aspect of the Malaysian school system. However, if we are aware that such groups of professionals function (more often than not) within a closed network of peers who grew up in the same milieu; share strong religious backgrounds and political affiliations; have in many cases attended the same elitist schools; and were university colleagues, it is possible to understand how they can support and reinforce each other's decisions and outputs to the exclusion of all other groups.

It is ironical that public outcry, however justified in specifics, was levelled at the ME curriculum as it was the first time that CDC, aware of the emotivism that any curriculum focused on values brings in its train, had sought the opinion of the public from the outset and was receptive to suggestions from diverse quarters about the syllabus. Currently curriculum officers are hosting writing workshops from time to time which teachers, principals and State Curriculum Officers attend in an attempt to harness a wider-based participation in the preparation of materials. The planning and writing teams presently include a number of non-Muslims and their inclusion has lent greater credibility to the ME curriculum where the public is concerned.

Teaching–Learning Strategies

Where teaching approaches and strategies are concerned, at the elementary level, planners are mindful of what Peters (1981) calls the "paradox of moral education" in that morality has its foundation in reason but children need to be inducted into it before they have developed the capacity for reasoning. The Malaysian ME syllabus takes the stand that children need to be morally socialized early in life for their own social well-being. They need to learn socially approved behavioural roles as well as the relevant moral language which will be required as tools for moral growth and expression when they reach the age of reason. For these reasons, during the first six years of the syllabus and especially at the lower primary level the major focus is on habit-forming and the building up of a relevant vocabulary.

At the secondary level (to be implemented nationally in 1989), the major focus is the problem-solving group discussion, choosing from alternative solutions and studying their possible personal and social consequences. The main aim there is to provide pupils with the tools of moral reasoning leading to moral judgement, using previously learnt content/values as a platform while at the same time assisting them to give reasons based on universal moral principles and not on relativistic codes of conduct. The syllabus as it stands does not provide, however, principles that indicate to the moral decision-maker how competing value claims are to be prioritized in moral conflict situations. Without such guiding principles, the classroom teacher faces difficulties ..ot only while reconciling competing claims but also in the giving of reasons which is a major objective of the syllabus (Leventhal and Fry, 1980).

The absence of any kind of ordering or clustering among the sixteen core values, hierarchically or otherwise, leaves the teacher ill-equipped conceptually. Furthermore, if the ME teacher is perceived as a neutral facilitator in stimulating discussion and keeping it alive, aiming at an examination of values held, then the syllabus may stand (Raths *et al.*, 1978). However, the teacher is seen in Malaysia as a moral authority. If the moral grounds for decision-making are not made explicit at the level of curriculum planning, it is difficult to see how moral interaction dialogues are to be developed and handled meaningfully. Unless restructuring of curriculum content and rethinking of strategy are attempted, it is more than likely that the five-year secondary school syllabus, when implemented will be an extension of the six-year primary school syllabus, i.e. with the values presented in discrete compartments, their interrelationships and their role in everyday interactive moral situations undisclosed.

Considerable thought needs to be given to the problem-solving, group discussion strategy. Participating in a moral dialogue is risky because it exposes the innermost self. In Malaysian society, representative of many Asian cultures, it is not common practice to speak about oneself, revealing innermost thoughts and feelings especially if they conflict with accepted norms. The recommended group discussion strategy may highlight obstacles such as the inability of pupils to respond in group discussions (not a major problem); the difficulty of recruiting support from teachers, parents and the general public (more complex); and the societal consequences of overturning traditional social norms (most complex).

Moral Values and the Total School Programme

Recent initiatives have been taken by the Ministry of Education to reinforce values taught during *Akhlak* and ME classes throughout the school's mandatory programme of co-curricular activities. This programme, now being trialled, has five components all of which earn the pupil points over the school year. Points are awarded for academic work and participation in games, athletics/sports; school clubs/societies/uniformed groups; beautification projects related to the school environment; and discipline.

Early reports on outcomes have not been particularly encouraging (*New Straits Times*, " 'Pointless' system in Negri Sembilar Schools", 16 May 1986, p. 9). Several essential features of the programme need to be thought through if programme objectives are to be accomplished. One of the most significant features is the manner in which points are awarded. What seems to defeat the *raison d'être* of the programme is that winning the points is more important than the participatory process. The Ministry of Education's evaluation format itself sets this in motion. For instance, checklists that provide guidelines to teachers for filling in progress reports award more points to pupils selected as school representatives for sports meets than regular participation. Similarly, pupils who attend annual general meetings of clubs and societies gain more points (especially if elected to committees) than do pupils who are consistent participants throughout the year as ordinary members. Pupils, with their usual canny ways of figuring out the reward system, have learnt the rules of this game very quickly!

Apart from the point-awarding system, there are other practical factors that make pupil participation problematic and reduce public support for the programme. Included among these are increased expenses, inadequate school facilities and teacher preparation.

Although fees charges for extracurricular activities are nominal, total expenditure for parents mounts up when the number of children per family is considered as well as expenses required for meals after school and added transportation costs. Next, most schools in Malaysia are double-session schools implying shared facilities which are insufficient to start off with. A particular school in one state with an enrolment of 2700 pupils, for example, has no school hall; has two basket-ball courts; one table-tennis table; two badminton courts and three floating classes (no homeroom) that may occupy any available space they can find. Pupils end up waiting around for quite a while for facilities to become free. Finally, the programme was trialled (and is about to be launched nationally if politicians have their way) without giving considered thought to teacher preparation. The result is that teachers lead organizations such as the Red Cross (Red Crescent in Malaysia) and Girl Guides using information sheets as guides and little else. Intensive in-serive courses are unable to provide training for all who require it in the short-term.

That the total school curriculum's role in the development of values has been recognized is an important step forward. Most important, perhaps, is that pupils of all ethnic and religious backgrounds come together for out-of-class activities and projects. But planners obviously have to hark back to programme objectives and rethink essential features of implementation if "Program Bersepadu" (Programme of Integration) is to make an impact on the development of values. Some careful evaluation of programme details would also not go amiss.

Commendations, Rewards and Recognition

At the national level, there are commendation days for young heroes, man of the year, mother (not woman) of the year and teacher of the year as well as child hero of the year. These receive a great deal of publicity through the media. Apart from these there are lists of commendations announced almost monthly on the birthday of the king, the sultans of nine states and the four state governors (a carry-over of the pre-independence Queen's birthday honours list). These commendations are generally intended for government servants who have served the country or individual state well and depend on recommendations made by heads of government departments.

Many of the awards carry titles with them and these are much sought after. Private individuals also may receive awards and titles, especially those from the business sector, for contributing to the wealth of the state/country. Titles are much desired as they provide an added boost where securing of business licences and permits are concerned. It is common knowledge that these titles can also be purchased and this often injects a strain of cynicism evident in the response given by the public to the announcement of awards. In recent years this cynical attitude seems to have been given support by the number of major financial scandals that have rocked the nation. Not only in terms of the amounts involved and their country-wide impact but also in terms of the titled and powerful personages implicated.[2]

At the local community level, there are efforts to promote public-spirit-edness, a sense of cooperation and healthier interaction by organizing "self-help" projects spearheaded by officials from the Ministry of Youth, Sport and Culture of Town/City Councils. The local press highlights them and raises awareness of relevant issues through their recognition. A variation of

[2] Two examples that have rocked the nation are the Bumiputra Malaysia Finance affair which surfaced in Hong Kong in 1983; and the more recent Pan-Electric stock market incident. The cases involved well-known titled personages as well as prominent political figures.

these activities is the youth work-camp, which may be organized by student groups and voluntary organizations. Apart from stimulating interaction between individuals from various backgrounds, the objective is to focus on projects that will raise the quality of life in disadvantaged communities. Again considerable recognition to these activities is given by the press. In many cases, if applications are made to the relevant sources those actively engaged in these activities may be awarded national commendations.

Conclusion

Malaysia has made much progress in developing and implementing a moral education curriculum, but these achievements have to be assessed against the tensions inherent in such an enterprise.

(1) Many have pointed out the contradiction that exists between the ME syllabus and the first, principal tenet of the national ideology (*Rukunegara*), "Belief in God". Although "Good Conduct and Morality" is expressed as another principle, its meaning is subsumed under the first. With its thrust on developing skills which lead to the making of independent moral judgements where the ultimate court of appeal is not a "God" or revealed religion, the ME curriculum may be seen as resting uneasily within the common curriculum structure.

(2) The specific values highlighted in the ME curriculum will always be subject to review in the light of changing conditions in Malaysia and the ability of teachers to convey the specified values. Already it is apparent that teachers are encountering difficulty with the notion of value hierarchy implicit in the current formulation, and hence some changes are in order.

(3) Especially problematic is the ME syllabus stress on autonomous moral judgement which some perceive to be a liberal Western bias, inconsistent with the hierarchical and somewhat formal nature of Malaysian family, community and political organization.

(4) While the achievement of national unity is an oft-stated primary educational goal, the division in Malaysia between Agama for Muslims and ME for non-Muslims, is perceived by some to give tangible expression and legitimacy by the schools to the cleavages evident in society. Future generations emerging from our schools will be expected to participate as adults who are policy-makers, managers, decision-makers, tax-payers, politicians, voters and your average citizen. However, they will have had little overt interaction at school level with peers from all backgrounds in the important domain of moral values although these are the people they will have to work shoulder to shoulder with. Recent developments in the planning of the New Secondary School Curriculum seem to reveal that these concerns are being given some attention. A new "Citizenship Education" syllabus as well as a "Personal and Social Values" syllabus are on the drawing board. These are being planned for both Muslim and non-Muslim pupils.

(5) The Cabinet Committee Report (1979) recommended that ME should be an examinable subject. Within the context of the Malaysian education system this means that it will be part of national public examinations, both at the end of the ninth and eleventh years, as is the case with Agama. Since the report was published, however, strong objections have been voiced by academic groups as well as professional teachers' bodies pointing out the negative features of formal summative evaluation (Mukherjee, 1983, 1985).

(6) Directly associated with the implementation of ME in schools is the issue of teacher training. Most teachers teaching the curriculum have had brief two- to ten-day in-service briefing sessions on the new primary school curriculum (of which ME is but one subject). At pre-service level, only three or four out of the twenty-eight teacher training colleges in the country have lecturers (one in each college) who have received formal training in the content and pedagogy of ME. While the capacity for training is modest, the objectives of the ME curriculum are not, and this does not bode well for the curriculum's implementation in the schools.

At the Moral Education Workshop held at the National Institute of Educational Research (NIER), Tokyo in early 1980, an issue that dominated many discussions was the existence of disjunctures between moral precept and practice. A great divide yawns between the moral education curriculum and the real world where success in life is equated with monetary achievements and status. Fraud in the corporate world has eaten its way into many homes and schools while pupils regard the efforts of the ME teacher with growing cynicism. Pupils are aware also of the ethos of schooling where a "good" pupil is one who performs well in examinations. Pupils from upper class backgrounds are favoured and anyway have a headstart in the occupational stakes. Schooling as a whole promotes competition and, as in the corporate world, "one-upmanship". How effective can ME programmes be in such an environment?

To add to the problems of planning and implementation, the affective impact of ME programmes is neither readily assessed while pupils are in school nor can their subsequent behaviour in life after school be attributed to ME and similar programmes. Moral action is the only authentic criterion of the success of socialization in the moral domain and its arena stretches beyond the purview of the school. Schools and the public need to remember, however, that schooling is only one agent, albeit an important one, in the socialization of the child. The family, the community, society at large as expressed through the media and other interactions, all play significant roles in the moral development of the child. The pursuit of ME programmes is not to be reduced in significance as it must be seen within the context of human endeavour within the moral domain. In any domain of knowledge progress is spurred on by images of excellence. The new global focus on the overt teaching of ME or its equivalent should be seen as part of modern man's attempt to re-create and rediscover images of excellence related to educated man, living in a society of men.

References

Baier, K. (1958) *The moral point of view*. Ithaca, New York: Cornell University Press.

Cabinet Committee Report on the Review of the Implementation of the National Education Policy (1979) Kuala Lumpur: Government Printers.

Chai Hon Chan (1977) *Education and nation building in plural societies: The West Malaysian experience*. Canberra: Development Studies Centre.

Ho Seng Ong (1952) *Education for unity in Malaya*. Penang: Malayan Teachers Unions.

Leventhal, K. and Fry, W. W. (1980) Beyond fairness: a theory of allocation preferences. In G. Mikula (Ed.), *Justice and social interaction*. New York: Springer.

Loh Fook Seng, P. (1975) *Seeds of separatism: Educational policy in Malaysia*. Kuala Lumpur: Oxford University Press.

Moral Education Syllabus (1982) (*Sukatan Pelajaran Pendidikan Moral*) Kuala Lumpur: Curriculum Development Centre, Ministry of Education.

Mukherjee, H. (1983) Moral education in a plural society: Malaysia. *Journal of Moral Education*, **12**.

Mukherjee, H. (1985) Moral education and the new secondary school curriculum. Paper presented at the Seminar on the New Secondary School Curriculum, 29 July, 1985, Kuala Lumpur.

Mukherjee, H., Ahmad, K. *et al.* (1984) *The lower secondary school curriculum and national unity*. Report presented to the Department of National Unity, Prime Minister's Department, Kuala Lumpur.

NIER (1981) *Moral Education in Asia*, Research Bulletin no. 20. Tokyo: National Institute of Educational Research.

Peters, R. S. (1981) *Moral development and moral education*. London: George Allen & Unwin.

Raths, L. E. *et al.* (1978) *Values and teaching: Working with values in the classroom*. Columbus, Ohio: Merril.

Report of the Education Committee (Razak Report) (1957) Kuala Lumpar: Government Printers.

Second Malaysia Plan 1971–75 (1971) Kuala Lumpur: Government Printers.

Third Malaysia Plan 1976–80 (1976) Kuala Lumpur: Government Printers.

Wong Hoy Kee, F. and Ee Tiang Hong (1971) *Education in Malaya*. Kuala Lumpur: Heinemann.

PART 4

Conclusion

CHAPTER 10

Policy Options for Values Education

WILLIAM K. CUMMINGS

Values education is possibly the most fundamental concern of society, yet much of the task of values education is carried out by the institutions of the family, the community and the Church, which are relatively insulated from the affects of public policy. What then are the options available to those in positions of public authority who seek to affect values education?

The case studies presented in earlier chapters reveal wide variety in national emphasis and practice. These differences indicate the complexity of the field of values education and the hazards involved in attempts to transfer practices developed in one national context to another. Yet at the same time, the differences help to stimulate thinking about the range of possible approaches to values education. In this chapter, drawing on examples from the case studies, I will provide at least the beginning of an outline of policy options accessible to public authorities for the promotion of values education.

Policy Formation and Policy Analysis

As a prelude to the discussion of policy options, it will be helpful to introduce a few observations about the nature of policy formation and its relations to policy analysis. Policy, at least in the discussion below, refers to actions taken by governments. The governments receive the authority to take these actions from their constituents in the broader society, and usually seek through these actions to return some benefit to these constituents. By benefiting the constituents, the government strengthens its authority. In democratic societies, the constituencies tend to be extensive, approaching the entirety of the societal community. In authoritarian regimes, the constituencies are usually narrower; in the extreme case, the government itself is the principle constituency.

The actual process of policy formulation is complex, involving the interaction of a diverse range of factors that no single actor ever fully comprehends. In this chapter I view the political leaders as the arbitrators of that process. These leaders operate from a set of givens: their cultural heritage, the com-

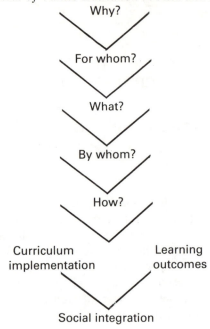

FIG. 10.1. *Analytical model of policy options.*

plexity of their socio-political and economic system, the resources they can mobilize to achieve educational objectives.

At the risk of over-simplification, six critical questions can be identified which policy-makers must confront when formulating a policy for values education, as illustrated in Fig. 10.1. Their answers to the Why and What questions (at the top of the diagram) tend to shape their approach to the remaining questions.

Political leaders are not always able to articulate the calculus they employ in identifying and supporting particular policies. They draw on experience, hunches, biases and the suggestions of their advisers. However, insofar as political leaders are able to approach these questions in a rational manner, I see them weighing at least two major considerations: what will be the political impact of their policies and what will be the benefit–cost in a more narrow economic calculus?

The implications of these two forms of assessment can be illustrated in terms of a policy decision on primary level enrolment expansion (Uphoff and Ilchman, 1972). A government policy for universal primary education has the potential both for enhancing regime popularity and for increasing the productivity of the labour force. However, the national context will condition the nature of political and economic benefits. Rapid expansion of primary education in a context of limited government funds may enhance regime popularity, at least in the short run. However, overly rapid expansion may result in low-quality primary education, with marginal economic returns. Slowing the rate of expansion might increase the economic benefits while reducing the political benefits. With this two-dimensional framework, the policy analyst is, in principal, equipped to evaluate the differential political and economic consequences of various strategies of expansion.

Most of the existing analytical work on educational policies is restricted to cost–benefit and related economic considerations. However, especially in the case of assessing values education, a broader framework is required, for as we have seen in most of the case studies the primary objective of these policies is to somehow affect the social and political fabric. In none of the cases was there explicit mention of the cost of proposed policies, and only in the cases of Korea and Malaysia was there an explicit expectation that the policies would improve economic performance.

But the task of evaluating political consequences is more ambiguous than that of evaluating economic consequences. The enrolment expansion example I have just summarized assumes a monolithic government which seeks support from an atomized public; but usually neither governments nor publics are so simple, and hence it is difficult to arrive at a single measure of political consequences. Policies are usually the result of compromises among different bureaux and constituencies. Each may have a different objective in mind in supporting a policy. Hence, where one bureau realizes success from a policy another may experience defeat. And what benefits one constituency may harm another.

The case studies we have reviewed suggest a variety of political objectives. In some cases, an actual learning outcome seems to be the objective. In the American case, the objective seems to be an enhancement of popular understanding of principles of government which will contribute to the maturity of the political process and hence to the benefit of all. Similarly, in Japan the objective is to strengthen the character of young people so that they cope with the contradictions and temptations of a rapidly changing world. In these cases, learning outcomes are a proximate criterion of policy success, as both the case studies on Japan and Western Europe remind us, social integration and the reduction of juvenile delinquency are more distal criteria.

In other cases, the discussion of moral education seems to be a proxy for a more basic struggle between contending ethnic and political groups. In Malaysia, the urgent push for a moral education curriculum for non-Malays appears to be a strategy for restraining the pressure from Muslim extremists who might otherwise urge Islamic education for all in a newly constituted Islamic state. Similarly, in Singapore the development of a course of Confucianism is a symbolic expression of Chinese identity. In these cases, success is realized simply by overcoming opposition in getting the new curriculum implemented.

Recognizing the complexity of objectives concerning values education, we propose an analytical model which includes both curriculum implementation and learning outcomes cum social change as complementary criteria of evaluation, as illustrated in Fig. 10.1.

Why Values Education?

At the outset, it is appropriate to state the obvious: differences in the respective national contexts have important bearing on the approach to values education.

Asia and the West

The major contrast in this book is between Asian states, which forthrightly assert a positive role of the state in values education, and Western states that are more reserved. Both within Asia and the West, there is wide variation in national practices. Nevertheless, it is the case that the Western states all achieved their present political structures between the late eighteenth and the mid nineteenth century. During this period of modern state formation, there emerged several common themes in educational policy. Perhaps most influential was the Enlightenment scepticism with respect to religious authority and the related proposal of the separation of church and state. Given the prominent role of Western churches in articulating moral standards, the implication was that the state should also play a limited role in monitoring or shaping the nation's moral life. Thus over time, even as public schools came to be expanded, the Western state evidenced much reserve with respect to common morality. While exercising restraint with respect to moral standards, the Western states were charged with the responsibility for teaching citizens how democratic governments functioned and inducing a sense of commitment to participation as citizens in this process. Thus in Western states, a major stress has come to be placed on civic education. John Meyer and his colleagues in the introductory chapter remind us that the trend towards narrowing the value agenda of schools went furthest in the United States, and hence the American example might be treated as exceptional rather than exemplary.

Modern Asian states, Japan being the first, rose in the wake of Western Imperial power, and felt genuinely threatened by the West. Japan, the first Asian state, made this concern explicit in one of its early development slogans, Western Science but Eastern Morality. Following a brief period of experimentation with Western institutions, Japan set about developing a unique national identity combining the best of both worlds. Notable in the Japanese model is the reliance on schools to teach loyalty to the state along with a code of behaviour for everyday life. Korea, China and Taiwan, and the other Asian states considered in this book parallel the Japanese example by looking to the schools to inculcate loyalty to the state and a moral code.

Homogeneous versus Pluralistic Societies

Distinct from geographic location and historical development is a society's cultural complexity. Japan, while politically divided at the dawn of her modernization drive, had a strong sense of common tradition and language. In contrast, the other Asian societies taken up in this study are characterized by varying degrees of cultural complexity. Both Malaysia and Singapore were composed of Malay, Chinese and Tamil sub-groups, and used English as the official language of instruction. In Indonesia, at the time of independence, at least three major languages and some 300 dialects were in use by significant numbers of people. In the West, the United States formed by immigration from all corners of the world is certainly the most complex, but other Western nations easily rival the US in this regard. The more complex a nation, the more difficult it is to develop a values education programme acceptable for or appropriate to all the members.

Established Religion or Not

Moral standards and concepts of national purpose are closely intertwined with the teaching of the great religions, and where these religions gain an institutional footing in the fabric of government then state-promoted values education will inevitably take on a religious dimension. The American republic, founded so that persecuted European sects could achieve freedom of religious practice, is unique in its disavowal of a public role in religious education. In contrast, several of the European societies accord special recognition to a particular Church, and in most of these cases policy-makers are inclined to include religious education as part of the publicly sponsored portfolio of values education.

Modern Japan, at the time of the Meiji restoration, experienced sharp conflict between competing religious groups, but as restoration of the descendent from the Sun God was a major theme in the new government's victory, Shintoism became the state religion. Until World War II, Shinto authorities played an important role in values education, and even after World War II when the American-imposed Peace Constitution stressed separation of religion and state, religious themes have been evident in official educational programmes. All of the South-East Asian states reviewed in this book acknowledge the importance of religion, though in Malaysia the recognition is to the single religion of Islam whereas in Indonesia, though a greater proportion of the population are Muslims, the recognition is to the Supreme Being.

Old States versus New States

In the early stages of nation-building, national leaders evidence the greatest concern for values as this is the time when future directions are being set. Their concerns achieve formal status in key documents such as constitutions, educational laws, principles of the national polity. In the fervour of national foundation, values education is prominently featured in various spheres including the schools, the media, community organization and public events. Over time this fervour is likely to fade as sectoral differences are smoothed over and traditions take root. Periodically, older states may experience revivals of values education, and in cases of major dislocation may even launch a major reform of their values education goals.

Economic Rise versus Decline

Yet another factor that seems to influence public interest in values education is the general state of welfare, both relative to earlier times and to other nations. Nations that sense they are doing well usually express confidence about their value system and the contributions of their members. In contrast, when nations enter a period of hard times, they begin to question their values and/or the popular adherence to the time-worn value standards that once guided the nation to glory. Judith Torney-Purta and Carole Hahn in their case study of Western Europe suggest that the concern to revitalize economic life has been a major impetus behind the European revival of values education.

Democratic and Authoritarian Regimes

Regardless of the nature of a regime, it cannot be denied that stage-promoted values education is clearly intended to set some bounds on the way citizens evaluate issues and conduct their daily lives. However, governments do vary in the extent and nature of control they seek to impose. Authoritarian regimes appear more interested in imposing extensive control. Also authoritarian regimes generally promote a conformist mode of values education. Of the case studies in this book, Korea and China provide the best examples of state monopolization of educational channels to bring about conformity, especially in regard to loyalty to the state. In contrast, in democratic societies there is likely to be bias towards providing individual citizens with the capacity to clarify values issues and make wise choices from a range of value possibilities.

What Should Be the Scope and Content of Values Education?

The national context which we have already reviewed generates the over-all impetus for particular directions in values education. These directions, often specified in national constitutions and educational laws, set the boundaries for decisions on the scope and content of values education.

Scope

Scope refers to the range of value areas that are included as objectives of educational policy. Some governments stress only one area, others several. The case studies identify several broad groups of values: moral values including family and social values, religious values, work values, civic values and for more authoritarian regimes a variant which might best be termed "commitment" to the national identity. Table 10.1 indicates the particular combinations that are currently stressed by policy-makers in the countries selected for this book.

TABLE 10.1. *Scope of Values Education Programmes*

Country	Value area				
	Moral	Religious	Work	Civic	National
US				x	
UK	x	x		x	
FRG	x			x	
Japan	x		x	x	
Singapore	x			x	x
Malaysia	x	x	x		x
Indonesia	x	x			x
Korea	x		x		x
Taiwan	x				x
China	x		x		x

Western countries place relatively singular stress on civic values. In the United States, the Constitutional separation of church and state reflects the historical sentiment that moral education is the responsibility of the family and church. A similar sentiment prevails in Western Europe; nevertheless, in most European countries educational institutions also devote attention to moral and/or religious values.

In contrast to the narrow scope of Western value education programmes, in East Asia the Confucian tradition provides clear legitimation for schools to assume a positive role in all spheres of values education. In the early throes of Japanese nationalism, the state's ambition for values education was comprehensive, only to be cut back following the World War II defeat. Most of the younger Asian societies, notably Korea, mainland China and

Indonesia, as well as many developing societies in other regions look to education to convey a comprehensive array of values. This ambition is a reflection of the concern among national leaders to foster national integration around a common set of values, and the ability of the national leaders to contain significant opposition against their particular definitions of national values. In Malaysia, following British precedent, the state initially did not seek to assume a major role in value education, but especially in recent years the state's ambition has increased.

So-called authoritarian societies tend to stress a wider scope of values than do democratic societies. Socialist states are notable for their stress on work values, and this stress has also been adopted by other societies, often of opposite political persuasion. For example, the dignity of labour and conscientious work are given considerable emphasis in the values education curricula of Japan and Korea. Currently Malaysia is involved in a "Look East" values campaign which primarily is concerned with learning the Japanese and Korean work ethic.

Implications

The more comprehensive the state's policy with respect to the scope of values education, the greater the resources it will need to devote to the realization of its objective. Also, the greater the scope the greater the political implications, both in terms of challenging opposition groups and in gaining converts to the government's interpretation of correct values.

Content

While policy-makers turn over the task of developing the content of most educational programmes to technicians, concerning values education they evidence much interest. In all of the case studies, senior political leaders have been continuously involved in the formulation of the new values education curricula. For example, in Singapore the Deputy Prime Minister drafted the programme on moral education, and in the United States the Secretary of Education is an articulate and persistent advocate of enhancing the values education curricula of public schools. Top politicians become involved because they recognize the content extends beyond knowledge to include judgements of what is good, true and beautiful, and on these matters there can be major differences. Policy-makers are concerned to see that the judgements featured in the curricula will be presented accurately and in a manner likely to gain approval from the general public, or at least not to provoke undue opposition.

The concern for content seems most acute with respect to the definition of national identity. The task of defining identity is simplified in nations that are relatively homogeneous. Commonly shared symbols and events become the raw material for constructing the curriculum.

Culturally diverse nations have the option of emphasizing either their unity or their diversity. A unifying focus is easiest when the diverse groups have participated in a common struggle, such as a war of liberation or against a foreign aggressor, as in the case of post-independence America or Indonesia. But even this revolutionary symbolism has its limitations when a new regime succeeds the old: Suharto's new order government during the first fifteen years of its rule suppressed recognition of Sukarno. Where national heroes are too controversial (or scarce), it sometimes is possible to use great men from other countries: Abraham Lincoln and Martin Luther King, though American, have universal stature as fighters against slavery and discrimination, Albert Schweitzer against sickness and poverty. Pre-revolutionary political and cultural symbols can also be highlighted, so long as these are not particular to a particularly sub-group. In the absence of political and cultural symbols, it is possible to highlight commonly shared natural wonders like Mounts Fuji and Merapi, the River Solo and old Mississippi.

Nations such as the US and India chose to strike a balance between unity and diversity. These nations allow both multilingual and multicultural education. Where the different cultural groups are geographically segregated, this is a relatively efficient policy to implement. However, in the American case where the groups are relatively well integrated, it can prove quite costly.

Finally, Malaysia and the Netherlands are examples of countries where diversity receives greater stress than unity. In Malaysia, as Hena Mukherjee relates, different programmes of value education are devised for Malays and non-Malays, the former studying Islam and the latter moral education, the former subject to Islamic law and the latter to civil law. And in the Netherlands, the policy of pillarization recognizes separate schools for the Catholic and Protestant communities.

Another set of content issues concerns the extent to which contrasting values should be introduced. For example, a major current issue in the United States is the amount of information that should be provided about other ways of government and other cultures in civic education, and whether this content should be prepared in such a manner as to present the foreign system in a favourable or unfavourable light. Similarly, proponents of religious education face up to the issue of emphasis on a single religion or a comparison of religions.

Implications

The more complex the context the greater the cost in developing the curriculum and the greater the difficulty likely to be encountered in its implementation.

For Whom?

Two broad choices concerning target groups need to be addressed by policy-makers: to what social groups and what age groups should the values education programme be addressed? The first question follows from the political objectives of the programme whereas the second is more related to content.

Most values education programmes promoted by contemporary states expect to convey a common message to all social groups. Achieving such a broad impact is potentially an expensive proposition if attempted as an independent activity. In periods of revolutionary change such as the early years of the Sandinista regime or the Cuban revolution, it may be possible to capitalize on the enthusiasm for the revolution to recruit volunteers to the education programme: in this manner impressive politically slanted literacy campaigns can be launched (Arnove, 1981). However, in normal times, it is difficult to recruit large numbers of unpaid workers for educational programmes; rather these programmes have to become additions to conventional institutions.

In the early stages of the industrial revolution it was not uncommon for governments to promote values education programmes to uplift the moral level of the working class. Also in some contemporary states, programmes are directed to specific sub-groups either with the intentions of assimilating them into the larger societal community or of conveying the official intent to keep these sub-groups permanently subordinate to the dominant group. Malaysia's school-based moral education, among the cases considered here, is the clearest example of a values education programme tailored to a specific minority group. Group-specific programmes are more feasible when the groups are geographically concentrated.

Somewhat distinct from decisions regarding the target group is the particular age level within that group to be designated for primary attention. It is generally regarded that programmes focusing on basic moral values are best begun at an early age, as moral development achieves its basic patterns during the early years (Maccoby, 1968). The moral education programmes of Japan, Malaysia and Indonesia begin in the first years of primary education. In contrast, programmes focusing on civic values and/or national identity are generally begun in the early years of adolescence or later, for until that stage young people usually lack the foundation in experience and intellectual background to digest the content of such programmes. Exceptions to either of these generalizations are readily available. The Sandinista literacy campaign achieved its greatest success with young children, and it is reported that the revolutionary Khomeini regime is placing special emphasis on the political education of primary school children in anticipation of their future role in the armed services and other roles.

While content is usually the major consideration when selecting the age group to target, the availability of facilities may also bear on the decision. Public schools are one of the few institutions to reach such a large cross-section of the public that are under the direct control of governments. Because public schools serve the young, values education is often directed to the young even in instances where policy-makers believe adults might be a more appropriate target group.

Pupils versus Teachers

While the early stages of values education policy focus on pupils, once the outlines of programmes are set it becomes important to identify and train teachers. In some countries, teacher training is given first priority as it is recognized that poor teaching will have a deleterious effect on the programme. Meiji Japan was notable for its extreme measures in teacher training: tuition-free education was made available to recruits who came primarily from rural areas, special full-time schools with dormitories were set up in isolated rural areas, former military officers were recruited to provide drills and dogmatic instruction on national values and morality to the recruits (Passin, 1965, p. 91ff.). Only after a sufficient number of teachers had been through this programme, did the government advance its programme of moral education in the schools.

Education or Political Assertion as the Outcome

The above observations assume that educational outcomes are the major objective of educational programmes, but in some instances other outcomes may be at least as important. For example, in the Malaysian, Singapore and Indonesian cases, it would appear that a major concern of the respective governments is to gain broader acceptance of their particular interpretations of national identity, and the educational arena has been selected as a convenient setting for carrying out this struggle. In these cases, the authorities may be less concerned with selecting the optimal age group.

Implications

Clearly there is wide variation in the target groups for value education. The more that are targeted, the more costly will be the programme and the more difficult to implement. On the other hand, once a programme gains a certain degree of pervasiveness, there are benefits of consistency and scale. Values learned in one setting are reinforced by those learned in other settings. Teachers in one setting can serve as consultants in others.

By Whom?

Thus far, no reference has been made to the particular agencies targeted for the conduct of values education. Public schools are one possibility, but there are others.

A general distinction can be made between public channels, those directly under the supervision of government, and private channels, those juridicially and financially autonomous though subject to public law and opinion. A second distinction concerns the groups and/or organizations relied on to convey values education. Homes have always played an important role in values education. Modern states recognize schools, voluntary organizations, work organizations and the media as additional agencies for values education. Table 10.2 illustrates the possible combinations of agencies available for the conduct of values education.

TABLE 10.2. *Agencies of Values Education*

Agencies	Sector	
	Private	Public
Family	xx	—
Primary schools	—	xx
Secondary Schools and universities	xx	xx
Youth organizations	x	x
Military education	—	x
Adult institutions	x	x
Campaigns and public events	—	x
Media	x	x

Key: xx = important in most societies; x = important in some societies.

It is conceivable that an officially defined programme of values education could be carried out exclusively by private agencies. A government might seek the cooperation of private agencies through exhortation, through passing laws requiring their observance of certain procedures believed necessary for the programme, or through providing monetary and other incentives to the private agencies. Authorities in Western societies often appeal to private institutions, even for the delivery of public educational programmes. For example, in both the US and the UK private institutions have been contracted for job-training programmes, programmes with a very substantial component of values education. And especially in the US, private associations

have taken the lead in promoting global studies and other related programmes aimed at raising American public consciousness about trade and
foreign policy issues as well as the difficulties faced by the third world.

Despite the availability of appropriate channels, governments decide to
implement some, if not all, of their values education programmes through
publicly controlled channels. The extreme cases come from the socialist
camp, where it is not uncommon for the government to nationalize all
agencies of education except the family; China even took steps through
the formation of farm and factory communes to penetrate the socialization
function of the traditional family.

The government of Meiji Japan tried to nationalize the private agencies
of education, but met resistance especially from the schools established by
well-regarded private dissidents such as Waseda's Okuma Shigenobu or
Keio's Fukuzawa Yukichi. Thus the government allowed the private institutions to stand but introduced laws requiring them to teach morals classes
with government-appointed teachers; also, as the graduates of private institutions were not allowed to compete for civil service jobs, their attractive-
ness to the general public was curtailed. The Japanese government also took
impressive steps to control other media. It penetrated youth and community
associations by sponsoring former military officers to become members of
the governing boards. It limited the number of radio stations and newspapers, and exercised gentle control over the content of these media. And
it censored foreign books and magazines before allowing their entry into
the country (Mitchell, 1983). These various measures are characteristic of
many contemporary governments who have values education programmes
of broad scope. New states in Asia have tended progressively towards a
strong public role in these various ways.

Implications

An extensive public role in values education is more costly to the state,
but fosters expectation of greater success. At the same time, states that have
once encouraged a more libertarian atmosphere and then seek to expand
their role are likely to encounter persistent resistance. Such currently seems
to be the case in Korea and possibly Singapore.

How

Linked with decisions on the agencies or values education are the objectives and methods of instruction. Several options are apparent.

Clarification versus Inculcation

First, concerning objectives, one school of thought seeks merely to help pupils clarify their current values (Purpel and Ryan, 1976). This approach assumes that the values pupils possess, rather than being questioned and possibly altered, should be accepted and used as a basis for clarifying the range of applications. In opposition is the view that values should be taught to pupils. This approach assumes that pupils may not have been exposed to the best influences and hence need to be taught appropriate values.

Cognitive Instruction versus Experience

A second difference concerns the manner of instruction. Some values educators believe that values can be taught in essentially the same manner as history or a related subject, through the use of lectures, textbooks and related assignments. In contrast are those who believe values education requires a special experience-based approach where students are placed in real-life situations and given the opportunity to test out their values in interaction with peers and other members of society.

School or Later

Most of the formal literature on values education assumes a school setting, but out-of-school settings are also appropriate for values education, especially where the experiential approach is favoured. Out-of-school settings range from relatively unstructured outings to the highly structured totalistic environments of military boot camps, prisons and mental hospitals.

While out-of-schools settings are usually preferred for experiential education, this can also be worked into the school routine through, for example, turning over a greater variety of school responsibilities to pupils, developing special field trips, and through careful revision of the school's hidden curriculum to strengthen the value lessons for pupils. Tomoda in Chapter 5 explains how Japanese primary schools make use of groups, both within classes and after school, to promote the values of cooperation and mutual respect; he also indicates how the austere climate in secondary schools is developed to reinforce the values of hard work and discipline.

Formal versus Informal Evaluation

Most educational programmes involve some form of assessment of pupil progress. In the case of values education, some educators believe that the process of interaction between students and teachers includes a type of assessment through group consensus or criticism, and that it would be undesirable to attempt anything more formal. Those who resist formal evaluations argue that the use of formal tests might reduce values education to a cognitive subject with students learning the correct answer but not believing it. In contrast are those who believe formal evaluation in values education, as in other subjects, is essential to motivate and ensure correct learning. The advocates of formal evaluation sometimes acknowledge that exams may only measure external conformity, but once a student acts out correct values in exam questions there is the prospect for this behaviour to influence his attitudes and beliefs. Of course, distinct from exams are other measures of values acquisition, such as teacher and peer evaluations or records of participation in community projects.

The disputes over assessment are sometimes no more than double-talk for a more basic concern, the control of the value formation process. If there is no formal assessment, then teachers will have full authority to do whatever they wish in the classrooms. Introducing class-based assessment can strengthen the authority of teachers. Social-based assessments strengthen the hand of principals. External assessments strengthen the hand of the state. In Korea and mainland China, the inclusion of values tests among the criteria for admission to higher educational institutions provides the state with a means of screening those destined for elite status in society.

Implications

The hows of values education are sharply constrained by other options. Value clarification is more likely to be emphasized in democratic societies that assume their citizens have a right to their own personal values whereas in authoritarian societies value instruction is more characteristic. Similarly, external testing is more characteristic of authoritarian societies. The more liberal approaches doubtless help individuals to achieve greater control of the state. In contrast, the more directive approaches offer potential dividends to the state in terms of greater mass conformity, and, when the people react negatively to state educational programmes, an indication of those sub-groups who resist state leadership. There are no obvious differentials in cost associated with any of these options, except that the liberal approaches may require more highly trained and hence higher paid instructors.

Conclusion

Clearly, policy-makers have a wide range of options to choose from in developing their values education programmes. Certainly, the first question that policy-makers need to address is their purpose: are they simply trying to publicize their own value preferences through educational programmes or are they genuinely interested in affecting the beliefs and thought processes of the broader society? And if they are striving for significant social impact, are they concerned to sharpen the intellectual and evaluative skills of the public or rather to shape popular values in particular directions? These concerns, along with the scope of values that are targeted, influence the level of public commitment in terms of power, funds and surveillance-monitoring. Once the discussion of values education moves beyond those activities in schools to the full range of activities undertaken by the state, it becomes apparent that there is wide variation in national practice.

In general, Asian states appear less constrained by law and custom in their review of policy options, and thus are more inclined to holistic pro-grammes of values education. In contrast, Western states tend to focus on a relatively narrow scope of values and mobilize fewer options for their realization. The aim here has been to identify the full range of options open to policy-makers as well as some of the implications of these options. In view of the current revival of interest in values education, it is hoped that this survey will provide educational leaders with insights into the full range of options now in place in Asia and the West.

References

Arnove, R. (1981) The Nicaraguan national literacy crusade of 1980. *Comparative Education Review*, June, 244–260.

Maccoby, E. (1968) The development of moral values and behavior in children. In J. Clausen (Ed.), *Socialization and Society*. Boston: Little, Brown.

Mitchell, R. H. (1983) *Censorship in Imperial Japan*. Princeton, NJ: Princeton University Press.

Passin, H. (1965) *Society and education in Japan*. New York: Columbia University Teacher's College Press.

Price, R. F. (1979) *Education in modern China*. London: Routledge & Kegan Paul.

Purpel, D. and Ryan, K. (Eds.) (1976) *Moral education: It comes with the territory*. Berkeley: McCutchan.

Uphoff, N. T. and Ilchman, W. (1972) The new political economy. In N. T. Uphoff and W. Ilchman (Eds.), *The political economy of development*. Berkeley: University of California Press.

Index

Aesthetic values 36, 111
Agama classes (for Malay pupils) 154
Allied Occupation 78
American case as an exception 13
American parents 69
American Revolution 59
Anti-communism 93, 94, 100
Armed forces, service in 136
Art classes 36
Asia 24, 142, 168, 180
Assessing results 40, 75, 88, 106, 118, 179
Authoritarian and democratic regimes 16, 170

Balhetchet, Dr. (Rev.) R. P. 138
Being and Becoming moral education
    program 138
Benefit-cost 166
Bennett, William J. 3
Bilingual school policy 131
Biographies 76, 112
Bloom, Allan 3
British colonial government (in
    Malaysia) 148
British colonies (former) 25, 135, 148
British public schools 41
Buddhism 147
Bullying 75

Canadian provinces 3
Capitalist class 95
Catholic private schools 41
Censorship of foreign books 177
Centralized system 42
Charity drives 39
Chiang Ching-kuo 115
Children's play-groups 90
China, Republic of 109
Chinese majority 131
Chinese-medium schools 136, 150
Christian heritage 31
Christian mission schools 151
Christmas 36
Church 7
Citizen 59
Citizen soldier 61
Civic consciousness 60
Civic education 35, 59, 69
Civic values 171
Civics 19, 84

Clan associations 142
Clarify current values 178
Class (capitalist) 95
Class council, Sweden 43
Class meeting, *klassens-time* 42
Classroom process 143
College level 106
Colonies
    British 25, 135, 148
    French 25
    Japanese 93
    Spanish 25
Common curriculum 149
Community and youth associations 177
Competition 119
Comprehensive programmes, school-
    wide 83
Compulsory free public education 31
Conceptual model of values education 32
Confucian ethics programme 139
Confucian societies 93
Confucianism 93, 112, 133, 171
Conservative government 49, 78
Conservative views 48
Content 172
Content analysis 93, 98
Cooperation 119
Core values 39, 152
Countries likely to employ moral or
    religious instruction 23
Cuban revolution 174
Cult of personality 125
Cultural policies 6
Cultural Revolution 122
Culture-carrier, language as 137
Cummings, William K. 84
Curriculum 12, 17, 43, 96, 109, 144, 155
Curriculum Development Centre
    (CDC) 151
Curriculum Development Institute of
    Singapore 139
    common 149
    hidden 36, 38

Decline of civic education 59
Decline of morality 16, 134, 142
Democracy 31, 104, 132
Democratic and authoritarian regimes 16,
    170
Demonstrations 39

Deng Xiaoping   125
Denmark   42, 48
Deviancy   75
Discovery method   86
Discussion questions   37, 115
Dore, Ronald P.   79
Drugs   134
Durkheim, Émile   96, 131

Easter   36
Eastern and Western values, contrasts   142
Eastern European countries   24
Economic development   22, 102, 132, 170
Economic factors, global   51
Economic values   52
Education reform report   136
Egalitarian values   84
Elementary educational timetables   17
English-medium education   132, 150
Enrolment rate, Japan   85
Established religion   15, 53, 169
Ethics programme, Confucian   139
Ethnic groups   167
Evaluation   178
Examination system, General Secondary
    Certificate of Education   40
Examinations   40, 75, 88
Experience   178
Extracurricular activity   109

Family 8, 33, 45, 53, 93, 133
Federated system   41
Filial piety   113
FRG, federated system   41
Friedman, Milton   66
Fundamental Code of Education of
    1872   76

Geography   84
GI bill   66, 71
Gilligan, Carol   118
Global economic factors   51
Goh Keng Swee   138
Government as educator   136
Group discussion   157
Guest workers   48
Guidance system   38

Heavenly mandate   93
Heroism   36, 112, 159
Hidden curriculum   36, 38
Hierarchical organization of school
    systems   143
Hindus (in Malaysia)   147
Hippie   134
History, subject of   77, 84
Holidays   36

Ideology   47, 94, 98
IEA Civic Education Survey   35
Immigrants   4, 47, 48, 54, 62, 134
Impact of values education   52
Imperial Family   77
Indirect approach   112
Individualism   13, 87
Industrial revolution   174
Integration
    national   172
    social   131
Islam   7, 25, 147, 155

Japan   168
Japan Teachers' Union   78
Japanese public opinion   77

Khomeini regime   175
Kinship   93
Kohlberg, Lawrence   33, 37, 118, 155
Koran   151
Korean independence   94
Korean War   62, 93

Latin American countries   24
LEA [local education authority]   40
Lee Kuan Yew   133
Liberal democratic tradition   37
Lippman, Walter   3
Loan and scholarship programs   70
Lutheran beliefs   43

Malay community, moral crisis in   134
Malay culture, dominance of   156
Malay-medium schools   150
Malaysian identity   150
Mandarin, campaign   137
Mao Ze-dong   120
Materialism   129
Media   7, 61, 89, 136, 177
Meiji Restoration   75
Meyer, John   168
Migrant mentality   134
Militarism   103
Military officers   94, 175
Military service   8, 61, 136
Modernization   126
Moral authority of teachers (Malaysia)   157
Moral education   12, 15, 19, 23, 32, 82, 93,
    128, 131, 138, 141, 152, 157, 171
Moral education programme, *Being and
    Becoming*   138
Mukherjee, Hena   173
Multi-ethnic societies   6
Multicultural society   46, 132

National character (Singapore)   145
National education system   148

National guard   61
National integration   11, 132, 172
National service   61, 172
Nationalism   61, 63, 77, 101
Neo-Marxist theory   96
Netherlands   41, 173
New order government   173
New states   15, 170
Newspapers   177
NIER (National Institute of Educational
   Research)   152
Northern Europe   36

Official languages (Singapore)   131
Ong Report on Moral Education,
   1979   138

Parsons, Talcott   3
Participation in school life   14
Pastoral system   38
Patriotism   60, 113
Peer groups   136
Personality cult   125
Pillarization   47
Pluralism, protection of   7, 148, 169
Point-awarding system   158
Policy formation   15, 52, 165
Political education   45
Political groups   167
Political objectives, variety of   167
Problem-solving approach   86
Public campaigns   8, 136

Relativism   49
Religion (established)   169
Religious education   12, 15, 21, 23, 36,
   139, 169
Religious institutions   53
Religious pluralism   31
Religious values   171
Report of the Education Committee
   (1957)   148
Report on Moral Education, 1979 (Ong
   Report)   138
Results, assessment   118
Revival of values education   45, 49
Revolutionary change   174
Rock music   134
Rukunegara   150

Sandinista regime   174
Scholarship and loan programs   70
School Education Law of 1947   81
Scientific spirit   114
Self-help projects   159
Shintoism   169
Shushin   76, 93

Singapore   131, 172
Singleton, John   79
Social integration   104, 131
Social movements   47
Social studies   19, 93
Socialist states   172
South-East Asian states   169
Speak Mandarin campaign   137
Sports   41, 89
State and statism   16, 93, 98, 105
State religion   15
Student attitudes   55
Student clubs   89
Student council   39, 82
Sun Yat-sen   114
Surveys   3, 62
   of life values   134
   of student attitudes   55, 70
Sweden   43
Syngman Rhee   94

Taiwan   109
Tamil-medium schools   150
Teacher recruitment   107
Teacher status   127
Teacher training   144, 149, 154, 175
Teaching methodology   128
Textbooks   96, 106, 110, 112
Thatcher, Margaret   45
Third Republic (1963–1979)   94
Third World societies   132
Tradition   15, 31, 37, 45, 48, 59, 76, 77,
   136, 143, 149, 165, 171, 175
Traditional values   45

Unemployment   48
UNESCO-NIER workshops on moral
   education   6, 152
United States   11, 59, 173
Urbanization, rapid   131

Values clarification   5, 47, 138
Values education   45
Vietnam War   62
Violence   75
Vocational courses   41
Volunteer army   65

Western countries   25, 142, 168, 180
Western European tradition   31
Work ethic   41
World society   11

Youth and community associations   8, 177
Youth work-camp   160
Yushin Regime (1972–1979)   94